CRATERS!

A Multi-Science Approach to Cratering and Impacts

Unless noted here, all photographic images appear courtesy of NASA (full credit lines are provided on *Craters!-CD*), and all line art was created by Ron Miller (Black Cat Studio, King George, VA).

Figs. 2.1, 2.2, 2.5; photo p. 37 courtesy of Ewen Whitaker.

Figs. 2.3, 2.4 are original illustrations from Galileo Galilei, 1610, *Sidereus Nuncius*.

Photos pp. 25, 88; illustrations pp. 52, 192, 197; figs. 11.2, 11.3, 12.1A, 12.1B courtesy of William K. Hartmann.

Figs. 4.1, 4.4 courtesy of the Lunar and Planetary Laboratory, University of Arizona.

Fig. 4.3 created by Sergey Ivanov.

Illustration p. 43 (and used elsewhere) is redrawn after Fig. 24.1 in W. Kenneth Hamblin, 1992, *Earth's Dynamic Systems*, 6th ed. (New York: Macmillian).

Fig. 12.5; image p. 81 courtesy of NASA and Calvin J. Hamilton, Los Alamos National Laboratory.

Figs. 11.1, 12.3, 12.3-Key, 13.1, 14.1, 14.2, 14.3, 14.4, 15.2, 16.1, 16.3, 18.1, 18.5, 20.1 were created by Gregg Sekscienski.

Fig. 11.4 courtesy of the Lunar and Planetary Institute.

Fiddler crab p. 105; illustrations pp. 108, 111 are originals created by Stacey Stevenson.

Illustrations pp. 107, 123, 126 from H.F. Osborn, 1916, *Bulletin of the American Museum of Natural History*, vol. 35, pp. 733–771.

Illustration p. 125 from H.F. Osborn and C.C. Mook, 1921, *Memoirs of the American Museum of Natural History*, vol. 3, pp. 245–387.

Stegosaurus p. 105; illustration p. 127 from C.W. Gilmore, 1914, *Bulletin of the U.S. National Museum*, vol. 89, pp. 1–143.

Illustration p. 109 from O.C. Marsh, 1880, *Odontornithes: A Monograph on the Extinct Toothed Birds of North America* (Washington, DC: Government Printing Office).

Fig. 16.4 (unshocked quartz) is Fig.1 A in B. French, "Shock Metamorphism as a Geological Process," and (shocked quartz) Fig. 1, W.V. Engelhardt, et al. "Observations on Quartz Deformation..." both in B.M. French and N.M. Short, 1968, *Shock Metamorphism of Natural Materials* (Baltimore: Mono Book Corp.). Courtesy of NASA.

Figs. 16.5 and 17.1 redrawn after Alvarez, et al., 1980, *Science*, vol. 208, pp. 1095–1108, Fig. 5. Redrawn by Gregg Sekscienski.

Image p. 189 courtesy of Naval Research Laboratory.

Image p. 204 courtesy of Max Planck Institut fur Astronomie and others.

Library of Congress Card Catalog Number 95-67462

ISBN: 0-87355-132-X

NSTA Stock Number: PB120X

Printed in the U.S.A. by Automated Graphics.

CRATERS!

A Multi-Science Approach to Cratering and Impacts

William K. Hartmann
with
Joe Cain

A Joint Project of the
National Science Teachers Association,
The Planetary Society,
and the
National Aeronautics and Space Administration

TABLE OF CONTENTS

INTRODUCTION

ACTIVITIES

DISCOVERING CRATERS

MAKING CRATERS

IMPACT DISTRIBUTIONS

KINETIC ENERGY AND IMPACTS

NO SPECIAL TREATMENT: IMPACTS ON EARTH

APPENDICES

Moon 608.tif

ABOUT THE COVER PHOTOGRAPHS:

FRONT COVER:

◆ The background image is Yuty crater on Mars. This impact site has a well developed central peak and displays a type of ejecta blanket seen only on Mars. Planetary scientists believe substructure ice deposits melted during impact, creating a muddy, liquefied ejecta that flowed over adjacent features. Unusually high bluffs are found on the far edge of each lobe of the ejecta. JPL/NASA image P-16848. This image is in the public domain.

◆ The three inserts are original paintings by William K. Hartmann. From the upper right to the lower left, these paintings are titled: *Two seconds before the end of the Cretaceous Period, One minute after the end of the Cretaceous Period,* and *1,000 years after the beginning of the Tertiary Period.* Together, these images represent the artist's interpretation of the cause of the K/T boundary and the extinctions that occurred at the end of the Cretaceous, including the final extinction of dinosaurs. The perspective is an orbital position 100 kilometers above Earth's surface. The approaching asteroid is traveling at a speed of 18 kilometers per second. The resulting crater is 200–300 kilometers wide. Used with the artist's permission.

BACK COVER:

◆ Original painting by William K. Hartmann, *The collision that made the Moon.* The artist has played a central role in developing the widely accepted theory that explains the origin of Earth's moon as the result of a collision between Earth and another large interplanetary body approximately 4.5 billion years ago. According to this theory, a small fraction of Earth's interior was blasted out, went into orbit, and later aggregated to form the Moon. This painting is based on a computer simulation of the event and shows the view one-half hour after the collision took place. Used with the artist's permission.

ACKNOWLEDGMENTS

Many people—scientists, educators, and writers—contributed to *Craters!*. This volume was created as a pilot module for the Scope, Sequence, and Coordination (SS&C) curriculum project, with generous support from NASA. It resulted from a cooperative agreement between National Science Teachers Association (NSTA), The Planetary Society, and the National Aeronautics and Space Administration.

The framework and initial scheme for this pilot module were created at a workshop in December 1992, chaired by William Hartmann (The Planetary Society's SS&C project coordinator, Tucson, AZ). The following people participated in that workshop: Russell Aiuto (NSTA), Bill Aldridge (NSTA), Rich Alvidrez (Jet Propulsion Laboratory), Ronald Armstrong (middle school teacher, Gansevoort, NY), Ghassem Asrar (NASA Headquarters), Pamela Mountjoy (NASA Headquarters), Richard Binzel (Massachusetts Institute of Technology), Geoff Briggs (NASA Ames Research Center), Linda Crow (Baylor College of Medicine), Linda French (Wheelock College), Louis Friedman (The Planetary Society), Doris Grigsby (NASA/AESP, Oklahoma State University), Martha Hanner (Jet Propulsion Laboratory), Gayle Hartmann (The Planetary Society's SS&C project editor, Tucson, AZ), Nancy Horn (SS&C teacher, Houston, TX), Garth Hull (NASA Ames Research Center), Andrew Ingersoll (California Institute of Technology), Ralph Kahn (Jet Propulsion Laboratory), Jim Kasting (Pennsylvania State University), Bob Kolvoord (Lunar and Planetary Laboratory, University of Arizona, Tucson), Larry Lebofsky (Lunar and Planetary Laboratory, University of Arizona, Tucson), Victor Mayer (Ohio State University), Ellis Miner (Jet Propulsion Laboratory), Wendell Mohling (NSTA), George Pinky Nelson (University of Washington), Frank Owens (NASA Headquarters), Myra Philpott (high school science teacher, Buena Park, CA), Carl Pilcher (NASA Headquarters), Lisa Rossbacher (California State Polytechnic University), Carl Sagan (The Planetary Society & Cornell University), Carol Stadum (The Planetary Society), and Gregory Vogt (NASA Johnson Space Center).

William Hartmann and Carl Sagan developed original concepts for the document in consultation with NSTA Executive Director Bill Aldridge. William Hartmann created the preliminary version of *Craters!* in 1993. This manuscript was circulated to various content experts, and additional writing and editorial contributions were made at The Planetary Society by Carol Stadum, Michael Reeske, Myra Philpott, Christine Clark, and Steve Reed. India Wadkins (The Planetary Society) and Elaine Owens (Planetary

Science Institute) assisted in the preparation of the preliminary manuscript. Gayle Hartmann edited the original document.

With additional support from NASA, a *Craters!* author/teacher workshop was held in August 1994. Pamela Mountjoy (NASA Headquarters) and Wendell Mohling (NSTA) coordinated this workshop, with assistance from Lisa Henderson (NSTA). Participants in this workshop were Dolores Willoughby Choat, J. Charles Floyd, Myra Halpin, Sue Cox Kauffman, Jo Anne Reid, and Len Sharp. These teachers also contributed to the review and revision process. Other educators who contributed to the review and revision process included Sharon Stroud, Nancy Ridenour, Frank Zuerner, Frank Watt Ireton, Sophia Clifford, Betty Paulsell, Linda Preston, Roger Rea, Linda Knight, Jan Woerner, Margery Lawson, Linda Stroud, Art Kimura, Carol Denicole, Richard Garner, and Henrietta Pane.

To expand interdisciplinary connections, additional materials were added to the original manuscript. Elaine Friebel created Appendix 2. Frank Watt Ireton created Activity 14 and contributed substantially to Activity 16. Joe Cain created Activities 12, 13, 15, 17, 18, 19, and the Resources List. Michelle Eugeni created Appendix 4. Information for the Dino Data Sheet in Activity 15 was compiled from 27 summary tables in David Weishampel, Peter Dodson, and Halszka Osmólska (eds.), *The Dinosauria* (Berkeley: University of California Press, 1990).

Gregg Sekscienski (NSTA) and Michelle Eugeni (NSTA) developed *Craters!-CD*, including concept design and locating suitable images. Leonardo Loureiro (MMedia, Hallandale, FL) graciously permitted use of *L-View*, and Wayne Rasbank (National Institutes of Health) graciously permitted use of *NIH Image*. All images on this CD-ROM are in the public domain and may be printed in multiple copies or otherwise duplicated for classroom use or teacher workshops without further permission.

Craters! was produced by NSTA Special Publications: Shirley Watt Ireton (managing editor), Gregg Sekscienski and Joe Cain (associate editors); Jennifer Hester, Glen Fullmer, and Ann Bustamante (editorial assistants); and Michelle Eugeni (program assistant). Joe Cain was NSTA's project editor for *Craters!*; Gregg Sekscienski produced the layout. Unless otherwise noted, illustrations were created by Ron Miller (Black Cat Studio, King George, VA), graphs were created by Gregg Sekscienski, and photographs appear courtesy of NASA. The book cover and inside design were created by Graves Fowler Associates. *Craters!* was printed by Automated Graphics.

PREFACE

Craters! has a short but dense history. In 1992, The Planetary Society, the National Science Teachers Association, and the National Aeronautics and Space Administration jointly agreed to create materials for the Earth and space sciences curriculum in NSTA's Scope, Sequence, and Coordination project (SS&C). In December 1992, with generous support from NASA, The Planetary Society hosted a two-day workshop that brought together 33 of the country's leading planetary scientists and science educators. Their charge was to build an outline for this curriculum and to set priorities for cooperative projects in the future. By workshop's end, this group had generated schemes for several possible SS&C modules in planetary science, and a consensus was reached about what planetary science information all high school students should have by the time they graduate.

Additional NASA funding supported development of a pilot SS&C module. That module—on cratering and the evolution of planetary landscapes, a topic originally suggested by Carl Sagan—was selected for its richness in interdisciplinary connections and its potential for applying SS&C principles. *Craters!* is the culmination of this pilot project, which has come a long way in a short time. William and Gayle Hartmann created a preliminary version of the module, which was reviewed for both content and pedagogy. Next, a team of SS&C teachers, working with Earth and planetary scientists, expanded the lessons to balance materials from the four disciplines— physics, chemistry, biology, and Earth and space science—especially *vis a vis* connections to extinctions at the Cretaceous-Tertiary boundary. A second round of reviews followed. To maximize teacher- and classroom-friendliness, another team of science teaching professionals and NSTA editors worked with the author to produce the final version of the activities included here. A number of activities have been presented in workshops and demonstrations at NSTA conventions.

Craters! provides a complete SS&C teaching module. First, craters are introduced as a generally observable phenomena. Second, by making craters themselves and by investigating the results, students gain close-up, hands-on experience with impact events and their products. Real crater examples from the Moon and elsewhere allow students to connect their laboratory experiences to phenomena space scientists investigate every day. Third, interdisciplinary connections are developed. Using cratering as a foundation, students launch investigations into topics traditionally found in separate disciplines. The mechanics of kinetic energy and energy transfer are studied while unraveling the connections between meteorites and craters. (It's like sifting through a crime scene from evidence left behind.) Studying impacts on Earth raises questions about the effects they have produced on the history of life and the history of Earth's surface. Was an impact involved in the mass extinction at the end of the Cretaceous Period? What about other mass extinctions in Earth's history? Is an impact likely in the near future? What do the Shoemaker-Levy 9 impacts on Jupiter tell us about possible impacts on Earth? These are just a few of the questions raised as part of the interdisciplinary study in *Craters!*

CD-ROM

A picture is worth a thousand words, the old saying goes. This certainly is true for those who study cratering. Many of the lessons created for this module have students examine images of craters from Earth, the Moon, or other planetary bodies. Within this book are many ready-to-photocopy images that fit these needs. To provide teachers with a way to produce the high-quality copies of the images they'll need (and with additional images for supplemental activities), *Craters!-CD* is included. NSTA developed this CD-ROM as a storage device for more than 200 images related to impacts and cratering. Appendix 4 provides simple instructions for using *Craters!-CD*. While *Craters!-CD* is not necessary for the activities, it increases the scope of this book and provides a jumping off point for further study. The CD-ROM icon (left) signals that images can be found on *Craters!-CD* to supplement that activity.

CURRICULUM MATRIX

Craters! is a multi-science, interdisciplinary book that introduces key concepts in many areas of science. Its 20 activities are designed to be presented either as a whole curriculum or in smaller, more focused units. To assist you, we have prepared a matrix that provides the subject and emphasis of each activity. Use the matrix as a quick reference for where each activity may fit into your lesson plans. You may find that cratering—the universe's building method—builds new interdisciplinary bridges for your students.

CURRICULUM MATRIX

ACTIVITY	SUBJECT AND EMPHASIS	BIOLOGY	CHEMISTRY	EARTH SCIENCE	ASTRONOMY	PHYSICS	MATH	ARTS	TECHNOLOGY
Discovering Craters									
1. You're Seeing Things	Optics and telescope construction				◆	◆	◆	◆	◆
2. Facing the Moon	Moon observations			◆	◆		◆	◆	◆
Making Craters									
3. Do It Yourself Cratering	Simulate crater formation			◆	◆	◆	◆		
4. Long Distance Detective	Geometric measurement of craters			◆	◆	◆	◆		◆
5. Anatomy of an Impact	Evaluate models and photographs			◆	◆	◆	◆	◆	◆
Impact Distributions									
6. Crater Count	Examine crater size distributions			◆	◆	◆	◆	◆	
7. Going to Pieces	Explain crater size distributions			◆	◆	◆	◆		
Kinetic Energy and Impacts									
8. Shaking Things Up!	Examine kinetic energy, energy conversion		◆		◆	◆	◆		◆
9. Just How Big is BIG?	Energy involved in bolide impacts			◆	◆	◆	◆		

ACTIVITY	SUBJECT AND EMPHASIS	BIOLOGY	CHEMISTRY	EARTH SCIENCE	ASTRONOMY	PHYSICS	MATH	ARTS	TECHNOLOGY
No Special Treatment: Impacts on Earth									
10. Craters, Craters, Everywhere	Study impacts on all planets			◆	◆				◆
11. A Hole in Arizona	Investigate Barringer Crater			◆	◆	◆	◆	◆	◆
12. There's No Place Like Home	Survey impacts across North America			◆	◆	◆	◆	◆	◆
Impacts and the History of Life									
13. That's Life	Survey the history of life and mass extinctions	◆		◆				◆	
14. Layer by Layer	Stratigraphy basics			◆		◆	◆	◆	◆
15. Discovering Dinosaur Diversity	Explore dinosaur extinctions	◆		◆			◆		
16. On the Path of Discovery	Investigate the K/T boundary	◆	◆	◆	◆	◆		◆	◆
17. Putting it to the Test	Test the K/T impact theory	◆	◆	◆	◆	◆		◆	◆
Impact Implications									
18. What are the Chances?	Probability of future impacts on Earth	◆	◆	◆	◆	◆	◆	◆	◆
19. Right on Target	Defend Earth against a future impact	◆		◆		◆	◆	◆	◆
20. One in a Million	Probability basics					◆	◆		◆

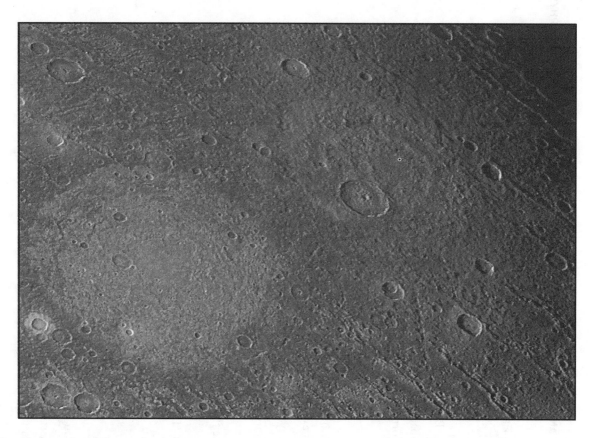

Close-up view of Ganymede,
a moon of Jupiter. On
Craters!-CD this is image
OtherM21.tif.

ACTIVITIES

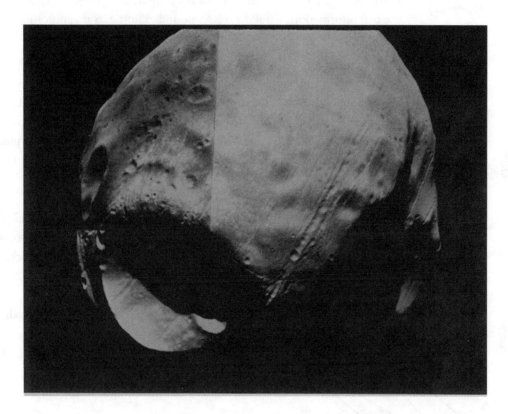

The Martian moon, Phobos, showing several enormous impact craters. On Craters!-CD this is image OtherM27.tif.

YOU'RE SEEING THINGS

MATERIALS

Each group (3 or 4 students) will need

◆ an assortment of lenses

◆ a pair of cardboard tubes

◆ sheet of blank, white paper

◆ marker or dark pen

◆ ruler or meter stick

◆ scissors

◆ tape

◆ clay or lens holder

OBJECTIVE

In this activity you will study some of the properties of lenses, such as focal length, and use that information to build a telescope and examine its magnification.

BACKGROUND

Telescopes use lenses or shaped mirrors to magnify images. These lenses and mirrors gather light and focus it into a small area. There are two basic types of telescopes: a *refracting* telescope uses only lenses, and a *reflecting* telescope uses shaped mirrors and a lens for an eyepiece (Figure 1). In this activity, you will explore how pieces of a refracting telescope function, then you will put these pieces together into a basic telescope.

The lenses used in basic refracting telescopes are convex in shape: thicker in the middle of the lens than at the edge. When light passes through the lens, it is bent. This bending is called *diffraction*. The thicker the glass, the more light is diffracted.

A telescope focuses light from distant objects so they seem larger and nearer. The larger the diameter of a lens, the more light it can gather. One measure of a telescope's performance is how much light it can gather.

Why are some of the world's best telescopes found on top of mountains? It's to get away from problems caused by the atmosphere. Earth's atmosphere absorbs certain wave-lengths of light, which means that some parts of natural light never reach the telescope. Also, Earth's atmosphere is constantly in motion. This blurs the viewing. Thus, the higher up a telescope is placed in the atmosphere, the less these problems affect observations. This is one reason NASA's Hubble Space Telescope, operating above most of Earth's atmosphere and in a microgravity environment, is such a success. There is essentially no atmosphere to obscure its data collection.

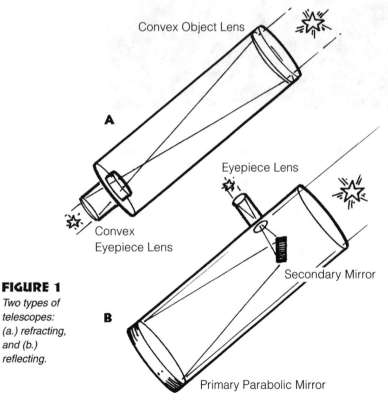

FIGURE 1
Two types of telescopes: (a.) refracting, and (b.) reflecting.

Convex Object Lens

A

Convex Eyepiece Lens

Eyepiece Lens

Secondary Mirror

B

Primary Parabolic Mirror

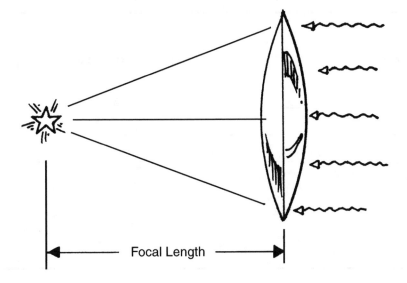

Focal Length

FIGURE 2

PROCEDURE

Studying Focal Length

1. Different lens shapes focus images at different distances. The distance from the lens (or mirror) to the point where the image comes into sharp focus is called the *focal length* (Figure 2). Using the lenses provided, you and your lab partners will take turns determining the focal lengths for the different lenses in your set. You will also build a simple refracting telescope.

2. Tape a piece of blank white paper on the wall opposite your classroom's window or another light source provided by your teacher. Turn out the lights and cover other windows.

TABLE 1

LENS NUMBER	FOCAL LENGTH (IN MM)	DIAMETER (IN MM)	F VALUE
1	_____	_____	_____
2	_____	_____	_____
3	_____	_____	_____
4	_____	_____	_____
5	_____	_____	_____
6	_____	_____	_____

TABLE 2

LENS NUMBER	F VALUE	OBSERVATIONS ABOUT IMAGE
1	_____	_____
2	_____	_____
3	_____	_____
4	_____	_____
5	_____	_____
6	_____	_____

3. Choose one lens from your assortment. Hold the lens by its sides and place it against the paper. Then slowly move the lens away from the paper. Have a lab partner watch the paper and signal you when the image of the light source comes into sharp focus. Have another lab partner carefully measure the distance between the lens and the focused image on the paper. This is the focal length for the lens. Record this value (in millimeters) in Table 1. Repeat this step for each of the lenses in your assortment.

4. Focal length is affected by many factors. Optical properties of the lens are crucial. Another factor is the absolute size of the lens. Because you are interested here in optical properties, cancel out the effect of lens size by dividing the focal length by the diameter of the lens. (This value is called the *f value* for a lens.) Determine the *f value* for each of the lenses you have, recording your results in Table 1. Make sure all your measurements are in millimeters before doing your division.

5. What properties of your lenses seem to determine their *f values*?

_____

_____

_____

6. Investigate the *kind of image* each of your lenses produces. Create an image of the light source as before using any of the lenses in your assortment. Describe the image to your lab partners and record your observations in Table 2. Compare this image with that shown in other lenses and with the original object. Note the size of the image, the image clarity, and whether the image is upside down or reversed.

7. Simple refracting telescopes use two lenses: an *objective* lens and an *eyepiece* lens. What lenses make the best parts for a telescope? Investigate this systematically using combinations of lenses from your set. Start by using the objective lens with the largest *f value* to the objective lens with the smallest *f value*.

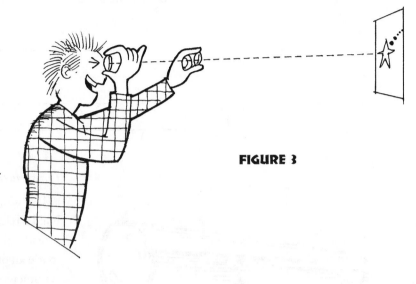

FIGURE 3

 ◆ Draw an asymmetrical image on the paper you taped to the wall (Figure 3).

 ◆ Choose two lenses from your assortment and record their *f values* in Table 3. Place one lens near your eye. This is the eyepiece lens.

 ◆ Align the second lens, the objective lens, with an image you created and move the objective lens toward or away from the eyepiece until the image is in focus (you may need to move across the room). In Table 3 record your description of the image you see—e.g., its size, quality, and orientation.

 ◆ Calculate the magnification (power) of your lens combinations by dividing the *f value* of the objective lens by the *f value* of the eyepiece. Record your results in Table 3. Magnification measures the number of times larger the image appears in the lens than the actual object appears without using the lens.

TABLE 3			
OBJECTIVE LENS F VALUE	**EYEPIECE LENS F VALUE**	**POWER**	**IMAGE QUALITY**
_____	_____	_____	_____
_____	_____	_____	_____
_____	_____	_____	_____
_____	_____	_____	_____
_____	_____	_____	_____
_____	_____	_____	_____

8. How does adding a second lens affect the size and quality of your original image?

_____

_____

_____

_____

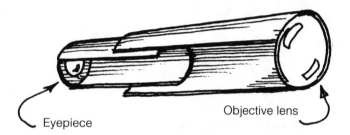

Eyepiece

Objective lens

Constructing a telescope

9. Use what you have discovered about your lenses to build a telescope. Select the combination of lenses that provides the *most* magnification. Your only constraint is to use an objective lens with an *f value* of 20 to 30 centimeters.

The next step in building a telescope is to build a sliding mechanism (for adjusting the focus). Cut one of your cardboard tubes along the entire length of the tube.

TABLE 4

OBJECT	ESTIMATED DISTANCE	POWER	IMAGE QUALITY
_____	_____	_____	_____
_____	_____	_____	_____
_____	_____	_____	_____
_____	_____	_____	_____
_____	_____	_____	_____
_____	_____	_____	_____
_____	_____	_____	_____
_____	_____	_____	_____

Overlap the cut so the tube will fit inside the other tube. Slide the cut tube partly into the other tube. Next, tape the lens you have chosen for the eyepiece to the end of the inner tube. Tape the objective lens to the other end of the outer tube. If the lenses do not fit inside the tubes snugly, wrap tape or cardboard around the outside of the lenses until they fit snugly in the tubes.

10. Focus your telescope on objects at different distances. You will probably need to move the tubes to change the distance between the eyepiece and objective—this adjusts the focus. Record the object and its estimated distance in Table 4. Record your observation about the telescope's performance and the adjustments you had to make. How are the images different from the actual objects you are observing?

QUESTIONS

1. What relationship did you find between lens shape and focal length (*f value*)?

2. Why do you think you were constrained in the focal length (*f value*) of the objective lens when you built your telescope?

3. What is the orientation of images projected onto cards by lenses?

4. Is the strongest power combination the *best* telescope? Explain why or why not.

5. What would you do to improve your telescope?

YOU'RE SEEING THINGS

MATERIALS

Each group (3 or 4 students) will need

◆ an assortment of lenses

◆ a pair of cardboard tubes

◆ blank sheet of white paper

◆ marker or dark pen

◆ ruler or meter stick

◆ scissors

◆ tape

◆ clay or lens holder

Caution!

Once students have constructed telescopes, you may choose to have them look at objects outside. If so, caution them to *never* look at the Sun through their telescopes. Immediate and permanent eye damage might result.

WHAT IS HAPPENING?

In this activity, students explore how the size and shape of a lens affects the images it produces. This will lay a foundation for understanding some of the fundamental principles of optics. It also will introduce the topics discussed in later activities. Students will be working with simple devices, and they should understand that important observations can come from even the most basic equipment. Lens-making, for instance, was relatively new when Galileo combined lenses together into his first telescopes. The observing devices he worked with were 10–30X, no better than the telescopes made by your students. Rather than always needing the most sophisticated tools, excellent research is built on the foundation of sharp observational skills.

IMPORTANT POINTS FOR STUDENTS TO UNDERSTAND

◆ Lenses come in all shapes and sizes. Different lens qualities (like shape) affect what a lens does.

◆ Every lens has a characteristic focal length—a measure of the distance between a lens and the image it forms of a distant light source.

◆ A telescope's usefulness—as measured by its magnification—depends on the lenses or mirrors used.

◆ A telescope's usefulness is limited by the materials it is made from and the environment in which it operates.

PREPARATION

Many suppliers offer inexpensive sets of lenses for student investigations. Ideally, each group's lens set should include at least one large lens (2 to 5 cm in diameter and a focal length of 20 to 50 cm) and several smaller lenses (1 to 2.5 cm in diameter and 1 to 5 cm in focal length). Label each lens. Labels are only used for identification purposes and should not reveal information about lens properties. Sequences such as A,B,C,D or 1,2,3,4 are sufficient. For the telescope, each cardboard tube should be 2 to 5 cm in diameter and up to 30 cm long. As an alternative to having students hold lenses, the can use clay or lens holders set on a table and focus the image on paper that is propped against a pile of books (see the book by Kipnis in the Resources List). Use cardboard tubes—cardboard sheets can be substituted and rolled into tubes by your students. You might also have commercial telescopes or binoculars available for comparison.

SUGGESTIONS FOR FURTHER STUDY

The eye contains a lens. How does it function? How does the eye's lens adjust so that a person can focus on objects at different distances? Eyeglasses use lenses, too. Why would you want to add a lens to the lens your eye already has? What kinds of vision differences are they intended to change? What is the difference between nearsighted and farsighted vision? What kinds of lenses are used to adjust for each of these kinds of vision abilities? (Perhaps an eye doctor can visit your classroom to talk about how eyes work and how to take good care of them.)

At their most basic level, cameras are simple combinations of lenses that feed light into a box containing film. Camera lenses vary widely. Students can investigate the different properties of those lenses.

NASA's Hubble Space Telescope operates without danger of atmospheric interference and in a microgravity environment. *Craters!-CD* contains images made from Earth-based telescopes (e.g., file: Othert03.tif) and images of the same objects taken with the Hubble telescope (e.g., file: Othert06.tif). Compare the quality of these images. What accounts for the differences? What has the Hubble telescope discovered that astronomers did not know before? What flaws were found in the Hubble telescope after it was first launched, and how were these problems corrected? Who runs this device, and how can you get information about what it discovers?

CD-ROM

Investigate devices such as radio telescopes, designed to collect information from wavelengths beyond the visible spectrum. Not all telescopes use visible light.

CONNECTIONS

Students can investigate the history of telescopes. These devices came into wide use first in the early 1600s, when their appearance caused a sensation. The largest early market for telescopes was not astronomy. Their nickname, "spyglass," says a lot about their most popular early use. Soldiers and sailors used spyglasses beginning before 1600. Spyglasses were also used by merchants in ports. Merchants who could see incoming ships first had the most time to position their buyers at the docks and thus gain a commercial advantage. The magnification of those devices was rather low, 3 to 4 times. Galileo Galilei (1564–1642) was the first person to turn the telescope toward the sky and to report systematically on what he saw. His report, *The Sidereal Messenger* (1610), has been translated into English and can be read by high school-level students. (Galileo's work is discussed in Activity 2.)

Microscopes are similar to telescopes. Students can investigate these similarities—and differences. What is the difference between simple and compound microscopes? This may lead students to investigate general principles of optics. Several solid curriculum units in optics are listed in the Resources List.

ANSWERS TO QUESTIONS FOR STUDENTS

1. Lenses that are thicker in the center have shorter focal lengths.

2. If the focal length is too long it becomes difficult to build a steady instrument.

3. Simple lenses all invert images.

4. Not always; it depends on the application. For instance, a higher power telescope has a smaller field of view. If you want to survey an area, the highest power telescope might not be the best choice. Also, the higher the power, the less bright the image looks in a given telescope with a given objective lens.

5. Possible answers: Design a sturdy mounting system to hold it steady. Design a better focusing system to allow finer focus.

FACING THE MOON

OBJECTIVE

In this activity you will make direct observations of the Moon and begin to examine its geology.

BACKGROUND

The Moon is so familiar to us that we notice it only on rare occasions—on bright, moonlit nights or when dust in Earth's atmosphere causes it to appear in a different color. But when was the last time you really looked closely at the Moon? What do you remember about its surface?

In this activity, you will use a telescope or other magnifying device to make observations of the Moon and its surface. In doing so, you're part of a grand scientific tradition going back in time to the famous Italian scientist, Galileo Galilei (1564–1642). Galileo experimented with lenses, just as you did in Activity 1. In 1609, Galileo turned his 30X telescope toward the Moon. Galileo may not have been the first to look at the moon with this new combination of lenses, but he was the first to widely report what he saw. Galileo's report caused a sensation when it was published because it was the first proof that other worlds had geological features like those found on Earth. Maybe what you'll see will surprise you, too.

MATERIALS

- telescope or binoculars
- paper and pencils for sketches

PROCEDURE

1. Your assignment is to make a set of observations of the Moon. Report your findings in Data Sheet 1.

2. On the reverse side of Data Sheet 1 or on a separate piece of paper, create a page-sized sketch of the Moon, including as many of the details as you can see. On your drawing, label prominent surface features and examples of items you mentioned on Data Sheet 1.

3. Compare your observations with those of other members of your group.

Galileo Galilei (1564–1642) at age 60.

QUESTIONS/CONCLUSIONS

1. What are the most noticeable features on the Moon's surface?

2. Based on your observations of the Moon and photographs you have seen of the Earth from space, how does the Moon's surface vary from the Earth's? (Provide at least three comparisons.)

3. How would you explain these differences?

4. When Galileo observed the Moon through his telescope in 1609, many expected him to see a smooth, uniform surface. If you were Galileo, what would you be telling your colleagues? Write a short newspaper article or letter to a friend telling of your discoveries. How would you describe what you learned about the Moon's surface?

DIRECT OBSERVATIONS OF THE MOON

Name: _____

Date: _____

Time: _____

Viewing device used: _____

Magnification: _____

Observing conditions: _____

_____

Describe features of the Moon's surface as best you can.

For example: Are there color differences on the surface or obvious terrain features? Do you see evidence of water (e.g., blue oceans or white ice at the poles)? Are some features rougher than others? Are some regions older than others? How can you tell?

_____

_____

_____

_____

_____

_____

_____

_____

_____

_____

FACING THE MOON

MATERIALS

- telescope or binoculars
- paper and pencils for sketches

Caution

Strongly warn students about the hazards of using magnifying devices to view the Sun. This should *never* be done. Immediate and permanent eye damage might result.

CD-ROM

WHAT IS HAPPENING?

Making direct and accurate observations is a crucial skill in science. These skills can be developed effectively by asking students to observe objects with which they are familiar. The Moon is an obvious choice for developing observation skills: it is an object frequently seen but rarely examined in detail.

Studying the Moon firsthand also provides an introduction to cratering. The Moon's surface is covered with craters of many sizes. From their Earth observatories, students will be able to see some of the largest of these craters. (Those using telescopes with higher magnification will be able to see more of the Moon's features.) The Moon is hardly the *only* planetary body with craters. In fact, most solid bodies in the solar system are heavily cratered. Craters are the solar system's most common landscape feature! However, the Moon probably is the only planetary body (other than Earth) that your students have *seen* firsthand.

Timing is essential for this activity. Best results are obtained near first quarter moon, which appears conveniently in the evening sky. At full moon, craters are difficult to see because the angle of solar lighting produces no shadows. It can also be painfully bright to look at the full moon through a telescope or binoculars. Observations of the Moon can be completed at night as homework. Binoculars and simple commercial telescopes are entirely adequate for this activity, as is the telescope assembled in the previous activity. Students with similar equipment at home can work in teams. Lunar observations using class-made telescopes also can be completed during the day, as the moon is observable in the day during certain parts of its cycle. Many calendars or farmer's almanacs give the phases of the moon. You may want to consult a local observatory (most state universities have these facilities) or a local astronomer about the best time to make lunar observations. If you prefer not to assign this project as homework or use daytime observations, images of the Moon are provided here (Figures 1, 2, and 5). On *Craters!-CD*, these are files: Moon214.tif (crescent phase), Moon215.tif (full), and Moon608.tif (half).

There are four primary features students may observe about the Moon in this activity: light areas, dark areas, craters, and rays extending out from the craters. The light areas are highlands, or mountains. Dark areas, once thought to be ancient oceans, are actually lava flows. Craters are obvious features; careful examination may reveal overlapping craters, indicating that one bolide (any falling body, such as a comet or meteorite) landed on a crater left by an earlier impact. More difficult to see are rays, which are streamers of bright dust extending out from the craters. Rays are best seen under high lighting, near the time of full moon.

IMPORTANT POINTS FOR STUDENTS TO UNDERSTAND

◆ Direct observation takes time, but it provides an important way to gain new information.

◆ The Moon's surface is covered with craters of many sizes, as well as mountains and plains.

◆ The Moon is not the only planetary body with craters.

PREPARATION

Telescopes or binoculars that are 10–30X are entirely adequate for this activity. (Galileo's telescopes were no better.) Holding these magnifying devices in a fixed position—e.g., on a tripod or table—steadies the telescope and improves the viewing.

Because the intention of this activity is to generate fresh observations, be sure to remove any images of the Moon that might be posted around your classroom. Tell your students that they are assuming the role of Galileo, as the first person to make systematic observations of the Moon using a telescope. At the conclusion of this activity, you may choose to circulate photographs or maps of the Moon's surface made at higher magnification. This will help your students develop a better appreciation for what they saw (and didn't see!).

Remember, simple telescopes like the ones constructed in Activity 1 might show the Moon upside down. Students will need to make appropriate adjustments. Binoculars will not require such corrections. Encourage students to double-check the orientation of the image their equipment produces by focusing on a nearby object and noting how it appears relative to its orientation.

FIGURE 1
Moon in crescent phase. On Craters!-CD this is file Moon214.tif.

FIGURE 2

Half Moon. On Craters!-CD this is file Moon608.tif. (Note: This image has been rotated 90° counterclockwise.)

SUGGESTIONS FOR FURTHER STUDY

Present a map of the Moon for students to study after they've completed their observations. (The Resources List includes several sources for maps, globes, and film footage pertaining to the Moon.) Can students locate the features they just observed?

Students can investigate the Moon landings of the Apollo missions. Several television documentaries, many books and articles, and several biographies are available as resources. To get a sense of what these landings meant to Americans, students might locate newspapers and popular magazines from the time. (The first *Apollo* landing on the Moon occurred on July 20–21, 1969.) The United States and the Soviet Union have also launched robotic spacecraft to the Moon. What have we learned from these projects about the Moon, about the history of our solar system, and about the potential for living on other planets?

CONNECTIONS

By observing the Moon and reporting their results, students are replicating what Galileo did in the early 1600s. Students can learn more about Galileo's work by reading translations of his famous 1610 book, *The Sidereal Messenger*. This book was written for a general audience and can be read by high school-level science students. Many biographies of Galileo are available as well.

Students may want to place Galileo's studies within the context of his time. Galileo's telescope work was important, not only because he was the first to systematically observe the Moon with a telescope, but also because he widely reported what he saw. Appreciating the larger significance of his work requires going back in time more than two millennia.

Science in ancient Greece was grounded more in philosophy than in observation. Aristotle (384–322 BCE) was a philosopher of nature, and his theories of the universe dominated thinking about nature for thousands of years. Aristotle reasoned along the following lines: (1) the heavens are perfect and eternal, (2) so everything in the heavens also must be perfect and eternal; (3) the only perfect solid is a perfectly smooth sphere, (4) so all heavenly bodies (which are themselves perfect) *must be* perfectly smooth spheres.

FIGURE 3

One of the watercolors Galileo made of the Moon based on observations through his telescope. From The Sidereal Messenger, 1610. Can you match the surfaces drawn by Galileo with those in the photograph in Figure 2? On Craters!-CD this is file Galileo1.tif.

When supporters of Aristotle's view described the Moon, they talked about it being a perfectly smooth sphere—it was, after all, a heavenly body. Anyone saying otherwise had to contend with these supporters and Aristotle's powerful reputation. They also had to explain how Aristotle could have gotten this point wrong when he seemed to make good sense in so many other areas.

Galileo was a philosopher of nature living at the end of the Renaissance. He was one of a group of people placing more emphasis on experience and observation and less on philosophy. He also was highly critical of Aristotle's influence over the study of nature. Galileo's observations of the Moon were part of a larger, more fundamental attack against Aristotle's system. In his 1610 book, *The Sidereal Messenger*, Galileo launched the first round of his attack on Aristotle by attacking what followers of Aristotle said about the Moon. From what he saw, Galileo believed the Moon was far from a perfectly smooth sphere. The paintings of the Moon he produced for that book (shown in Figures 3 and 4, and on *Craters!-CD*—these are files: Galileo1.tif and Galileo2.tif) were intended to provide dramatic evidence that it had a rough surface. By implication, Galileo was arguing that Aristotle's theories of nature were wrong. After all, how could the Moon—a heavenly body—not be perfect? Publishing this work was the first of many attacks on Aristotle that Galileo produced during his life. (The Resources List provides sources on Galileo's life and work.)

CD-ROM

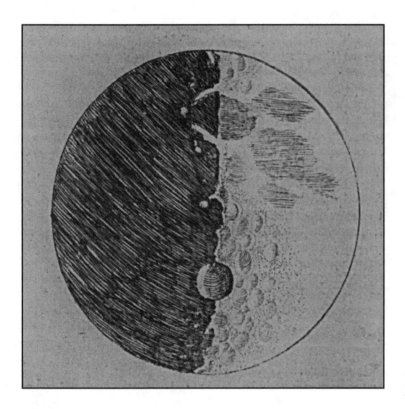

FIGURE 4

Another watercolor Galileo made of the Moon using his telescope. From The Sidereal Messenger, 1610. Can you match the surfaces drawn by Galileo with those in the photograph in Figure 5? On Craters!-CD this is file Galileo2.tif.

Soon after Galileo published *The Sidereal Messenger*, astronomers placed heavy emphasis on telescopes and the new observations this device made possible. Johannes Hevelius was a pioneer in this effort. By the 1640s, he had built in Danzig (now in Poland) a 150-foot-long telescope and used it to produce an extraordinary atlas of the Moon (in his 1647 book *Selenographia*). Students wanting to explore the history of studies of the Moon should closely examine Hevelius' work. (In other books, Hevelius reported observations on comets and other planets.) Hevelius played an important role in establishing the term "seas" for the flat, dark areas on the Moon—he wrote in Latin and used the words "mare" (MAH-ray, singular) and "maria" (MAR-ee-ah, plural). In addition, Hevelius' friend, Giovanni Riccioli, began the practice of naming lunar features after great scientists and prominent people in history, a practice that continues today. (See the book, *Landmarks of Science*, in the Resources List.) How many names can your students recognize on a lunar map?

ANSWERS TO QUESTIONS FOR STUDENTS

1. Noticeable features include light areas (highlands, or mountains), dark areas (maria, or dark plains), craters, and rays extending out from the craters.

2. Answers will vary, but encourage detailed observations. For example, the Moon has more craters, it is not as colorful, it has no clouds.

3. The Moon has no atmosphere, therefore there are no clouds or water.

4. Answers will vary.

FIGURE 5

Full Moon. Compare this image with Figure 4. On Craters!-CD this is file Moon215.tif.

DO IT YOURSELF CRATERING

MATERIALS

Each group will need:

- bag of simulated planetary bedrock (light colored)
- cup of simulated planetary surface (dark colored)
- broad, shallow box, such as a pizza box or lid from a paper box
- sieve or large spoon
- simulated bolides (labeled and of assorted masses)
- drop cloth or floor cover
- ruler
- leveling device
- chair or step ladder
- string (2 meters long), weight on the end
- balance

OBJECTIVE

To observe crater formation and to identify distinctive features of impact sites.

BACKGROUND

What does a crater look like? What happens to a planet's surface during an impact? In this activity, you will investigate these questions using a model planet surface.

PROCEDURE

Preparing Your Planetary Surface

1. Clear a working area by removing desks, chairs, and other objects. Open your drop cloth and lay it down smoothly on the ground.

2. Place the box in the center of your workspace. Fill this container with simulated planetary bedrock up to several millimeters below the rim. Lightly pack it, then smooth the surface with your leveling device.

3. Using a sieve or large spoon, sprinkle over your bedrock a thin layer of simulated planetary surface. Use the leveling device to create a smooth surface, but *be careful not to mix* the two layers.

DATA BOX 1

BOLIDE #	MASS (G)	CRATER DIAMETER (MM)	OTHER OBSERVATIONS
——	——	——	————————————————
——	——	——	————————————————
——	——	——	————————————————
——	——	——	————————————————
——	——	——	————————————————
——	——	——	————————————————

Simulating A Bolide Impact

4. Move a chair or stepladder next to your test surface. (You'll want to be able to look down on your test surface.)

5. Have one member of your group climb on the chair—*be careful to keep balanced!* This person will be the bolide dropper. (A bolide is any falling body, such as a comet or meteorite.) A second member of your group should hold the measuring string vertically next to the test surface and position the bolide dropper's hand at 2 meters above the test surface.

6. Give a bolide to the dropper. Work systematically starting with the largest bolide you have. When repeating this experiment use progressively smaller test bolides. Position other members of your group along the drop cloth's edge so that they can observe the impact from a safe distance.

7. With the experiment arranged so that the bolide will fall from a height of 2 meters and hit somewhere on the test surface, have the dropper release the bolide.

DATA BOX 2

_____

_____

_____

_____

_____

_____

8. Discuss what each member of your group observed during the impact, and record these observations on Data Box 1. *Without touching anything on your test surface*, examine the changes resulting from your simulated impact. Describe the crater. Has there been mixing of the different layers? Was debris scattered uniformly in all directions? Where did the debris come from? How large is the hole created by the bolide?

9. Repeat this experiment using different bolides. You do not need to repair your planetary surface between impacts. Continue to record your observations and comparisons in Data Box 1.

10. When you have completed your testing of different bolides, make some comparisons. Is there a connection between features of the impact site and the mass of the bolide? Describe your comparisons in Data Box 2.

11. The difference between this model and real bolides is that real bolides fall at a much higher velocity. The objects you are dropping move at velocities measured in *meters* per second. Real bolides move at velocities measured in *kilometers* per second. Repair your planetary surface, climb up on the chair, have people stand back, and throw one of your bolides onto the test surface. Examine the resulting crater. Does it look any different from the ones you have been making? In what way?

DATA BOX 3

_____

_____

_____

_____

_____

_____

12. Using a movable lamp to represent the Sun, illuminate one or more craters first at a low angle from the side (representing dawn light) then at higher angles, and finally from above (noon). Comment on how shadows change. Are shadows more visible at low light or high light? Which light reveals rough areas that might be dangerous during a landing? Are different features prominent at high light?

Modeling an Old Planetary Surface

13. On your test surface, simulate the effects of many impacts by repeatedly dropping bolides of different masses on the surface many times. In no particular order, drop large bolides one dozen times; drop medium mass bolides two dozen times; and drop small mass bolides four dozen times. Stop several times during this procedure to observe the test surface and the mixing of your different layers. Notice how this mixture of sizes produces features more like the Moon's. Is there a point at which your surface has so many craters that new ones don't seem to affect its surface very much? Record your observations in Data Box 3.

QUESTIONS/CONCLUSIONS

1. In this experiment, you created a model to simulate a real phenomenon. Models are extremely useful for experimentation, but models are never perfect representations of natural phenomena. Name three ways this model is different from real cases of bolide impacts. How could you create a more realistic model?

2. Planetary scientists study impact sites to learn more about bolides, especially how many exist of different sizes and how often they collide with planetary bodies. What kind of information would you be able to extract from the data you created in this experiment?

DO IT YOURSELF CRATERING

MATERIALS

Each group will need:

- bag of simulated planetary bedrock (light colored)

  Choices for this include mortar powder, white flour, or grout.

- cup of simulated planetary surface (dark colored)

  Choices for this include dark-colored grout, yellow cornmeal, or chocolate powder.

- broad, shallow box, such as a pizza box or lid from a paper box

- sieve or large spoon

- simulated bolides (labeled and of assorted masses)

- drop cloth or floor cover

- ruler

- leveling device

- chair or stepladder

- string (2 meters long) with a weight on the end

- balance

WHAT IS HAPPENING?

This activity develops two skill sets. First, students learn about craters and crater formation, both in the laboratory and in nature. Second, they use models for building inferences about processes beyond their direct experience.

On every solid-surface planetary body explored so far, there is evidence of bolide impacts. Some impacts were large, others were small. All occurred according to a basic series of physical principles. An extensive background to cratering is provided in Appendix 1.

Surfaces exposed to cratering for a long time show two characteristics. First, as craters become more numerous, the original surface layers will be mixed. Sometimes called *gardening*, this mixing occurs on surfaces such as the Moon's and is simulated in the model by the mixing of bedrock and surface layers. This mixing tends to make a surface more uniform in color than in areas where distinct, fresh, unmixed geologic rock units are exposed. The longer the planetary body is exposed to impacts, the more these different layers will be mixed. Second, once a surface becomes completely covered with craters, it is said to be *saturated*. Only the oldest surfaces in our solar system appear to be saturated; however, once a surface becomes saturated, new impacts are difficult to identify. This is because new craters tend to obliterate older craters. As a result, the total number of craters remains roughly the same.

Only geologically inactive planetary bodies ever have a chance to become saturated with craters. If a planetary body is geologically active, as Earth is, craters are erased as rifting, erosion, volcanic eruptions, and other events modify the surface (see Activity 12). Detection of geologic events on other planets, such as the lava flows seen on the surface of Venus by the Magellan satellite, can be roughly dated by their interaction with existing craters.

IMPORTANT POINTS FOR STUDENTS TO UNDERSTAND

♦ Impact craters have distinguishing characteristics that make them different from volcanic craters.

♦ Studies of craters can provide considerable information about the history of the solar system.

♦ Craters are found on all solid-surface bodies in the solar system.

♦ Younger, more geologically active surfaces have fewer craters.

PREPARATION

You may choose to run this activity inside or outside. Containers can be a pizza box, or baking pan, or a wooden box at least 30 cm in diameter and 2 cm deep. Larger (but not deeper) containers are preferable.

For the simulated bedrock, any light-colored, fine-grained material will work: sifted dirt or builder's sand work adequately, but flour, grout, or mortar powder work best. For the simulated surface, any fine-grained powder of a darker color—e.g., gray tile grout or corn meal—should be used. As a result of contrasting colors in the layers, light colored ejecta from the "bedrock" can be easily distinguished from the darker surface layer. Leveling devices can be any rigid object with a straight edge—e.g., a ruler, index card, piece of wood—that students can use to run over the surface of the layers to create a smooth test surface.

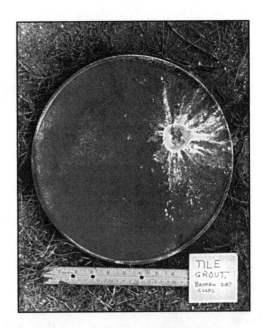

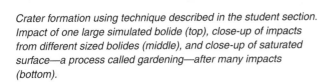

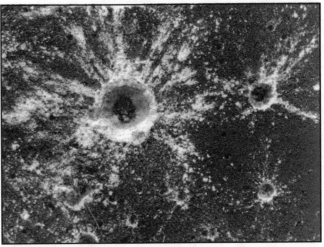

Crater formation using technique described in the student section. Impact of one large simulated bolide (top), close-up of impacts from different sized bolides (middle), and close-up of saturated surface—a process called gardening—after many impacts (bottom).

For the simulated bolides, marbles or other spheres such as steel shot, ball bearings, or golf balls work well. In nature, bolides travel at such high velocities that they usually disintegrate on impact. To make this activity more realistic, hand-packed clods of dry dirt can be used as well. If created properly—this requires practice—clods will leave a crater and disintegrate at the same time. Because projectiles will create a splash of debris, *require the use of safety goggles.* You may wish to have students find the mass of their bolides before use to allow comparison between mass and crater size. (This will be investigated in Activity 9.) The important point of this activity is to examine crater formation.

SUGGESTIONS FOR FURTHER STUDY

The simulated bolides that students create for this activity fall at a velocity considerably slower than do bolides in nature. Students can vary the velocities of their bolides by throwing rather than dropping them onto the test surface. Higher velocities produce better results; however, *increased supervision and safety measures will be required* if students are asked to throw objects in the classroom. Better approaches would be to drop the test bolides from different heights or perform higher velocity tests as a teacher-led demonstration.

Shoemaker-Levy 9 produced multiple impacts on Jupiter because the original object broke into fragments before falling onto Jupiter's surface. If students use dirt clods at some point in their investigation, they might create a clod that is 10 centimeters in diameter and then break it into fragments of different and irregular sizes. Studying the resulting impacts will provide a launching point for investigating Shoemaker-Levy 9 (see Appendix 2).

CONNECTIONS

Bolide impacts can be compared with other kinds of falling bodies. Compare this student activity to a raindrop hitting a pond surface. High speed films show this kind of event in slow motion. Such films are commercially available, or your students might be challenged to create a similar record using still photography or a video camera.

Impacts are a kind of collision. The physics of colliding bodies is well known and students can investigate both basic principles and additional examples of collision phenomena (see Activities 8 and 9).

Science is not the only human activity that notices bolide events. Students can investigate the use of meteorite and comet imagery in poetry or literature. Halley's Comet, for example, is shown in the Bayeux tapestry. Students also might compare how bolides are recorded and studied in non-Western cultures and in historical times. For example, the sacred stone in the Islamic shrine at Mecca is believed to be a meteorite. Meteorites were often preserved in medieval Christian churches in Europe. Materials in the Resources List, such as Ursala Marvin's paper, provide good starting points for such investigations.

ANSWERS TO QUESTIONS FOR STUDENTS

1. Answers will vary with the model created. The main differences are those of scale: speed of impact, size of bolide, structure of planetary surface. You may extend the studies by constructing a deeper, multilayer surface that can be excavated in cross-section to look at subsurface impact results. Mixing grated paraffin with sand layers, then baking the "impact" before excavation is one method. Adult supervision needed. In general, the main value of laboratory impact craters is to simulate certain features, such as throw-out of ejected material, buildup of rims, overlap, etc.

2. Lunar crater numbers plotted *versus* size, show something of the size distribution of the bolides, which shed light on their origin, as you'll see in Activities 6 and 7.

Basic features of impact craters.

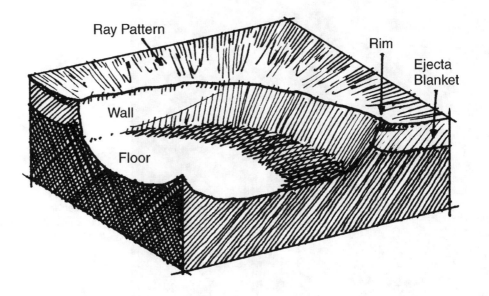

Ray Pattern

Rim

Ejecta Blanket

Wall

Floor

LONG DISTANCE DETECTIVE

MATERIALS

Each group will need

- crater sample
- modeling clay
- cardboard base
- ruler
- lamp or spotlight
- protractor
- calculator with tangent function or tangent tables

OBJECTIVE

To develop techniques for measuring topographic features at a distance.

BACKGROUND

Here's the problem: you're a planetary scientist working for NASA's new Moon explorer project, in which a robot vehicle will land on the Moon's surface to collect information about possible mineral deposits. You're part of a team charged with finding a location for the explorer to land. This is an important assignment. If the explorer lands in a crater that is unsuitable, it won't be able to climb out and do any exploring. If your explorer got stuck, you'd have a *very* expensive and embarrassing mistake to explain.

Geologists think the area shown in Figure 1 is a good place to look for valuable minerals. Mission planners want to know whether or not it's a safe place to land the explorer. Your task is to prepare a report for them about the depth of large craters in the area. In particular, they want to know about the depth of craters labeled A, B, and C. (To give you a sense of scale, crater A is about 56 km wide.)

Moon 405.tif

FIGURE 1

Potential landing site for new Moon explorer. You've been asked to decide whether or not this location is a good choice.

PROCEDURE

Part I—Testing Your Idea

1. Discuss possible methods for measuring crater depths with members of your group. Is there a solution that immediately comes to mind? Describe your solution in your Plan of Action box.
2. Have a member of your group collect the tray of materials.

PLAN OF ACTION

How would you remotely determine crater depth?

_____

_____

_____

_____

_____

---

3. Place the crater example in front of your group. Examine it closely to identify its key features.
4. Using modeling clay, construct an accurate crater model on your cardboard base. Your model should be at least several centimeters deep and should replicate as many features from your sample crater as possible. Also compare what you build with photographs of craters.
5. Test your solution for measuring crater depths using your model. How well does it work? Evaluate your plan in the Evaluation box.
6. There are several ways to solve the problem you've been assigned. After the evaluation of the technique you developed is complete, obtain from your teacher the procedure for Part II of this activity.

EVALUATION

How well did your plan work?

_____

_____

_____

_____

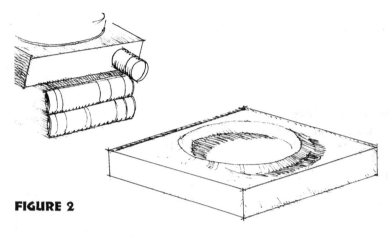

FIGURE 2

PROCEDURE

Part II—A Technique for Remote Investigation

One technique to solve the problem you've been assigned involves simple geometry. After the evaluation of the technique you developed is complete, try this approach.

7. Place your model crater at the center of your workspace. Set a lamp nearby, arranging it at an angle between 5 and 15 degrees off the table (as shown in Figure 2) so that a shadow will be created by your crater.

8. The crater's depth can be determined if you know the length of the shadow it casts and the angle of the incoming light source (Figure 3). Use the following mathematical relationship:

depth of crater (d) = [length of shadow (L)] multiplied by [tangent of angle of incoming light (α)]

FIGURE 3

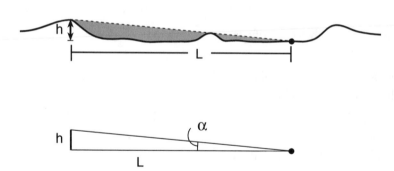

For example: if the angle of incoming light is 15 degrees and the measured shadow length is 18 cm, the crater depth will be

$$
\begin{aligned}
d &= L \cdot \tan(\alpha) \\
\text{depth} &= 18\ \text{cm} \cdot \tan(15\ \text{degrees}) \\
\text{depth} &= 4.8\ \text{cm}
\end{aligned}
$$

(This can be checked against measurements using your clay model.)

9. Measure the length of the shadow cast by *your* model crater. Record your result in Data Table 1.

10. Measure the angle of your light source.

11. Follow the formula in Step 8 to determine your model crater's depth. Record your determination in Data Table 1.

12. Repeat this experiment using different angles for the incoming light. Record your measurements in Data Table 1.

13. Verify your calculations by directly measuring the depth of your model crater. How do the results compare?

DATA TABLE 1

	Trial 1	Trial 2	Trial 3
Length of Shadow Cast	____	____	____
Angle of Incoming Light	____	____	____
Calculation of Crater Depth	____	____	____
Directly Measured Depth (top of rim to floor)	____	____	____

PROCEDURE

Part III—Advice for the Moon Exploration Project

14. Now that you have a technique for remotely determining crater depth, you are ready to calculate the depth of craters in the possible landing site for the new Moon explorer (Figure 1). Obtain from your teacher a full page image of the site (Figure 4). This image will include data about scale and the angle of incoming light. Calculate crater depth according to the method described in Part II of this Procedure, recording your results in Data Table 2. (Remember to change the *scale* of your measurement by converting your answer to kilometers.)

DATA TABLE 2

	Crater A	Crater B	Crater C
Diameter of Crater	____	____	____
Length of Shadow Cast	____	____	____
Angle of Incoming Light	____	____	____
Calculation of Crater Depth (top of rim to floor)	____	____	____

QUESTIONS/CONCLUSIONS

1. Summarize the results of your investigations:

Craters:	A	B	C
Calculation of Crater Depth:	_____	_____	_____

2. Crater depth is not the only variable that might make it difficult for the new Moon explorer to climb out of a crater. What other problems could there be? How could you collect information about these hazards?

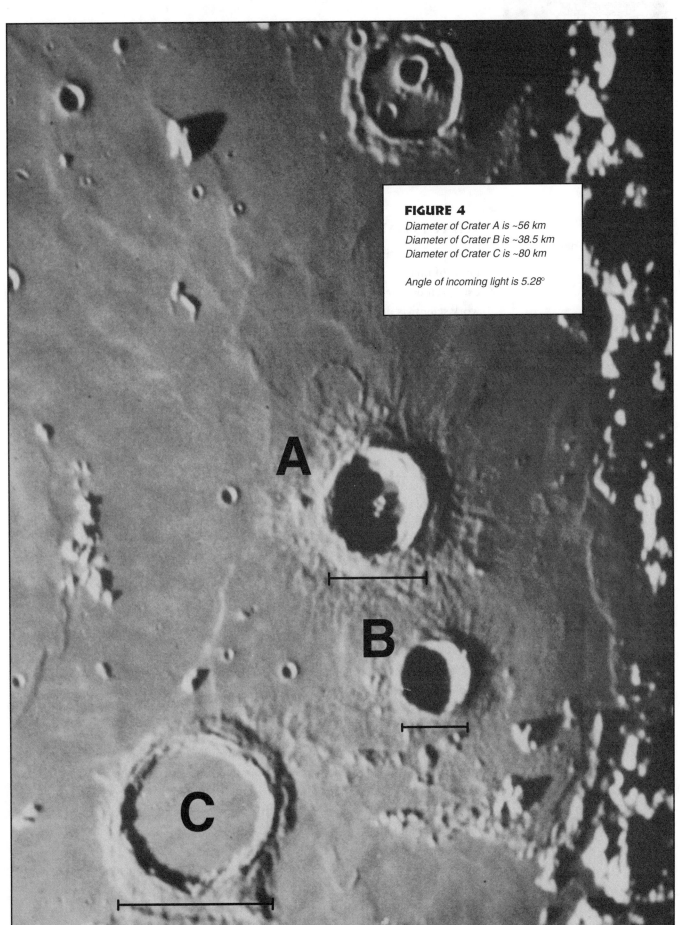

FIGURE 4
Diameter of Crater A is ~56 km
Diameter of Crater B is ~38.5 km
Diameter of Crater C is ~80 km

Angle of incoming light is 5.28°

A

B

C

Moon 405.tif

LONG DISTANCE DETECTIVE

MATERIALS

Each group will need

- crater sample
- modeling clay
- cardboard base
- ruler
- lamp or spotlight
- protractor
- calculator with tangent function or tangent table

WHAT IS HAPPENING?

Planetary scientists collect most of their information from photographs and other kinds of images created by remote means. Finding out how to extract information using remote techniques—such as telescopes—is an important part of the detective work scientists do. In fact, nearly all that we know about planetary and other solar bodies comes from what we can see and infer from information collected by remote means.

How can remote instruments provide so much information? In this activity, students learn some of the techniques planetary scientists use to draw information from the data their instruments collect. They also learn how models are used to double check the findings scientists make from these remote techniques.

Factors other than depth will determine whether a robot can climb out of a crater: steepness of the crater rim, whether the surface is covered by small or large blocks of rubble, and so on. Unfortunately, better photographic data is necessary before these subjects can be addressed.

IMPORTANT POINTS FOR STUDENTS TO UNDERSTAND

- Data collection often is done remotely.
- Considerable information can be extracted from relatively small amounts of data—but this requires ingenuity.
- Geometry has important applications in planetary sciences and in interpreting space photos or aerial photos of Earth.

PREPARATION

Before you begin this lesson, you need to create a simulated crater for each group to model. It is possible for several groups or a whole class to share one sample crater. These samples can be created using a streamlined version of the procedure described in Activity 3. Having students work with soft modeling clay will allow you to recycle the clay for additional classes.

This procedure is divided into three parts for a reason. First, students are given an opportunity for team discovery in solving the problem at hand. Because the second part of the procedure contains one solution to that task, distributing this part at the start will ruin that process. Give students some time to develop their own solutions (approximately 15 minutes). Students should be familiar with the mathematical concept of tangent. You might review this while Part II is underway. Be sure to have a calculator with a tangent function handy. An alternative is to have tables of tangent values ready to distribute.

CD-ROM

Figure 4 can be made available to students either by photocopying the image presented on page 33 or by printing the file of this image from *Craters!-CD*. The image on the CD-ROM (file name: Moon405.tif) is an unlabeled version of Figure 4. You will need to present the numerical information separately. In addition, you may choose to use other images. *Craters!-CD* contains two additional images where the angle of incoming light is known: Moon404.tif and Other617.tif (Gaspra). See Figures 5 and 6. Data about the angle of incoming light and crater diameter can be found in the text descriptions.

SUGGESTIONS FOR FURTHER STUDY

Challenge students to develop their solutions from Part I further. Have space scientists actually used such a technique in their work? How would your students go about testing their solution using the Moon? The technique students learn in Part II of this activity is analogous to one used by foresters to measure the height of trees and by surveyors to measure the height of mountains. Challenge students to explore these applications.

FIGURES 5 AND 6

Additional images useful for this activity: Moon404.tif (our Moon) and Other617.tif (Gaspra). Specific information about each image can be found on Craters!-CD.

Now that students know how to determine crater depth, they can compare depth to width ratios for different craters on the same and for craters on different planetary bodies. Is there a consistent ratio?

CONNECTIONS

Scientists use many techniques to investigate phenomena in locations too remote to visit easily. Such locations include other planets, deep space, the bottom of the ocean, and Earth's interior. Investigation of objects that cannot be studied directly is common to many fields of science—from the study of crystal structure to reveal molecular arrangement of molecules to the analysis of brain activity during human speech. Encourage students to examine these types of activities and the techniques used for remote investigation.

Students can investigate the use of photographic analysis in fields such as history, forensics, and anthropology.

ANSWERS TO QUESTIONS FOR STUDENTS

1. Students should obtain the results shown in the key to Data Table 2.
   Hint: tan(5.28°) is ~0.0924. Be sure to allow for variation in measurements and encourage attention to the number of significant digits. Note also that the angle of illumination cited, 5.28°, is an approximation; it actually varies slightly at different points in the picture and is a bit higher for Crater C. Using sophisticated techniques, astronomers have calculated the crater depths as: Crater A = 3.077 km, Crater B = 2.770 km, and Crater C = 1.850 km. Though large, Crater C is not deep. Ask students to investigate why. (It has been partly filled in by lava, which creates the broad, flat floor.)
2. Numerous factors can affect the explorer's ability to climb out of craters. Rubble on the crater's floor and the steepness of crater walls, for example, pose significant problems. Unfortunately, higher resolution photos would be necessary to assess these problems.

DATA TABLE 2 - KEY

	Crater A	Crater B	Crater C
Diameter of Crater	56 km	38.5 km	80 km
Length of Shadow Cast	34.7 km	26.3 km	81 km
Angle of incoming light	5.28°	5.28°	5.28°
Calculation of Crater Depth	3.2 km	2.43 km	0.75 km

ANATOMY OF AN IMPACT

OBJECTIVE

In this activity you will use photographs to examine basic features of craters and to develop skills for reconstructing events from evidence left behind.

BACKGROUND

In the previous two activities, you worked with models. Models are important tools in scientific research. When objects under study are too far away, too large, or too small to be investigated directly, models offer useful starting points for scientists. They provide a means for representing objects and phenomena so that research onto them can begin. Models also have important roles in verification. When objects cannot be tested directly, models can be used in their place. To test how a plane would react to certain atmospheric conditions, for example, engineers model those conditions in wind tunnels and test plane replicas in simulation. Likewise, to test what happens to people in auto accidents, crash test dummies are used as models. Because you could not go to the Moon to examine craters firsthand, in the last two activities you worked with crater models.

Always be aware, however, that no matter how useful models are, they are never *exact* replicas of the objects they simulate. Sometimes models are not reliable indicators of how the original object will react. Models in architecture are good examples. A tabletop replica of a bridge, for instance, can withstand more relative force applied to one spot than can a full-sized bridge. A *scale effect* occurs that makes the tabletop model unreliable. The best way to verify a model's appropriateness is to compare it as best you can to the original. Always proceed cautiously when drawing conclusions about an object from information gained through a model.

MATERIALS

Each group will need

◆ copies of crater photographs (two for each group)

◆ drawing paper

◆ pencils

◆ model craters

The face of the Moon contains many major impact sites. Five of these are located here using arrows.

Moon 215.tif

Moon 307.tif

Close-up of a relatively fresh crater. This view comes from looking down on the Moon at an oblique angle.

In this activity, you will apply the experience of working with crater models from Activities 3 and 4 to *real* cases of impact sites. Using photographs of craters provided here and by your teacher, you will investigate the anatomy of craters and compare them to a model—like the ones you made in earlier activities—that your teacher has on display. In the process of this close study, you should be thinking about how to use the evidence left behind to reconstruct the actual impact event. What happens to make a crater appear the way it does?

PROCEDURE

Observing a Crater

1. Working by yourself, examine the large craters in the images presented here and made available by your teacher. Identify the major features you observe. Also think about how you can reconstruct the original impact events given the evidence you have available.

2. In Observation Box 1, create a basic sketch of an impact crater based on your study of the photographs. Label key features. Be sure to look for patterns that can shed light on the impact process itself.

OBSERVATION BOX 1

Comparing Notes

3. Reassemble in your group and compare results. What features did everyone identify as part of the labeled craters? Discuss any differences between your general sketches. Also, discuss how the various features of a impact site could have been created. (Remember, members of your group may disagree about how features you observe were caused. Disagreements are a normal part of scientific investigations. If such differences occur, discuss how to design a test that would expand your understanding of the phenomenon.)

4. Look at photos of heavily-cratered surfaces. Can you find examples of a crater on top of another? Which crater formed first?

5. Use your generalized sketches to reconstruct the process of a crater's impact on a surface. Write a chronology of events taking place during an impact. Be sure to include processes that account for all the features identified on your generalized sketch.

Moon 6A05.tif

Comparing Reality to Models

6. At this point, look at the crater model your teacher has prepared. It was made in a similar way to how you made craters in earlier activities. Study the craters under different angles of lighting. Compare the photographs of real craters to the model and create a list of similarities and differences between your model and photographs of the real thing.

Heavily cratered surface on the Moon. This is an old region whose surface has been exposed for about 4 billion years. Therefore, it has accumulated many impact craters.

QUESTIONS/CONCLUSIONS

1. Being able to visualize natural processes is key to scientific research. Compare your crater with the diagram illustrating a bolide impact (your teacher will provide this) and write a paragraph describing a bolide impact and the cratering process as if you were narrating a film showing what happens during an impact event. Be sure to include in your narration explanations for how each of the elements in your generalized sketch was created.

2. Is the crater model a good representation of a *real* impact site? How is it realistic? How is it *unrealistic*?

3. Suggest ways for improving the model. How would you make it more realistic?

ANATOMY OF AN IMPACT

MATERIALS

Each group will need

- copies of crater photographs (two for each group)
- drawing paper
- pencils

You also will need to prepare model craters like the ones created in Activity 3.

Spectacular image of crater and ejecta blanket. All the radiating material was ejected from the crater and dumped on the surface. On Craters!-CD this is image Moon310.tif.

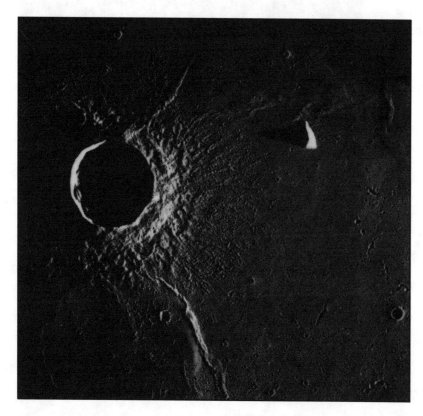

WHAT IS HAPPENING?

Scientific research involves models. For example, *scale* models represent objects in manageable sizes, and *dynamic* models simulate processes. Students need to appreciate how models are used in scientific research. They also must learn how to evaluate models for strengths and weaknesses. The best way to gain this appreciation for the role and limitations of models is to compare results directly from real and model circumstances. In this activity, students examine photographs of real impact sites for comparison with those produced in a model. With the memory of the model fresh (and additional ones on hand for study), comparison is effective and illustrative of both the benefits and limitations of modeling.

Although the model developed for Activities 3 and 4 is good in many respects, its main limitation involves the speed of impact for the falling body. Real lunar and planetary impacts occur at speeds much greater than the speed of sound. These speeds are called *hypersonic*. When bolides fall this fast, a pressure wave (traveling at the speed of sound) builds up in the rock. Just before the bolide would actually strike the surface, something peculiar happens. The pressure wave that builds up cannot carry energy away from the impact fast enough to "get out in front" of the bolide. As a result, the energy and heat created by the impact concentrate, and an explosion occurs! Thus, the effects of a hypersonic impact are really caused by an explosion and not by a collision. The explosion is frequently underground, after the bolide has punched a hole in the surface. In the model, impact speeds are much slower than the speed of sound. In fact, simulated bolides must be thrown relatively hard to create enough air pressure in front to throw out the powder representing the surface layer. This creates something of a "simulated" explosion, although the bolide itself is not destroyed.

Analyzing lunar photographs from orbital height, planetary scientists can compare features of real impact craters to features produced in models. Students should be able to identify a number of key features in their photographs. These features include

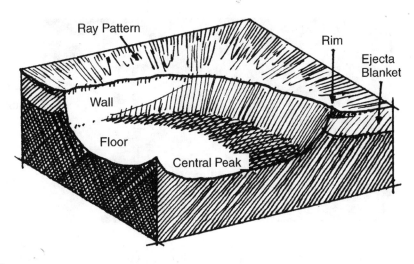

- ◆ Crater's raised rim

- ◆ Crater's central peak (if present)

- ◆ Ejecta blanket of debris, thrown out by the explosion and deposited outside the rim in a ray pattern outward in decreasing volume

- ◆ Overturned strata or rock layers

When examining their photographs, students might benefit from the following information:

Schematic of crater and key features. Note that only larger lunar craters, bigger than 10 km in diameter, have central peaks. This is because central peaks are caused by a rebound-like phenomenon that occurs only at larger scales.

Crater shape: Small craters typically have a smooth, bowl-shaped interior. In large impacts, the energy involved and the weight of the crater walls are so large that a *rebound* phenomenon occurs. After being pushed down by the initial explosion, the bottom center of large craters rebound upward again, assisted by the weight of the newly-created walls. This rebound produces a central peak. Students usually do not identify this peak as being part of the crater. They can confirm that the peak appears in large but not small craters for themselves, although later geological events, such as lava flows filling a crater, can obscure some peaks. (Students can simulate the appearance of this central peak using water droplets.) During impact, steep crater walls are created. These walls are then subject to landslides and slumping. A landslide will have an irregular surface; slump blocks will look like a series of terraces or steps on the inner wall of the crater.

Identifying the ejecta blanket: The material blown out from the crater during an impact flies outward and piles up on the outer rim and beyond. This scattering is largely responsible for the crater's raised rim. (The raised rim also results when the impact explosion bends the surrounding strata upward.) More debris falls closer to the rim than farther away. The debris field forms what is called an *ejecta blanket,* and this blanket usually forms a feather or ray pattern, thinning with distance. The ejected rays of fine, bright, pulverized material are one of the ejecta blanket features best simulated in Activity 3.

Composition of the ejecta blanket: Impacts disturb local geology. If a bolide falls on an undisturbed surface, the rock found under the ejecta blanket will be original—i.e., undisturbed—rock from the area. The ejecta blanket itself would consist of material blown out of the site of the explosion. Because the temperatures and pressures

produced during the explosion are so high, material in the ejecta blanket can include rock that was highly fractured, heated, or melted. These shocks produce distinct effects in rock, and geologists studying samples from ejecta blankets usually have little difficulty identifying them as such.

Stratigraphy: Because the ejecta blanket forms at the same time as the crater, it creates a widespread layer equal in age to that crater. Later craters lay down other ejecta blankets atop the first. These layers can be distinguished in photos from space or on the ground. Geologists study this layering and compare it to rock layers elsewhere to unravel the geological history of a region. This practice is called *stratigraphy*. Stratigraphy is presented further in Activity 14.

Additional impacts on the Moon. On Craters!-CD this is image Moon303.tif.

IMPORTANT POINTS FOR STUDENTS TO UNDERSTAND

- ◆ A surprising amount of information can be extracted by studying photographs only.

- ◆ Models are useful tools for research and verification.

- ◆ Models always are imperfect representations. Knowing their limitations is as important as knowing their advantages.

- ◆ Real and model craters have important differences. Studying cratering simply from models has its limitations.

PREPARATION

Students begin this activity working alone, then complete the activity in groups of three or four. Work with images of the Moon for this activity. Several are printed here for your use. Many others are available on *Craters!*-CD and elsewhere (see Resources List). You might consider assigning different images to different student groups.

CD-ROM

In advance, prepare crater models for each group, or one for the class that groups can take turns examining, following the method provided in Activity 3 and 4. Leave the models exactly as they are following the impact. For your convenience, Appendix 1 provides more background information about the cratering process.

SUGGESTIONS FOR FURTHER STUDY

Models are common in scientific research. Students can investigate the use of models both inside and outside planetary sciences. Models of molecules have enabled chemists to visualize chemical reactions better. Topographic maps are models of landscapes. In recent years, computer modeling and simulations have become widespread (e.g., in meteorology), and students can explore these applications. Models do not necessarily need to *look* like what they represent. But they must *act* like what they represent.

Students also can investigate how different technologies produce high resolution photographs of planetary bodies. Compare ground and space-based telescopes with planetary probes. Photographs also are produced during human exploration in space. Students can investigate the results of those projects. Especially interesting are the Apollo missions to the Moon.

CONNECTIONS

Models are common outside the sciences too. Ask students to compare the use of models in science to the use of metaphors and analogies in literature, film, and music.

ANSWERS TO QUESTIONS FOR STUDENTS

1. Answers will vary.

2. Answers will vary. General problems with the model's realism will be related to scale.

3. Answers will vary with the model created. The main differences are those of scale: speed of impact, size of bolide, structure of planetary surface. Possible ways to build a more realistic model: (1) use a higher velocity impact, made with adult supervision, or (2) construct a deeper, multilayer surface that can be excavated in cross-section to look at subsurface impact results. Mixing grated paraffin with the layers, then baking the "impact" before excavation is one method. Adult supervision is needed.

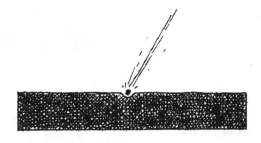

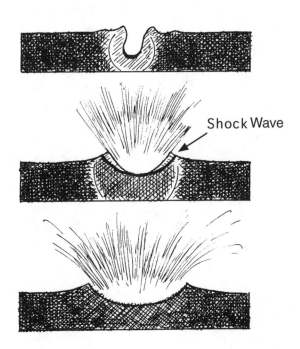

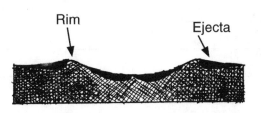

Schematic of impact with crater formation. Use this for Question 1 in the Student section.

CRATER COUNT

MATERIALS

Each group will need
- image of the Moon's surface
- ruler
- freshly-sharpened pencil
- graph paper (optional)

OBJECTIVE

In this activity you will examine the distribution of crater sizes on the Moon. In the next activity, you will investigate a process that could explain this distribution.

BACKGROUND

In a previous activity—when you measured a crater's depth using geometry—you learned how to derive information about distant places from photographs. That activity gave a hint of the kinds of analysis possible using photographs alone. In this activity, you will use photographs to study the *sizes* of craters. It turns out that studying the distribution of crater sizes provides clues about processes in space—processes that are far removed from the places where impacts actually occur.

To do this kind of study, space scientists are trained to look beyond the obvious in the photographs they examine. This calls for sharp detective work and creativity. In this activity, you first will look for patterns in your photographs. In the next activity, you will examine one process going on in space that might account for the patterns you find.

PROCEDURE

1. With your lab partners, examine the image shown in Figure 1. How much detail does it show? What surface features are most prominent? Are there any patterns on the surface? What features can you identify? Record your ideas in Observation Box 1. This is an image typical of most areas on the Moon's surface.

OBSERVATION BOX 1

44

Moon 6A04.tif

FIGURE 1

Heavily cratered lunar highlands. Is there a pattern to the size distribution of these impact sites?

PLAN OF ACTION

2. In this activity you'll be concerned primarily with *crater size*. Locate the largest crater on the photograph. Have everyone in your group separately measure its diameter by making pencil marks at the edges, then measure the distance (in millimeters) between the marks. Round off to the nearest whole millimeter.

3. Compare your measurements. If they vary, discuss ways to improve the consistency of your results. Develop a plan of action for creating accurate, *repeatable* measurements. Be sure to discuss how to measure craters that do not have clear edges. Write your plan of action in the box provided.

4. Once you have agreed on a plan, measure the size of *every* crater on the photograph. Divide this task within your group in a way that ensures *all* craters are measured and that each is measured *only once*. Record the data in Data Table 1. Expand the table if necessary.

5. Collecting data is the first step in understanding. Now condense your raw data into a summary form using Data Table 2. Place an "X" in the row for each crater with a

DATA TABLE 1 — Crater size data

	CRATER SIZE (MM)		CRATER SIZE (MM)		CRATER SIZE (MM)		CRATER SIZE (MM)		CRATER SIZE (MM)		CRATER SIZE (MM)
1	____	8	____	15	____	22	____	29	____	36	____
2	____	9	____	16	____	23	____	30	____	37	____
3	____	10	____	17	____	24	____	31	____	38	____
4	____	11	____	18	____	25	____	32	____	39	____
5	____	12	____	19	____	26	____	33	____	40	____
6	____	13	____	20	____	27	____	34	____	(extend if necessary)	
7	____	14	____	21	____	28	____	35	____		

DATA TABLE 2	Crater Size Count		TOTAL
SIZE INTERVAL (MM)	NUMBER OF CRATERS		
0–0.9			
1–1.9			
2.0–3.9			
4.0–7.9			
8.0–15.9			
16.0–31.9			
32.0–63.9			
64.0–127.9			

diameter falling within that size interval. Make your X's with the same size, shape, and spacing. When all craters have been added, count the number of X's in each row, and write the total in the space provided.

6. Graphs provide a visual means to summarize data. Sometimes patterns are easier to identify using graphs than using data tables. If you have been careful in the way you've drawn your X's in Data Table 2, you have made a histogram of your results. (Turn the page sideways to see it.) Create a graph for your results by plotting the number of craters on the Y-axis (vertical) and size of craters on the X-axis (horizontal). The axes should look like those in Figure 2.

7. Examine the total counts in Data Table 2 and in the graph you made. What can you say about the size distribution of craters in this image of the Moon's surface? Compare your results with other groups in your class. Record your conclusions in Observation Box 2 (on the next page).

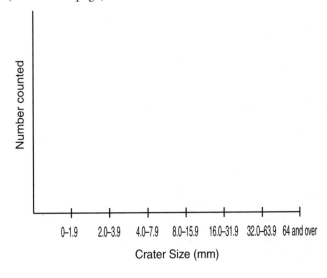

FIGURE 2

Template for bar graph to summarize data on crater size distribution. Note that the intervals are not uniform, but increase by a factor of 2 in each step. Extend graph to the right if needed.

OBSERVATION BOX 2

_____

_____

_____

_____

_____

_____

QUESTIONS/CONCLUSIONS

1. What is the area (in square kilometers) shown in your image of the Moon? What size (in kilometers) is the largest crater? the smallest?

2. Compare your conclusions in Observation Box 2 to what you wrote in Observation Box 1. What would you add to your report about this image following your analysis?

3. Form a hypothesis to explain why there are not the same number of large, medium, and small craters.

4. Discuss your answers to the first three questions with your group. Is the distribution pattern observed simply the result of random processes or is there something more? Write a 2–3 paragraph group report of your discussion and your collective observations.

CRATER COUNT

WHAT IS HAPPENING?

Activities 6 and 7 are closely linked. Together, they develop two skills: pattern recognition and the search for causal connections. This first activity emphasizes pattern recognition. Students are asked to find patterns in the distribution of crater sizes for typical areas of the Moon's surface. They will discover that this distribution follows a specific relationship in which small bodies far outnumber large ones. In the next activity, students will examine one process—the fragmentation that occurs when asteroids collide—as a possible explanation for this pattern.

In examining photographs, students will see that some craters are fresh and sharp, while others are old and battered, causing a "softer" appearance. Some craters even overlap other craters, indicating relative age.

IMPORTANT POINTS FOR STUDENTS TO UNDERSTAND

- The size distribution of craters follows a specific pattern.
- Finding a pattern in nature raises questions about its cause.
- Data collection is just one step of scientific investigation. Tables and graphs are efficient ways to summarize data and locate patterns.

PREPARATION

Students should work in teams of three or four, and each student should have a copy of the same image. For variety, you may ask different groups to analyze photographs of different areas on the Moon. *Craters!-CD* contains 29 additional images of lunar surfaces that can replace Figure 1. These files are stored in the directory Moon6. The image used for Figure 1 is file Moon6A04.tif on *Craters!-CD*.

Reliable and reproducible measurements of crater sizes are crucial, and students should not gloss over the Plan of Action portion of this activity. To appreciate the task, try this activity yourself prior to its assignment. Students working with images with high crater density may choose to create a grid system on their image. The group could divide the photograph into sections and assign one section to each person. Or, they could have one person measure all craters within a certain size interval. Students should realize that there are several ways to complete this task, and their goal is to form a plan and make it work.

MATERIALS

Each group will need

- image of the Moon's surface
- ruler
- freshly-sharpened pencil
- graph paper (optional)

CD-ROM

Because a pencil's graphite will leave a sheen on dark areas (whereas other markers do not), it makes a superb tool for this activity. A *freshly-sharpened* pencil is essential for marking crater edges with a high degree of accuracy. Calipers offer an excellent substitute for a ruler in this activity. You may choose to review the construction of histograms and other graphs during this activity.

SUGGESTIONS FOR FURTHER STUDY

After students have produced their graphs, ask them to consider different means of visual representation: change scales, choose different graphing styles (X-Y plots or pie charts), etc. The curve produced on a linear scale (using simple intervals such as 1, 2, 3, 4, 5, 6, and so on) will be different from one produced using a logarithmic scale (1, 2, 4, 8, 16, 32, and so on). Data Table 2 purposely uses logarithmic intervals. If you have access to graphing software, this is a good activity to use with it. Most graphing software will allow students to experiment with a variety of graphing styles.

FIGURE 3
Sparsely cratered lunar lowlands. This image can be retrieved from Craters!-CD as file Moon6B11.tif.

CD-ROM

Craters!-CD contains many images of planetary bodies other than the Moon that can be used for extensions of this study (see Activity 10). Students can be asked to look for the same patterns of crater size distribution on these different surfaces. Images useful for such a study include Other301.tif, Other610.tif, Other604.tif, Other633.tif, and Other640.tif. Additional images are located in the Folder Other6. Directions for measuring craters using the *Craters!-CD* images are available in Appendix 2.

CONNECTIONS

Discuss the subject of measurement *scales*, such as those found on maps, globes, and photographs. How do scale changes alter the *impression* given to a viewer? For example, change the scale of the X-axis in Figure 2 from logarithmic units to linear units. How is the impression of the data changed?

With a geologic map of the lunar surface, you may wish to do an analysis of the geologic history of the crater photograph area. For example, older areas have more impact craters; younger areas have fewer.

This activity offers a launching point for studying the relative age of different areas on the Moon or a planet. Figures 3 and 4 show two areas on the Moon. Figure 4 shows the heavily cratered lunar highlands. Figure 3 shows the sparsely cratered lava plains, or maria. The two photographs have roughly the same dimensions.

Obviously the highlands have received more impacts, and the reason is that they are older—and have been exposed to bolide impacts longer. In the lowland plains, lava flows have obscured previous impacts and left a clean slate to record more recent impacts. Of course, a similar-sized random area on Earth has many fewer craters still because typical Earth surfaces are still younger than the Moon's lava plains. (Planetary scientists have shown that craters appear on different worlds at roughly the same time, within a factor of perhaps two to four. Nevertheless, it is safest to compare provinces on the same world, where the cratering rate is uniform.) Apollo data and rock samples show that the highlands formed about 4.1 billion years ago and the lava plains formed about 3.5 billion years ago. Why do the highlands have 30 times more craters than the lava plains? This is unexpected because the lava plains are only a little younger than the highlands. The answer involves a changing *rate* of impacts over time. The planets finished forming about 4.5 billion years ago, at which time there was considerable interplanetary debris. The amount of debris decreased over time because collisions and impacts swept up the debris. As the amount of debris declined, so did the number of impacts. From the considerable difference between the two images in Figures 3 and 4, the rate of impacts must have changed dramatically in the 500 million years between the formation of these two areas. Planetary scientists use studies of impacts, such as this comparison, to locate and assign relative ages to different regions on various planets.

FIGURE 4
Densely cratered lunar highlands. This image can be retrieved from Craters!-CD as file Moon6A06.tif.

ANSWERS TO QUESTIONS FOR STUDENTS

Answers will vary depending on which images students examine. As we will learn in the next activity, the reason there are more small craters than large (i.e. more small asteroids than large) is that asteroids are fragments of larger "parent bodies" that shattered during collisions. When natural objects fragment, there are usually more small pieces than large. Thus, the craters guide us back toward more basic cosmic processes. Have your students think about the objects that caused the craters.

GOING TO PIECES

MATERIALS

Each group will need

◆ a box containing fragments from a simulated asteroid collision

◆ rulers (one for each student)

◆ graph paper

Artist's rendering of an asteroid collision in space. Is there a connection between these events and the size distribution of craters on the Moon?

OBJECTIVE

To examine a process that could explain patterns in the size distribution of craters as observed in Activity 6.

BACKGROUND

In Activity 6, you studied the distribution of crater sizes using photographs. You discovered there was a pattern to that size distribution. In this activity, you will begin developing explanations as to why a pattern exists in that data and why *that* particular pattern is the one you discovered.

Asteroids are small planetary bodies that orbit the Sun. Most are rocky in composition, but some contain large amounts of metal. Most can be found traveling between the orbits of Mars and Jupiter. Others travel in more oval-shaped orbits—these paths sometimes approach Earth. Thousands have been observed closely enough to have well-measured orbits. These are cataloged with names and numbers, but many other asteroids exist. No one knows exactly how many asteroids exist in our solar system, but to give you a basic idea of their numbers, consider this: about 30,000 asteroids are large enough to be photographed using a medium-sized telescope. The largest asteroids include Ceres (970 km in diameter), Pallas (580 km in diameter), and Vesta (540 km in diameter). New asteroids are being discovered all the time.

Asteroids have many shapes and sizes. They also change shape and size over their life history as the result of collisions. Gravitational influences from large planets—such as Jupiter and Mars—cause asteroid orbits to change. These changes sometimes put asteroids on collision courses with each other or with other planetary bodies. If one asteroid is hit by another one that is large enough, they both fragment into many pieces. The resulting fragmentation produces a large number of new, smaller asteroids. Asteroids that we see today are fragments of larger, original asteroids as old as the planets themselves. There is a connection between what happens to asteroids during collisions and the crater size distribution you investigated earlier. In this activity, you will explore that connection.

OBSERVATION BOX 1

_____

_____

_____

_____

_____

_____

PROCEDURE

1. Your teacher will lead a demonstration to simulate asteroid collisions in space. You will receive a box containing the remains of one simulated asteroid after it has suffered several collisions. These "asteroid fragments" were made by shattering a model asteroid.

2. Sort your asteroid fragments roughly by size. Record your impressions of the size distribution of these fragments in Observation Box 1. Are the fragments evenly distributed by size or are there many more of some sizes than of other sizes?

3. Make a _quantitative_ study of fragment sizes using the following procedure. Each member of your group should have a ruler and a copy of Data Table 1 for their individual data. Distribute the fragments among group members. Measure and record the size of

DATA TABLE 1	Fragment Size Count	
SIZE INTERVAL (MM)	**NUMBER OF FRAGMENTS**	**TOTAL**
0–0.9		
1.0–1.9		
2.0–3.9		
4.0–7.9		
8.0–15.9		
16.0–31.9		
32.0–63.9		
64.0–127.9		

DATA TABLE 2	Summary of Group Counts
SIZE INTERVAL (MM)	TOTAL NUMBER OF FRAGMENTS
0–0.9	
1.0–1.9	
2.0–3.9	
4.0–7.9	
8.0–15.9	
16.0–31.9	
32.0–63.9	
64.0–127.9	

FIGURE 1

Template for bar graph to summarize data on fragment size distribution. Note that the intervals are not uniform, but increase by a factor of 2 in each step. Extend graph to right if needed.

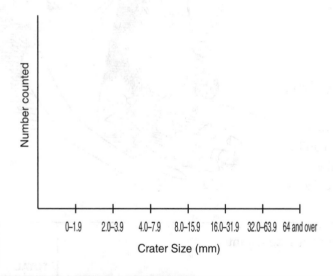

each fragment using Data Table 1. Place an "X" in the appropriate row for each fragment. Be sure you count each fragment *only once*, and be sure also to count all fragments regardless of size. Extend Data Table 1 if needed.

4. When the counting is complete, return all fragments to the box.

5. Begin your analysis of the data by adding together fragment size counts from each group member. Place the total counts in Data Table 2.

6. Now condense the data from your lab partners using Data Table 2. What can you say about this size distribution? Is there a pattern? Record your conclusions in Observation Box 2.

OBSERVATION BOX 2

7. Graphs provide a visual means to summarize data. As you did in Activity 6, create a graph for Data Table 2 using axes like those shown in Figure 1. Compare your results with other groups in your class.

QUESTIONS/CONCLUSIONS

1. Summarize the results of this investigation. What patterns exist in the size distribution of collision fragments?

2. Compare the results of this investigation with those in Activity 6. In particular, do you see any similarities between the crater size distribution and the fragment size distribution?

3. What conclusions would you, as a space scientist, draw about what happens to asteroids during their life history?

4. What connections might exist between crater size distribution on the Moon and the size distribution of collision fragments? Present evidence for your conclusions.

5. If collisions reduce asteroid sizes, why do large asteroids still exist?

6. Observers once claimed that Moon craters were all caused by volcanoes. What do you think? Use the data collected in Activities 6 and 7 to justify your view.

Moon 606.tif

The Moon's Schroeter's Valley and Aristarchus Crater, photographed during the Apollo 15 mission. The large, bright-appearing crater to the left of the head of meandering Schroeter's Valley is Aristarchus, approximately 35 km in diameter. Aristarchus is one of the freshest and best preserved large craters on the Moon.

GOING TO PIECES

MATERIALS

Each group will need

- a box containing fragments from a simulated asteroid collision
- rulers (one for each student)
- graph paper

For the collision simulation

- sledge hammer
- mat
- burlap or heavy canvas bag, with tie
- safety goggles for all participants
- simulated asteroids

WHAT IS HAPPENING?

Planetary scientists can extract an enormous amount of information from what otherwise might appear to be simple photographs. Your students learned this in Activity 6 and will extend that learning here, though in a less direct manner.

There is a connection between the size distribution of craters studied in Activity 6 and asteroid collisions. When asteroids collide, they fragment. Fragmentation occurs in predictable patterns. Usually a few large, some medium, and many small fragments are produced during collisions. The size distribution of these pieces follows a simple logarithmic pattern. That same pattern also is found in the size distribution of craters on surfaces such as the Moon's. This correlation has led most planetary scientists to agree that, in general, craters are caused by impacts of meteorites that are fragments of asteroids.

Asteroids typically collide at speeds of about 5 kilometers per second. When a small asteroid hits a large one, the result is merely a crater in the larger one. However, when asteroids of comparable size collide, they break each other into fragments. Fragments are cast in many directions and drift off into interplanetary space. Asteroid collisions and craters are related because some of these fragments are captured by a planetary body's gravitational field and become meteorites that crash into a planet.

It is crucial that students realize all the pieces they measure come from breaking one object. The point of the lesson is that any fragmentation event produces a roughly predictable and repeatable shape of size distribution, which has the same general character as that found for lunar craters.

IMPORTANT POINTS FOR STUDENTS TO UNDERSTAND

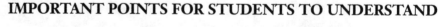

- Asteroids exist in many sizes, from very small to very large.
- Asteroid size distribution follows a predictable and measurable relationship, with many small bodies and few large bodies.
- This relationship exists because asteroids collide and fragment; many new, smaller asteroids result from these collisions.
- Planetary scientists agree that most craters are caused by impacts of meteorites that are fragments produced during asteroid collisions.

PREPARATION

Simulated asteroids can be molded from either concrete or plaster. (Adding dry paint to the mix will give variety to your samples.) Concrete block or a brick can also be used. The main criterion is that the body be solid and roughly spherical, cubical, or lumpy, but not flat or hollow. The ideal size for a simulated asteroid is 20–30 cm.

For safety reasons, shattering the simulated asteroid is done best as a teacher demonstration. If you believe they will act safely and responsibly, students can participate in the demonstration or do the shattering themselves. *If students are involved, be sure to emphasize the risk of serious injury and closely monitor their activity.* Require that safety goggles be worn during the shattering process. Keep those not involved in the demonstration at a safe distance.

To simulate asteroid collisions, follow these instructions.

1. Locate a place on the floor or outside that will serve as a hammering surface. Be sure it provides adequate room for safely swinging the hammer and is sufficiently removed from students so that the risk of flying debris will be minimized. Place the mat on the floor to protect the surface.

2. Place your simulated asteroid in the canvas bag. Tie the bag tightly, and set it on your mat. *Be sure to wear safety goggles.*

3. After students and assistants have moved to a safe distance, simulate an asteroid collision by striking the rock in the bag with a strong blow. Strike the mass *no more than* three times after it breaks; otherwise you will grind it into too many pieces.

4. Open the bag and *carefully* empty its contents into the collection box. These fragments are the materials students will use for their investigations.

An alternative to this large, dramatic exercise involves cookies or crackers. Give each student a hard-baked cookie or several crackers and a paper or plastic bag. After all students have these supplies, tell them to place the material in the bag, seal the bag, and slap it three times against their desk. This will simulate a collision as does the larger simulation, but it is less involved. You will need to adjust the scales used in the data tables if you use this variation.

SUGGESTIONS FOR FURTHER STUDY

Following this investigation, you may ask students to re-examine photographs of planetary surfaces and continue to study size distribution. This also is an ideal time to discuss asteroids in general, as well as the asteroid belt that exists between Mars and Jupiter. Shoemaker-Levy 9—which impacted Jupiter in July 1994—most likely was a comet or weak asteroid that fragmented into many pieces (although this probably was caused by gravitation when it passed very near Jupiter and was not caused by a collision).

Students may use Activities 6 and 7 to explore asteroid and crater size distributions and power laws. At the simplest level, the smaller the fragment size you consider, the more objects you count. At a more sophisticated level, you can notice that as the size decreases by a factor 2, the number of objects increases by about a factor 4. If your students are advanced enough, point out that the character of the size distribution is that as the size drops by a factor N, the number of objects goes up by roughly N^2. This kind of relation is called a power law because the number is inversely related to the size raised to the same power.

CONNECTIONS

Ask students to explore the asteroid belt between Mars and Jupiter. How many asteroids are there? Why does the belt exist? Is there a connection between the asteroid belt and the history of planetary formation? What forces in the solar system act most strongly on the asteroid belt?

ANSWERS TO QUESTIONS FOR STUDENTS

1. Summary results will vary. The pattern distribution should be a large number of small fragments and dust, some medium size fragments, and a few large fragments. The larger the range of fragment sizes, the better defined will be the graph.

2. Comparisons will vary but should draw the conclusion that the patterns are similar.

3. During the "life" of an asteroid it will collide with other asteroids until it is reduced to small fragments.

4. Hypotheses will vary, but they should recognize the connection between fragment size and crater size.

5. Large asteroids still exist because the number of collisions has reduced, asteroids have become more separated, and few have overlapping orbits.

6. The close match in distribution patterns of crater sizes and collision fragments is strongly suggestive that collision fragments caused the Moon's craters. If volcanoes were the cause, what explains the size distribution?

SHAKING THINGS UP!

OBJECTIVE

In this activity you will explore the connection between motion, friction, and heat. This connection helps explain what happens during an impact.

BACKGROUND

Rub your hands together and what happens? They begin to warm. Where does the warmth come from? Rub faster or harder, and your hands get hotter. Why? What is the connection between motion and the temperature change that just occurred?

PROCEDURE

1. Measure 200 grams of sand into your cup. Place the thermometer bulb halfway into the sand and measure its temperature. Record this value in the Observation Box under Column A. This is the initial temperature.

2. Place a stopper into one end of the plastic tube. Carefully pour the sand into the tube. Set the tube in a vertical position and allow the sand to settle evenly.

   Note: Timing is important in the next few steps. Read the procedure for steps 3 and 4 before continuing. Prepare to make the measurement in step 4 as quickly as possible.

3. Close the other end of the tube tightly with your second stopper. Holding the tube's ends in each hand, invert the tube so that the sand travels from one end of the tube to the other quickly. Your motion should be regular and smooth. Count to yourself "one-one-thousand" through the motion of each inversion. Repeat this motion exactly 25 times.

4. Quickly open the tube and pour the sand into the plastic foam cup. Place the thermometer bulb halfway into the sand and measure its temperature. Record this value in the

MATERIALS

Each group will need

- plastic tube (at least 50 cm long)

- stoppers to close both ends of the tube

- balance

- thermometer (-10° to 110°C)

- plastic foam cup

- 250 ml beaker

- 600 g dry sand, at room temperature

- balance

- graph paper

Observation Box under Column A as "after 25 inversions." Calculate the change in temperature caused by the motion.

5. Examine how temperature is affected by the *amount* of motion. Use your experimental setup to investigate. Repeat steps 1–4 using 10 and then 50 inversions instead of 25. Record your measurements in the Observation Box under Column B.

6. Examine how temperature is affected by the *intensity* of motion. Repeat steps 1–4 using fast and vigorous *versus* slow and gentle inversions. Record your measurements in the Observation Box under Column C.

7. Once you have completed your systematic observations, summarize your data in graph form. Plot temperature change on the y-axis and your independent variables (amount of motion and intensity of motion) on the x-axis.

OBSERVATION BOX

Column A:
Control
200g SAND

____ initial temperature
____ after 25 inversions
____ temperature change
    after 25 regular
    inversions

Column B:
Changing Amount of Motion
200g SAND

____ initial temperature
____ after 10 inversions
____ temperature change

____ temperature change
    after 25 regular inversions
    (from Column A)

____ initial temperature
____ after 50 inversions
____ temperature change

Column C:
Changing Intensity of Motion
200g SAND

____ initial temperature
____ after 25 vigorous inversions
____ temperature change

____ temperature change after
    25 regular inversions
    (from Column A)

____ initial temperature
____ after 25 gentle inversions
____ temperature change

QUESTIONS/CONCLUSIONS

1. Summarize your observations. What is the connection between motion and heat?

2. How can you explain these connections? How do these studies affect your understanding of heat?

3. Apply your answers to questions 1 and 2 to explain why your hands get warm when they are rubbed together.

4. What is the difference between heating your sand using a shaking motion and placing it in an oven?

5. Sand, which is mainly quartz, melts at a temperature of 1,400 degrees Celsius. How would you raise your sample's temperature to this level?

6. Calories are standard units of heat. One calorie is the amount of heat required to raise one gram of water one degree centigrade. The number of calories produced in the trials for this activity can be calculated by multiplying the change in temperature by the mass of the sand and what is called the specific heat of the sand. Sand's specific heat is 0.24. The resulting formula is

   Calories = change in temperature X mass X 0.24

   Be sure the temperature is given in degrees centigrade and the mass in grams. Calculate the number of calories produced in your experiments.

   You also may have encountered the unit "joule" before. This standard unit of energy also is used to count quantities of heat. One calorie is equivalent to 4.186 joules. Conversion to joules is useful because it allows you to compare different kinds of energy production—explosions and earthquakes, for example.

SHAKING THINGS UP!

MATERIALS

Each group will need

- plastic tube (at least 50 cm long)

- stoppers to close both ends of the tube

- balance

- thermometer (-10° to 110°C)

- plastic foam cup

- 250 ml beaker

- 600 g dry sand, at room temperature

- balance

- graph paper

WHAT IS HAPPENING?

Heat is a kind of energy, and energy can be transformed from one form into another. In this activity, motion (kinetic energy) of a mass of material (shaking sand) is transformed to thermal energy (motion of molecules within the sand grains). Activities 8 and 9 explore heat from this perspective. In this first activity, students work through a series of experiments to understand the connection between motion, mass, and heat. In the second, students apply this understanding to problems relating to bolide impacts. The kinetic energy of a bolide is transformed to heat and motion of debris during impact.

In this activity, the temperature change is caused by the transfer of the kinetic energy of the mass movement of the sand to the kinetic energy of the molecules in the individual sand grains. This transfer happens by friction—the process of one grain hitting another as the student shakes the tube. Students probably have learned that kinetic energy of an object can be calculated as the product of one-half the mass times the mass's velocity squared:

> Kinetic Energy = 1/2 m v²
> where *m* is the mass of the moving body in kilograms and *v* is its
> velocity in meters/second.
> Kinetic energy is expressed in terms of the standard unit, joules (J).

The temperature of a mass is related to the kinetic energy of its molecules in a simple way. When temperature is measured on the absolute scale of Kelvins, it is directly proportional to the av*erage* kinetic energy of the individual molecules making up the mass. Change the velocity and the kinetic energy changes. Change the kinetic energy and the temperature changes. Thus, the faster the molecules move, the warmer the sand becomes.

When we rub our hands together, we use the kinetic energy of our hands, and friction, to increase the motions of molecules in the cells of our palms. This increases the temperature of our skin. When an asteroid enters the atmosphere at speeds of several kilometers per second, molecules in the surrounding air pick up extra speed. As a result of the additional speed and friction, both air and bolide become extremely hot. When a bolide collides with a planet, a great deal of kinetic energy is transferred to the planet. Velocities of molecules increase suddenly and dramatically, converting much of the kinetic energy into heat. When air and water heat suddenly, they quickly expand. Superheating water and air causes an explosion. (An additional fraction of the kinetic energy is transformed into sound and into fragmenting the materials at the impact site.)

Calories are standard units of heat. One calorie is the amount of heat required to raise one gram of water (at a pressure of one atmosphere) one degree centigrade. The number of calories produced in the trials for this activity can be calculated by multiplying the change in temperature by the mass of the sand and the specific heat of the sand (0.24). In formula, this is expressed as:

Calories = change in temperature (°C) X mass (g) X 0.24

Calories can be converted to joules arithmetically using the standard that one calorie is equivalent to 4.186 joules. Conversion to joules is useful because this allows comparison with other producers of kinetic energy. (This kind of comparison will be done in Activity 9.)

IMPORTANT POINTS FOR STUDENTS TO UNDERSTAND

◆ Heat is a kind of energy and can be generated by motion.

◆ Motions of large masses can transform to heat through friction—the collision of constituent grains or molecules.

◆ Energy of a moving object depends on the *speed* of motion (velocity) and the *mass* of the object.

◆ Energy of motion (kinetic energy) can be transformed, but the total amount of energy remains the same.

PREPARATION

Clear plastic tubes work best for this activity. Clear plastic tubes for holding fluorescent bulbs are available from most hardware stores. Alternatively, the tubes used to separate golf clubs in golf bags are available from sporting goods stores. These tubes allow students to see what is happening inside, but a cardboard tube with secure plugs for the ends can also be used. The temperature changes may be small depending on the materials used. You may have to experiment to find the best system.

It is not necessary to have tubes exactly 50 cm in length. However, tubes must be *at least* this long to obtain significant results in a short time period. For comparison, you might provide tubes of differing lengths to different groups and ask them to explain variations in their results. If all groups use tubes of the same length, their results can be collected and jointly analyzed by the class. This provides the opportunity to discuss experimental variation.

SUGGESTIONS FOR FURTHER STUDY

This experiment uses the Celsius temperature scale but also makes reference to the Kelvin scale. Introduce students to the Kelvin scale, its connections to the Fahrenheit and Celsius scales, and its role as an absolute measure of motion. The Kelvin scale was named after William Thompson (1824–1907, given the title Lord Kelvin of Largs). Thompson carried out fundamental research in thermodynamics helped develop the law of the conservation of energy, and developed dynamic theories of heat, electricity, and magnetism.

The concept of specific heat also is introduced here. This is a standard measure that allows the heating properties of different materials to be compared. Specific heat is measured as the quantity of heat required to produce a one degree Kelvin increase in temperature. Specific heat is given in units of joules per kilogram. Water has a specific heat of 418, which means 418 joules of energy are required to raise the temperature of one kilogram of water one degree Kelvin.

CONNECTIONS

Relate what students have learned to the concepts of kinetic energy and the conservation of energy. Point out to the class that if a meteorite is approaching Earth, it carries a certain amount of energy at the moment it hits the ground. Energy is transformed into heat during the impact and mechanical motion causes debris to be blown out, thus excavating a crater. If humans excavated a crater of the same size, the energy would come from manual labor (chemical energy from food), or from burning fossil fuels (to run the machines that did the work). Students may have visited or seen pictures of open pit mines. Consider the huge equipment and time that have been used at these mines to make these craters.

ANSWERS TO QUESTIONS FOR STUDENTS

1. As motion is increased, heat increases as long as there is friction. This is because the sand grains hit each other (friction) and transfer their kinetic energy to the actual vibrational movements of the molecules.

2. Answers will vary. Encourage critical thinking in student answers.

3. When we rub our hands together, we use the kinetic energy of our hands, and friction, to increase the motions of molecules in the cells of our palms. This increases the temperature of our skin. Adding lubricants—for example, lotion to hands, oil or graphite to moving machine parts—decreases friction.

4. Shaking the sand transfers kinetic energy to sand molecules by making the sand grains hit each other. Heating sand in an oven works by heating the air and causing the air molecules to transfer kinetic energy into the sand grains as the air molecules hit the grains. This is called heating by conduction.

5. Answers will vary. An enormous amount of shaking would be required to melt the sand! Point out that impact craters often contain spherules of melted sand. Therefore, impact craters have transferred enormous amounts of kinetic energy into heat.

6. Answers will vary from one experiment to another. Be sure students pay attention to significant figures and check the appropriateness of their units.

JUST HOW BIG IS BIG?

MATERIALS

Each group will need

- bag of simulated planetary bedrock
- cup of simulated planetary surface
- container
- sieve or large spoon
- simulated bolides (assorted sizes)
- drop cloth or floor cover
- ruler
- chair
- string, weight on end
- graph paper
- safety goggles for everyone

FIGURE 1

OBJECTIVE

This activity explores the connection between crater size and the kinetic energy of impacting bolides.

BACKGROUND

In Activity 8, you explored the connection between heat and motion. You learned that temperature is affected by mass and velocity: shake the sand faster and its temperature rises. Measuring heat in Activity 8 was a way to measure the energy involved in the motion of that system. Kinetics is the study of motion. The *kinetic energy* of an object is the energy associated with its motion. You may already know that kinetic energy can be calculated as the product of one-half the mass of a moving body times its velocity squared:

kinetic energy = 1/2 mv^2

where m is the mass of the moving body, and v is its velocity. Kinetic energy is expressed in terms of the standard metric unit, joule (J). One joule is the amount of energy needed to move a mass (any mass) a distance of 1 meter using a force of 1 newton. One newton is defined as the force needed to accelerate a 1 kg mass by 1 meter/second^2.

Consider the relationship between these variables. Qualitatively, note that the kinetic energy increases as mass increases or as the velocity increases. Quantitatively, note that if the mass doubles, the energy also doubles. If the velocity doubles, the energy is *four* times greater. Why? You can see in the formula that kinetic energy is related not to v but to v^2.

Think about the kinetic energy involved in dropping water balloons. When you drop a light water balloon and a heavy water balloon, why does the heavy one make such a bigger splash? (Figure 1) Think about how the masses are different and how mass affects kinetic energy.

TABLE 1

Comparison of energy produced during different events

EVENT	ENERGY (KILOJOULES)	COMPARISON
One 1,600 kg (about 3,500 lb) car colliding with wall at 90 kph (55mph)	5×10^5	1
Two 1,600 kg (about 3,500 lb) cars colliding head on at 90 kph (55mph)	1×10^6	2
Explosion of 1 ton TNT	4.2×10^9	8,400
Typical lightning bolt	5×10^9	10,000
Average tornado	7.5×10^{11}	1,500,000
Explosion of 20-megaton fusion bomb	8.4×10^{16}	1,680,000,000,000
Total US electric power production in 1990	1×10^{19}	20,000,000,000,000
Typical 10-day hurricane	2.5×10^{19}	50,000,000,000,000
Earth's daily receipt of solar energy	1.1×10^{22}	22,000,000,000,000,000
Impact of a large bolide (the size that wiped out dinosaurs; 10km diameter, 20km/sec velocity)	7.5×10^{23}	1,500,000,000,000,000,000

— adapted from Ray Newburn, Jr., "The Comet About to Smash into Jupiter," The Universe in the Classroom, 1994, no. 27 (table is on page 5); Arch Johnston, "An Earthquake Strength Scale for the Media and the Public," Earthquakes and Volcanoes, vol. 22 (graph is on page 215).

Now imagine dropping water balloons of the same weight from different heights (Figure 2). If you drop a water balloon from close to the ground, it either won't pop or will create just a minor splash. But drop it from a window or throw it down, and it's sure to scatter water all over. You know the balloon dropped from higher up or thrown will have a higher velocity. Think about how these different velocities affect kinetic energy.

Compared to other events, impacts of large bolides involve an enormous amount of energy (see Table 1). Bolides move at high velocities (*kilometers* per second) and can be enormous in size. These features give the rarest, largest bolides huge kinetic energies. Look at the craters they form!

FIGURE 2

OBSERVATION BOX 1

MASS (G)	CRATER DIAMETER (MM)			
	TRIAL 1	TRIAL 2	TRIAL 3	AVERAGE
_____	_____	_____	_____	_____
_____	_____	_____	_____	_____
_____	_____	_____	_____	_____
_____	_____	_____	_____	_____
_____	_____	_____	_____	_____
_____	_____	_____	_____	_____
_____	_____	_____	_____	_____

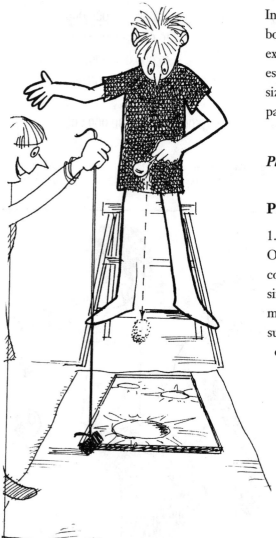

In this activity, you will explore the connection between the energy bolides carry and the craters that form during impacts. Through experiments and calculations, you will be able to build quantitative estimates about the energy bolides carry just from measuring crater sizes. You also will be able to predict the size of craters formed during particular bolide impacts.

Part I: Experimental Trials

PROCEDURE

1. Clear a working area by moving desks, chairs, and other objects. Open your drop cloth and lay it down smoothly on the ground. Put the container in the center of your workspace. Fill this container with simulated planetary bedrock (light-colored material) up to several millimeters below the rim. Lightly pack the bedrock and smooth the surface with your ruler so it is flat. Cover the bedrock with a thin layer of simulated planetary surface (dark-colored material).

2. Move a chair or stepladder next to your test surface. You'll want to be able to look down over your test surface. Have one member of your group climb on the chair—*be careful to keep balanced!* This person will be the bolide dropper. A second member of your group should hold the measuring string vertically next to the test surface and position the bolide dropper's hand exactly at the desired height above the test surface. The standard height is important, as you'll see in the analysis.

3. Give a bolide to the dropper. Start with the bolide of largest mass. When repeating this experiment use progressively smaller masses. Position other members of your group along the drop cloth's edge so that they can observe the impact from a safe distance.

4. With the experiment arranged so the bolide will fall from exactly the predetermined height and hit somewhere on the test surface, have the dropper release the bolide. In Observation Box 1, record the mass of the bolide and the diameter of the crater it formed.

5. Repeat this experiment two more times, using the same mass and height. After several tests you will need to smooth the surface again.

6. Repeat steps 1–5 using bolides with different masses.

QUESTIONS/CONCLUSIONS

1. When you have completed testing the different bolides, calculate the average diameter created for trials using each mass. What is the relationship between crater size and bolide mass?

2. Graph bolide mass *versus* crater diameter using graph paper. However, instead of using crater diameter directly, try plotting the *cube* of the diameter, D^3. Does the curve become more like a straight line?

3. What does the shape of the curve indicate? What causes it?

4. Why would the cube of crater diameter, D^3, provide this shape? Why isn't velocity counted here?

Part II: Predictions Based on Calculations

PROCEDURE

Graphing the mass against the cube of crater diameter, D^3, produces roughly a straight line. Why? You know that a bolide's mass affects its kinetic energy. (If everything else is constant, higher mass means higher kinetic energy.) You also know that kinetic energy influences crater size (increasing the energy increases the crater size.) In Part I, you experimented with these connections. In Part II, you will extend that work to build quantitative predictions about the relation between mass and crater size. Begin with this chain of reasoning:

a. When a crater is formed, the total amount of energy used is proportional to the *volume* of material excavated.

b. Because a crater is roughly a hemisphere, its volume is determined by the cube of the diameter (D), or D^3. (The volume for hemisphere is $2/3\ \pi(D/2)^3$.)

c. As a result, energy needed is proportional to D^3.

d. In an impact, the energy involved is kinetic energy, which is defined as $1/2\ mv^2$.

Moon 901.tif

e. If kinetic energy is proportional to D^3, then for an impact, you can predict

$$D^3 \text{ will be proportional to } mv^2$$

(In proportions like this, constants—such as the 1/2—can be dropped out.)

This prediction (D^3 will be proportional to mv^2) matches the results of Part I: increasing bolide mass causes a proportional increase in the volume of the crater. This explains the roughly straight line. Knowing this relationship, you can make quantitative predictions about a bolide's mass once you've measured its crater size.

The lunar farside photographed by Apollo 11 astronauts. The large crater is I.A.U. crater no. 308 (approximately 80 km in diameter). Think about the differences in mass required to create these different sized craters.

Quantitative predictions

INCREASE IN CRATER DIAMETER (D)		REQUIRED INCREASE IN MASS
2X		_____ times
5X		_____ times
10X		_____ times
20X	REQUIRES	_____ times
50X		_____ times
100X		_____ times
200X		_____ times

QUESTIONS/CONCLUSIONS

1. Use the formula in (e.) to answer the following question: In order to produce a crater twice (two times) as large as another, how much larger must a bolide be?

   _____ times as large

   (Hint: the answer is *not* two times.)

   Check the result you obtain with your teacher before proceeding.

2. Once you learn the basic rule for solving problems like Question 1, complete Prediction Box 1.

3. In applying the formula (D^3 will be proportional to mv^2) to Prediction Box 1, what are you assuming is constant for all impacts?

4. What additional factors could produce variations in the results compared to the predictions?

5. Compare your predictions to the results obtained in Part I. Does the prediction—D^3 will be proportional to mv^2—accurately estimate your results? Explain any variation you find.

JUST HOW BIG IS **BIG?**

MATERIALS

Each group will need

- bag of simulated planetary bedrock

- cup of simulated planetary surface

- container

- sieve or large spoon

- simulated bolides (assorted sizes)

- drop cloth or floor cover

- ruler

- chair

- string, weight on the end

- graph paper

- safety goggles for everyone

WHAT IS HAPPENING?

In Activity 8, students experimented with the connection between activity and energy. They learned putting more energy into their sand affected the energy (in the form of heat) of their system. This activity extends that work to a quantitative level. Students learn about kinetic energy and its numerical relation to mass and velocity:

$$\text{kinetic energy} = 1/2\ mv^2$$

Because Part II contains some of the results for Part I, don't hand out the Part II worksheets until Part I has been completed. In Part II, students experiment with the connection between bolide mass and crater size. Qualitatively, heavier masses leave larger craters. Quantitatively, as mass increases, crater volume (measured here as the cube of the crater diameter) increases proportionally. These results occur because as mass is changed in the experiment, so does the bolide's kinetic energy.

Because a numerical relationship exists between kinetic energy and crater volume, quantitative estimates are possible for impact sites. In Part II, students are introduced to the rationale for such estimates and are led to the prediction that:

$$D^3 \text{ will be proportional to } mv^2$$

In exploring this prediction, students gain an appreciation for the numerical relation itself—e.g., that a 10-fold increase in crater diameter requires a 1,000-fold increase in mass.

An extension provides the formula for making other quantitative predictions for impacts. Because crater size depends on both mass and velocity, students also might want to explore how changing velocity affects cratering.

The three elements of this activity (Parts I and II, plus the extension below) are designed with increasing levels of abstraction. Such a design allows you to tailor this activity to your students' ability levels and interests. Part I may be presented alone. Likewise, the extension may be passed over without major loss to the learning objectives.

IMPORTANT POINTS FOR STUDENTS TO UNDERSTAND

• Kinetic energy is the energy associated with motion.

• The kinetic energy of a bolide is determined by its mass and velocity, or 1/2 mv^2

• Because a numerical relation exists between a bolide's kinetic energy and crater size, quantitative predictions about impacts are possible.

PREPARATION

Part I

This activity uses a streamlined version of Activity 3. Whereas in Activity 3 the emphasis was on the anatomy of craters, here the point is to connect crater size with the bolide's kinetic energy. Several elements of the experimental design are crucial for good results. First, to keep velocity basically constant, bolides should be dropped from a standard height. Dropping height should exceed 2 meters, and higher drops (closer to 3 meters) are preferable. Students can stand on chairs or ladders if it is safe for them to do so. Create measuring strings of uniform length to standardize dropping height. To keep the string taut, tie a weight onto the bottom end of the string, or tie one end to the container of simulated surface. An alternative is to have students throw bolides to the surface; however, this practice prevents velocity from being controlled during the experiment.

More controlled results are obtained when bolides *differ in mass but not in volume*. Such bolides can be made by hollowing out small balls (table tennis balls, super balls, or reusable ice balls) and refilling them with lead weights or substances of varying densities. When resealed, these simulated bolides should be weighted. Various sizes of BBs can be cast in plaster molds, if enough preparation time is available. Slingshot ammunition also works well for weights.

Number the bolides. Students can measure the mass as part of the activity. Each group should use masses that range at least in one order of magnitude (e.g., 10–100 grams). The widest range of bolide masses for this experiment need not extend beyond 5–500 grams. Be sure to test the bolides you create prior to launching this activity in class; optimal weight ranges will vary depending on your choice for simulated planetary materials.

Photograph from Apollo 8 of Goclenius Crater (foreground). The three clustered craters (background, left) are Magelhaens, Magelhaens A, and Colombo A. Goclenius Crater is approximately 67 kilometers in diameter. This is image Moon907.tif on Craters!-CD. As an extension to this activity, students can be asked to estimate the size of bolides that created particular craters.

The lunar farside as seen by Apollo 11 astronauts. The large crater is I.A.U. crater no. 308 (approximately 80 km in diameter). This image is Moon 901.tif on Craters!-CD. It also is the same image as Figure 4 in the student section.

Part II and Extension

No equipment is required for these sections. You may choose to review algebraic manipulation with your students. Also, be sure to work through the answers to student questions prior to beginning these sections. Several steps require knowledge of basic algebraic rules, such as the principle of complementarity (a change to one side of an equation requires a complementary change to the other). Calculations in the extension require the use of power functions: squares, cubes, square roots, and cube roots. For numerical calculations, students are advised to have calculators or spreadsheets available. Remember: finding the cube root of a number, x, is equivalent to raising it to the one-third power, or $x^{1/3}$. Also remind students about the difference between manipulating equalities *versus* manipulating proportionalities.

SUGGESTIONS FOR FURTHER STUDY

Table 1 in the student section introduces scientific notation. Students can learn how to make computations using this shorthand. Likewise, the standard unit of energy, joule, is introduced in this activity. Students can explore the uses of this unit, its physical meaning (what does 100J feel like?), and its conversion to other energy units, such as calories and ergs.

Some of the largest impacts occur with such force that the raising of the rim actually produces a series of rings encircling the crater. (This is shown in the painting on this book's front cover.) The 150 kilometer, multi-ring Orientale basin on the Moon and crater Lise Meitner on Venus are good examples of such impacts.

CONNECTIONS

Bolides move at considerable velocities. How do they acquire those speeds? Planets' speeds in moving around the Sun typically range in the tens of kilometers per second. So even if two bodies collide at a fraction of that speed, they are likely to crash at kilometers/second. By comparison, a rifle bullet typically moves at a few hundred meters per second.

Students can explore the physics of gravitational attraction and the role gravity plays in altering the directions and velocities of meteorites and comets. Jupiter's massive gravitational field, for example, is responsible for diverting the path of many interplanetary bodies. Planetary scientists use the sling-shot effect of these gravitational fields to steer and accelerate spacecraft.

Although bolides involve complications to the basic approach, this activity provides a launching point into the physics of falling bodies. The modern study of this subject began with Galileo (whose telescope work was discussed in Activity 2), and it forms a basic element in any physics curriculum. Students can explore this topic and the ways bolides offer special cases of free fall.

You might ask students to examine this activity as an application for the principle of conservation of energy. Ask them to trace how the kinetic energy of the bolide is converted to other forms of energy during the impact.

ANSWERS TO QUESTIONS FOR STUDENTS

Part I

1. When students compare crater size to bolide mass directly, they should get a curve. If they plot bolide mass versus crater diameter cubed, the graph should be closer to a straight line. Such results have allowed scientists to say bolide mass (and energy) are roughly proportional to the cube of the crater diameter.

2. When students graph the cube of crater diameter against mass, their graphs should approximate a straight line. Variations in experimental conditions (e.g., differences in the compactness of the simulated bedrock) will produce noise in the graph. If so, you can discuss "noisy data" and extend the range of masses (and the care taken in the procedure) to clarify the shape of the plotted curve. It's a good chance to talk about how scientists have to work hard to get good data.

3. Students should connect crater size to the kinetic energy of falling bolides.

4. The answers to these questions are explored in Part II.

Part II

1. The mass must be increased 8 times. Why? Follow this chain of reasoning:

   a. For a crater diameter (D_2) twice as large as another (D_1):

$$D_2 = 2D_1 \qquad \text{and} \qquad m_2 = ym_1$$

   b. To predict the mass that made crater D_2, you begin with:

      $(D_2)^3$ is proportional to $(m_2)\, v^2$, or,
      $(D_2)^3$ is proportional to $(ym_1)\, v^2$, or,
      $(2D_1)^3$ is proportional to $(ym_1)\, v^2$

and solve for y, the proportional change in mass to compensate for the 2-fold increase in crater diameter. Remember: to maintain the principle of complementarity, equal changes must be made to both sides of the equation. Solving for y gives the value to add as a complement.

   c. Assume the two bolides move at the same velocity, so velocity becomes irrelevant:

      $(2D_1)^3$ is proportional to (ym_1)

   d. Expand the equation. This is the key step! Watch what happens to the *left* side of the proportion.

      $(2^3)\,(D_1)^3$ is proportional to (ym_1), or,
      $8\,(D_1)^3$ is proportional to (ym_1)

   e. To keep the proportionality constant, both sides of the equation must be changed equally, so solve for y:

      $8 = y$

Thus, to increase crater diameter 2X, mass must increase 8X. Substituting a variable, x, for 2 in this equation produces the generalization that change in mass will be equal to the cube of the change of the diameter, or $y = x^3$.

2. Once students are comfortable with the explanation for Question 1, they can use the cube relation for Table 1.

y	requires	x^3
2X	requires	8X
5X	requires	125X
10X	requires	1,000X
20X	requires	8,000X
50X	requires	125,000X
100X	requires	1,000,000X
200X	requires	8,000,000X
500X	requires	125,000,000X

3. Velocity is assumed to be constant in Question 1, as shown in step (c).

4. Beyond the equation, other elements of the impact are assumed to be constant. For example, it is assumed that both impacts occur on surfaces of the same density. If students are interested, they can identify numerous assumptions. Knowing what is assumed is an important skill for understanding models in science.

5. Answers will vary.

EXTENSION

If students are comfortable with the algebra involved, you can ask them to make additional predictions. This requires manipulating steps (a–e) in Question 1 as follows:

- If crater diameter increases by x, what will be the increase in velocity?
  Answer: for step (b), begin with the equation:
  $(xD_1)^3$ is proportional to $m (yv_1)^2$
  [Velocity will increase as the square root of x cubed, or $(x^3)^{1/2}$.]

- If mass increases by x, what will be the increase in crater diameter?
  Answer: for step (b), begin with the equation:
  $(yD_1)^3$ is proportional to $(xm_1) v^2$
  [Crater diameter will increase by the cube root of x, or $x^{1/3}$.]

- If velocity increases by x, what will be the increase in crater diameter?
  Answer: for step (b), begin with the equation:
  $(yD_1)^3$ is proportional to $m (xv_1)^2$
  [Crater diameter will increase by the cube root of x squared, or, $(x^2)^{1/3}$.]

CRATERS, CRATERS EVERYWHERE

There is no student section for this activity.

MATERIALS

♦ images of surfaces from different planetary bodies

♦ materials from selected previous activities

CD-ROM

OBJECTIVE

This activity offers a review and assessment of techniques developed in previous activities by studying planetary surfaces other than the Moon.

WHAT IS HAPPENING?

This activity has two purposes. First, it shows students that cratering occurs not just on the Moon but on other planetary bodies, too. A variety of images from other planetary bodies are provided in this activity. In addition, *Craters!-CD* provides for your students more than 200 images of planets, satellites, and asteroids. The same principles used to explore impacts and craters in earlier activities (these focused on the Moon) can be applied to impacts on *any* surface. The only planetary body not discussed in this activity is Earth. Impacts on our planet will be treated in Activities 11 and 12.

The second purpose of this activity is review. If your class has followed these lessons in sequence, students will have worked through nine activities that have introduced more than a dozen major concepts and skills. This activity provides a point for you to pause and take the time to reinforce these basic concepts and skills while also emphasizing integration. You will find that investigating the features of other planetary bodies carries with it a special excitement. Tapping into this energy brings an added strength to the review process.

IMPORTANT POINTS FOR STUDENTS TO UNDERSTAND

♦ Evidence of impacts have been found on all planetary bodies that scientists have examined closely.

♦ The principles developed in earlier activities for impacts on the Moon can be applied to impact studies on any surface.

♦ Earth and Moon are not unique in terms of being subject to impacts.

Extend Activities 3 and 5 using craters from Mercury's surface. The small, bright halo crater in the center of this image is 10 km in diameter, while the prominent crater below has a central peak 30 km across. The darker, lightly cratered area (upper left) may be an ancient lava flow. This image is Other301.tif on Craters!-CD.

PREPARATION

How best to review the different kinds of skills developed in earlier activities is a matter of preference. You might adapt previous activities to create stations for students to visit, assign projects that focus on particular planetary bodies, or ask groups to create comprehensive reports for particular images. Or, to tailor projects to your students' needs and interests, you might create specific assignments, such as the following two, for investigation:

1. Compare the cratering on several planetary bodies. Decide on a uniform area size, then randomly choose areas in which to count crater size distribution. Create a table to show the ratios of sizes in each area. Then, develop a table to show the ratio of impact sizes on each planetary body. Ask students to write up their discoveries as a newspaper article or present them in a seminar for their fellow students.

2. Using techniques from earlier activities, analyze depth-to-width ratios of craters on different planetary bodies. Are impact craters similar on different planets? Ask students to report their findings to the class.

In addition to the images reproduced in this activity, more than 200 planetary surface images are located on *Craters!*-CD. For other sources of planetary images, see the Resources List.

Extend Activity 9 with this image of Saturn's moon Tethys. The smoother, blurred area toward bottom center is caused by incomplete data analysis. This image is Other901.tif on Craters!-CD.

SUGGESTIONS FOR FURTHER STUDY

Students should be encouraged to investigate what planetary scientists know about particular planetary bodies and study the methods scientists use for creating that knowledge. If students concentrate on images created from one source—e.g., images from Voyager 2 or the Viking probes—have them investigate the project that built, launched, and used that device. NASA facilities are located throughout the United States. Perhaps a visit to one is possible. Students traveling on family vacations also may have the opportunity to visit large NASA facilities, such as Cape Canaveral in Florida, the Johnson Space Flight Center in Texas, or the Jet Propulsion Laboratory in California. In addition, a visit to Washington, DC, can include a tour of the Smithsonian Institution's National Air and Space Museum. See the Resources List for further information about NASA facilities.

Working with images produced by the Voyager spacecrafts, planetary scientists have produced three-dimensional images of surfaces in the outer solar system. If you use stereoscopes in your classroom, obtain an original copy of *Science News* for November 12, 1994 (volume 146, pp. 314–315), to view images of Uranus' moons Titania, Miranda, and Ariel, as well as Saturn's heavily cratered moon, Rhea. These images were produced by Paul Schenk at the Lunar and Planetary Institute in Houston, Texas.

Using images of volcanic craters and meteor craters as a starting point, investigate how the two types of craters can be distinguished. Generally, volcanic craters are less regular in outline and lack the hummocky ejecta blankets thrown out of impact craters. What can you infer from the presence of volcanoes about the geologic dynamics of a planetary object? (Hint: What does the presence of volcanoes tell about presence of heat inside the planetary body?) Are there volcanoes on our Moon? Mars? Venus? Io? Europa? Callisto? Pluto? A good volcanic crater to use as an example is Mars' Olympus Mons summit caldera.

CONNECTIONS

Students can investigate the discovery of particular planetary bodies: planets, satellites, asteroids, and comets. Like the four largest moons of Jupiter (which Galileo discovered using his telescope in 1610), each discovery has a unique and detailed history. Students should be easily able to see the four large moons of Jupiter with a small telescope or large binoculars, as Galileo did. Students might also investigate the search for Planet X, the possible tenth planet in our solar system. Why has its existence been suggested and what evidence exists for its presence?

Students might investigate the process of naming newly discovered planetary bodies or features of those bodies. Who gets to name these bodies? What do some of the names mean? Challenge your students to decipher the meaning of as many names as they can. By convention, for example, all features of Venus are named after prominent women. If your students discovered a new planetary body, what name would they choose for it? Investigate the community of astronomers that searches for new planetary bodies. How and where do they report their results?

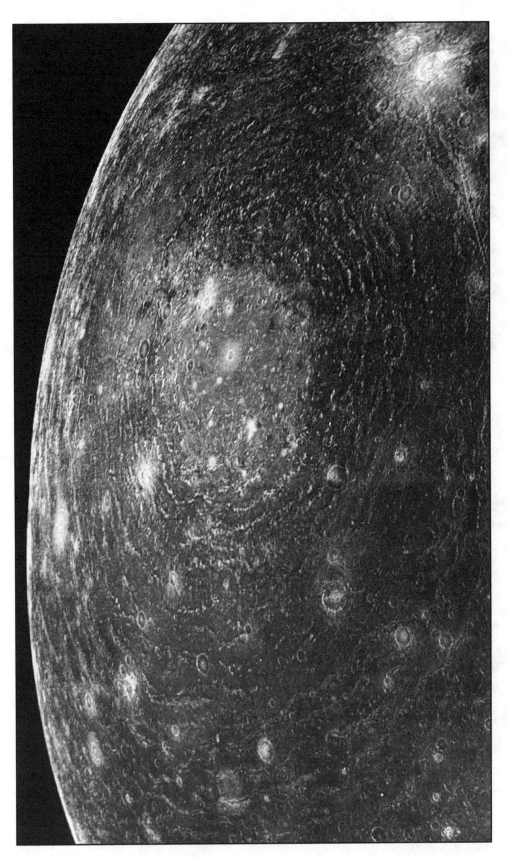

Voyager 1 image of Jupiter's moon, Callisto, shows the heavily cratered surface and the prominent ring structure known as Valhalla. Valhalla is an impact "crater" that has been filled in, flattened, and modified by the glacier-like flow of the ice that comprises Callisto's crust. Valhalla's bright central area is about 300 km across with sets of concentric ridges extending out to 1,500 km from the center. This image is Other304.tif on Craters!-CD.

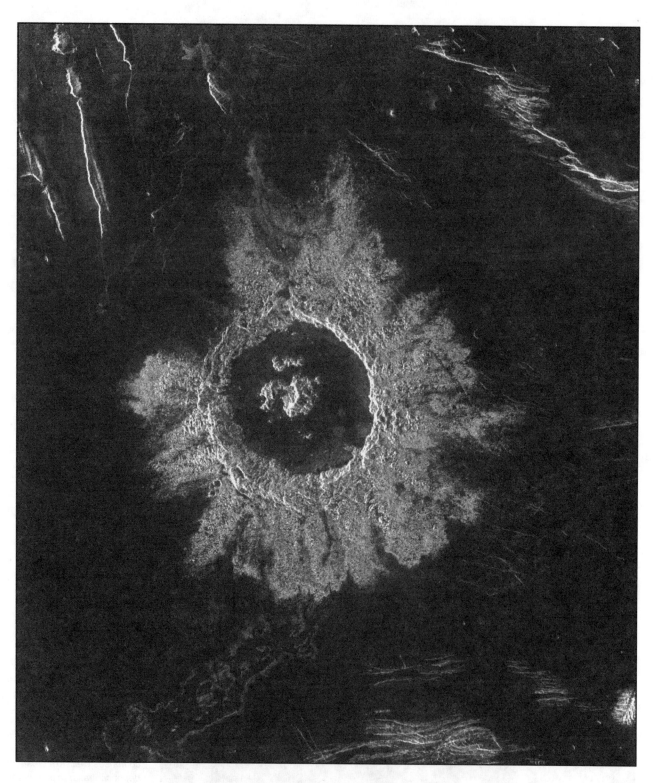

The surface of Venus is covered largely by geologically young lava flows (500 to 800 million years old). Impact craters such as this one are scattered across the planet but are rarer than on the Moon because the surface is younger. This example, imaged by radar from the Magellan orbiter, shows a well developed central peak and an outer, hummocky ejecta blanket. This image is Other313.tif on Craters!-CD.

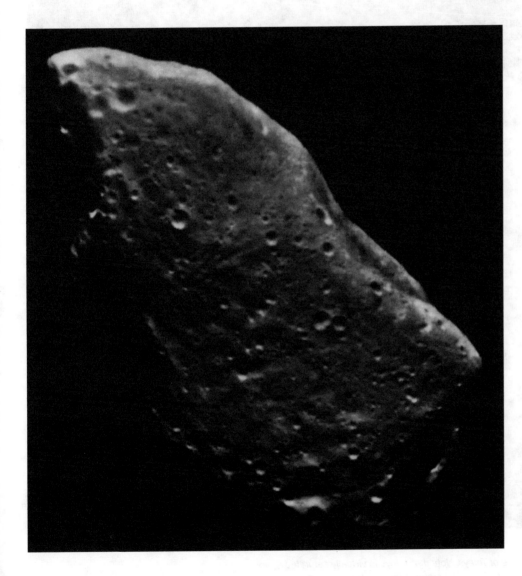

Asteroid 951 Gaspra, composite image. Notice that this asteroid is covered by craters marking impacts of still smaller asteroid fragments. This image is Other618.tif on Craters!-CD.

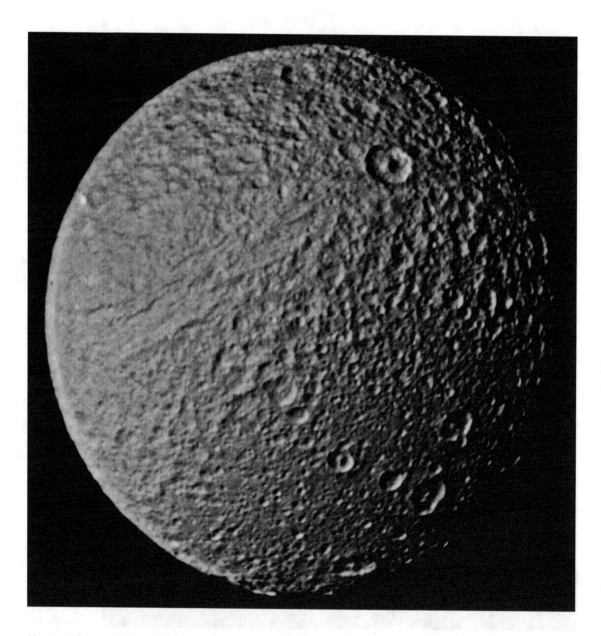

Voyager 2 image of Tethys. Note that Tethys is virtually saturated with impact craters. The large crater in the upper right lies at the edge of the huge trench system that girdles nearly three-fourths of the circumference of the satellite. This image is Other641.tif on Craters!-CD.

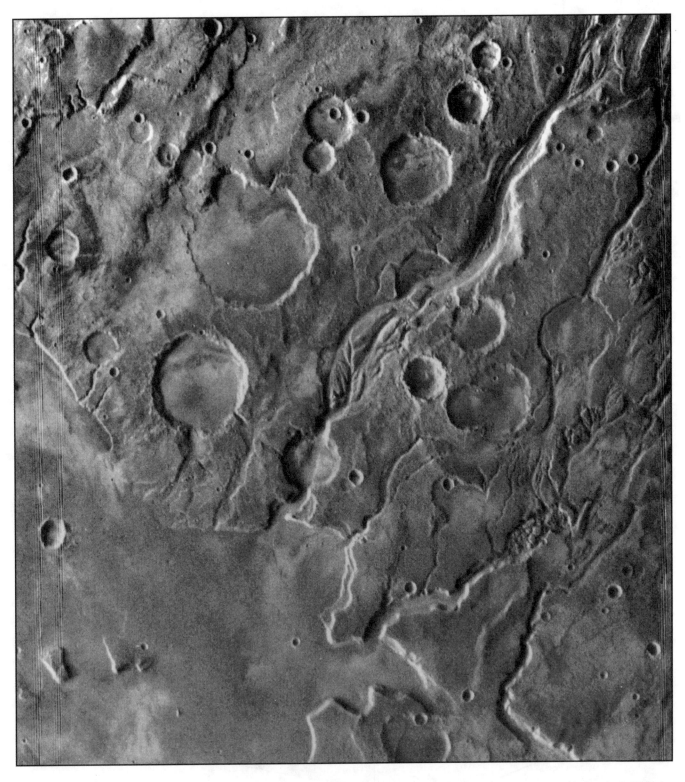

Cratered highlands on Mars are laced with dry arroyos marking ancient riverbeds. Mars is more like Earth than most moons and planets; erosion and even ancient river flow have obliterated or filled in craters to various degrees. Still, there are more craters on Mars than on Earth. This image is Other642.tif on Craters!-CD.

A HOLE IN ARIZONA

MATERIALS

♦ image of Barringer Crater

♦ instructions for research

OBJECTIVE

This activity introduces you to Barringer Crater in Arizona. Evidence of impacts can be found just about everywhere in our solar system. Earth is no exception.

BACKGROUND

If you're ever in Flagstaff, Arizona, head east on Interstate 40 (Figure 1). Travel about 80 kilometers and you'll be just north of an extraordinary site: Barringer Crater (Figure 2). This activity asks you to be a detective. Investigate this site. Learn what caused it and what it tells us about Earth's history.

PROCEDURE

Your teacher will describe what kinds of materials you are expected to locate, where you might find them, and what form your final report should take. Be creative in your search. There are many ways to locate the same information.

FIGURE 1

Location of Barringer Crater

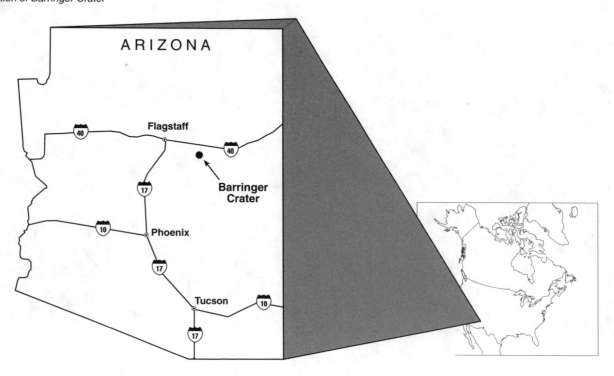

QUESTIONS/CONCLUSIONS

Descriptive Information: What Is It?

1. Locate this site on a topographic map. What is its latitude and longitude?

2. How big is this site?

3. Describe its features.

4. How old is it?

5. Were there any eyewitnesses?

6. Why hasn't it eroded away like many other impact sites on Earth?

7. What was the local environment like at the time this happened?

8. Describe the geology of this area. Does this hole stand out as unusual?

9. What happened to the material inside it?

10. Who owns this site? When was it recognized as an impact feature?

FIGURE 2

Aerial view of Barringer Crater. The meandering paths are roads. The Visitor's Center is on the left of the crater.

Earth 129.tif

Earth 120.tif

View of Barringer Crater from the rim.

Interpretation: How Was It Formed; Why Is It There?

11. What evidence exists to show that this is a crater formed by impact of an asteroid fragment?

12. What is the size estimate for the bolide?

13. If this bolide had fallen at 20 kilometers per second, how much kinetic energy was it carrying just before the impact?

14. Is what happened here a rare or common event for Earth? Can you identify another example of this phenomenon on Earth?

A HOLE IN ARIZONA

WHAT IS HAPPENING?

This activity is designed as a personal research project. Students can work alone or in groups. In the process of investigating Barringer Crater, students are asked not just to locate facts but also to describe interpretations about this hole in the ground. The process of scientific reasoning is thereby reinforced.

Barringer Crater—also known as Meteor Crater—is the best preserved bolide impact site in the United States. The crater itself is over 1.2 kilometers in diameter and more than 180 meters deep. The rim is raised nearly 50 meters above ground level. Barringer Crater formed 20–50,000 years ago when a nickel-iron meteorite—between 10 and 60 meters in diameter and weighing as much as 900 million kilograms—fell from the sky. The impact was approximately equivalent to an explosion of 15 megatons of TNT. Most meteorites are of rocky or icy material, and 10–60 meter meteoroids of this material seldom reach the ground, instead exploding or vaporizing in the atmosphere. Roughly one in 30 meteoroids is nickel-iron, a material dense enough to reach the ground. A collision that produces a crater like Barringer Crater happens roughly once every 30,000 years or so. Thus, while Barringer Crater is a rare feature by human standards, it is a common and normal feature by geologic standards. Others exist, but older ones in most climates are severely eroded. (To have students explore the frequency of bolide impacts on Earth, see Activities 18, 19, and especially 20.)

At first, scientists studying this site believed it was the cauldron of a volcano. Indeed, other volcanoes exist roughly 60 miles away, near Flagstaff. However, meteorite fragments composed of nearly pure nickel-iron alloy were found in abundance nearby. These were identified as fragments of the iron cores of asteroids, leading some geologists to suggest the site was an impact crater. Furthermore, mapping of the subsurface structure, using drill holes, showed it was a bolide explosion site, not a volcanic crater. Today the meteorite origin for Barringer Crater is undisputed.

IMPORTANT POINTS FOR STUDENTS TO UNDERSTAND

- Evidence of impacts can be found just about everywhere in our solar system. Earth is no exception.

- Barringer Crater, located in northern Arizona, is a large and well preserved bolide impact site.

MATERIALS

- image of Barringer Crater

- instructions for research

Earth 120.tif

FIGURE 3

Aerial view of Barringer Crater. On Craters!-CD, this image is file Earth129.tif.

CD-ROM

PREPARATION

Before launching this activity, review research techniques with your students. Tell them what kinds of materials you expect them to locate, where they might find them, and what form their final reports to you should take. Several guides to Barringer Crater are provided in the Resources List. *Craters!-CD* contains images for the views of Barringer Crater provided here.

SUGGESTIONS FOR FURTHER STUDY

For extra credit, a group can be asked to play the role of tour guide in a mock visit to the site. Have them "walk" through the crater's features and answer questions in the same way that guides do at tourist sites.

Students can use the list of questions in the Questions/Conclusions section for other impact sites, especially ones that exist (if any do) in your region of the country.

CONNECTIONS

Students might want to explore the history of research about Barringer Crater. Humans were not present in North America at the time the impact occurred, so eyewitness accounts do not exist. Native Americans seem to have found no reason to take special interest in what was located there. Through the 19th century, American geologists believed this site was produced in a huge steam explosion, the result of volcanic activity nearby. It can be found on maps of the time labeled as "Coon Mountain" or "Coon Butte." (To be fair, there *are* craters in the area caused by volcanic activity so this seemed to be a reasonable explanation at the time.) The first

FIGURE 4

Aerial view of Clearwater Lakes, Quebec. This pair of craters, 32 and 22 km in original diameter, may mark an impact by an asteroid and its satellite. The craters have been eroded by glaciers in the ice ages. On Craters!-CD, this is file Earth128.tif

to suggest this site represented an impact crater was Daniel Moreau Barringer (1860–1929), a Philadelphia lawyer, geologist, and mining engineer. Barringer sought to mine what he thought would be a "treasure" of nickel and iron he expected to find left over from the original meteor. He never found that treasure, however. For a variety of technical and personal reasons, Barringer's theory of a meteor impact was ridiculed by many geologists. The long process of theory conversion also can be a subject of student investigation. Useful readings are provided in the Resources List. You also can contact the state geological survey in Arizona for more information.

Barringer Crater is well preserved due to the region's arid climate. Processes of erosion still affect the crater, and this case provides a good launching point for investigating how erosion (and other processes) changes Earth's surface. Compare Barringer Crater (Figure 3), for example, with the twin Clearwater Lakes in Quebec (Figure 4). These lakes (32 and 33 kilometers in diameter) probably were formed by a pair of bolides nearly 300 million years ago. (See Figures 3 and 4 in Activity 18 for an example of a binary asteroid.) These craters show considerable erosion and demonstrate how impacts have occurred on Earth throughout its history even though the surface remains quite unlike that of the Moon.

THERE'S NO PLACE LIKE HOME, OR IS THERE?

MATERIALS

Part I

Work in small groups. Each student will need

- at least one topographic or geologic map of an area on Earth
- one sample image of the Moon's surface

Part II

Work in small groups. Each student will need

- blank map of North America

OBJECTIVE

In this activity you will investigate the frequency of impact sites on Earth and work to explain why Earth's surface is not as heavily cratered as other planetary bodies.

BACKGROUND

The Moon has an enormous number of impact craters, as do many other planetary bodies. Radiometric dating of rocks from the Moon indicates (a.) most of its surface is between 3 and 4 billion years old, (b.) the Moon itself is about 4.5 billion years old, and (c.) the Moon stopped being geologically active about 2 billion years ago. Identical dating techniques place Earth's origin around 4.6 billion years ago. Here is the paradox: if Earth is about as old or slightly older than the Moon, why does the Moon have so many impact craters and Earth have so few? Does Earth somehow avoid bolide impacts, or is there another explanation?

Part I: Investigating Samples

PROCEDURE

1. Ask your teacher for maps of different regions on Earth. Examine these maps closely. Make the following records in Observation Box 1: What location are you investigating? What is the scale—how many millimeters on the map are equal to one kilometer on the actual landscape? How many square kilometers are represented in the map you are studying?

2. Carefully search your map for craters and evidence of craters. In Observation Box 1, record the latitude and longitude of any craters or evidence of craters you find.

3. After each member of your group has examined at least one map, compile your team's results. How many craters were located? How many total square kilometers were examined? Calculate the number of craters per 1,000 square kilometers.

OBSERVATION BOX 1

Search for crater sites in North America

LOCATION

scale: _____ millimeters = 1 kilometer

size: _____ square kilometers shown on map

IMPACT SITES IDENTIFIED

1. _____
2. _____
3. _____
4. _____
5. _____
6. _____
7. _____
8 _____
9. _____
10. _____

11. _____
12. _____
13. _____
14. _____
15. _____
16. _____
17. _____
18. _____
19. _____
20. _____

QUESTIONS/CONCLUSIONS

1. Compare your results with a similar surface area on the Moon. Qualitatively, are craters on Earth more frequent, as frequent, or less frequent than craters on the Moon? If you can give a quantitative answer, by all means do so.

2. Within your group, discuss reasons for the results in Observation Box 1 and in Question 1 above. What could explain the differences in crater frequency? How would you test these possible explanations?

3. How is Earth's surface different from the Moon's? How could these differences help explain your observations?

4. Examine Figures 1 (Barringer Crater) and 2 (Clearwater Lakes). Where in North America are these craters located? Does the difference in their age or location provide clues to the explanation you are seeking regarding craters on Earth?

5. What different *physical and geological processes* do you suppose have acted on these two craters since their formation? Does this difference provide more clues about the absence of craters on Earth?

Earth 129.tif

FIGURE 1A

Barringer Crater, Arizona, is the largest and best preserved bolide impact site in the United States. The crater has a rim diameter of 1.2 kilometers, and is more than 180 meters deep. The rim is raised nearly 50 meters above ground level.

6. Think about the differences between these two statements:

a. *Craters* are much less frequent on Earth than on the Moon.

b. *Impacts* are much less frequent on Earth than on the Moon.

How are these statements different, as far as the observations in this activity are concerned?

Earth 128.tif

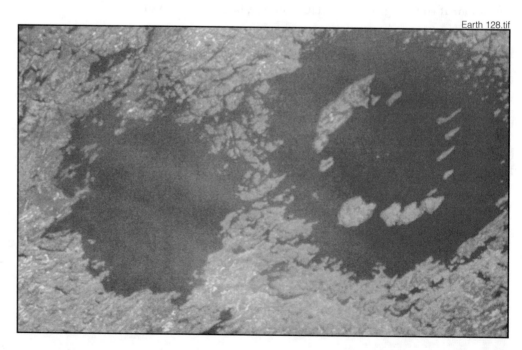

FIGURE 2

Twin impact craters of Clearwater Lakes, Quebec. These formed simultaneously by two separate meteorite impacts, probably an asteroid and its satellite asteroid. Asteroid Toutatis (Figures 3 and 4 in Activity 18) is an example of the binary asteroids that can explain double craters. The larger lake (right) has a diameter of about 32 kilometers.

Part II: Surveying North America

In Part I, you found that craters were much less frequent on Earth than on the Moon. You also suggested reasons to explain this difference. Looking for craters in Part I may have left you with the impression that very few craters are known on Earth. This would be wrong. Geologists have identified many impact sites around the globe. Of course, compared to the Moon, craters are relatively rare on our planet. Because it has no atmosphere, the Moon's surface does not weather. There is almost no erosion or deposition (except for "sand blasting" effects of small meteorites). Because it now has neither volcanic nor tectonic activity, the Moon has a static surface—craters are not obliterated by other geological processes. In fact, the surface that you see today on the Moon has been its surface for *at least* 2 billion years. As a result, the Moon's entire surface provides a chance to examine more than 2 billion years of accumulated impacts. Smaller bolides incinerate entering Earth's atmosphere.

Earth 120.tif

FIGURE 1B
Another view of Barringer Crater, Arizona, this time from the rim using a wide-angle lens.

Earth is different. Earth's atmosphere causes weathering and erosion on the surface. Volcanoes and tectonic activity also constantly change Earth's surface. Combined weathering, erosion, and tectonic activity remove most evidence of bolide impacts on Earth. This is also true of some other planetary bodies—e.g., Venus has violent windstorms and sandstorms.

In addition, because rocks on Earth's surface vary in age, impact rates are hard to study. The longer a surface is exposed to possible impacts, the more craters it should have. The oldest rocks so far found on Earth are 3.8 to 3.9 billion years old, but these are rare. Rocks from the Precambrian (before about 600 million years ago and as old as about 2.5 billion years old) are found on every continent. They are most abundant in eastern Canada, northern Europe, and sub-Saharan Africa. However, most of Earth's surface is covered by rocks that are relatively young. For example all ocean basins—this amounts to about 75 percent of the planet's surface—are less than 200 million years old. With all this change going on, existing impact sites can be removed from Earth's surface, and newer surfaces have less chance of showing an impact in the first place!

If you had trouble finding craters in Part I, don't think Earth is immune from bolide impacts. Most ordinary maps show virtually no impact features on Earth except for the Barringer Crater in Arizona. Does this mean none exist? In this part of the activity, you will work with a sample of known impact sites across North America. Many of these craters are nearly covered by sediments or eroded away. Most have been found only after careful geologic study. This will provide you with a sense of how many crater sites are known and where they are located. Please note, however, that the choice of North America for a study site is simply a matter of convenience. Craters have been found on all seven continents.

DATA TABLE 1

39 known or likely impact sites on North America

LATITUDE	LONGITUDE	DIAMETER (KM)	AGE (MILLION YEARS AGO)	LATITUDE	LONGITUDE	DIAMETER (KM)	AGE (MILLION YEARS AGO)
46°N	81°W	140	1850 ± 150	36°N	87°W	14	200 ± 100
44°N	76°W	2	550 ± 100	47°N	103°W	9	200
43°N	89°W	6	500	58°N	109°W	37	117 ± 8
46°N	78°W	3.8	450 ± 30	56°N	102°W	12	100 ± 50
60°N	111°W	6	440 ± 2	49°N	95°W	2.7	100 ± 50
57°N	66°W	8	400 ± 50	30°N	102°W	13	100
62°N	102°W	12.5	400	59°N	117°W	25	95 ± 7
47°N	70°W	46	360 ± 25	21°N	89°W	180	66
36°N	85°W	3.8	360 ± 20	49°N	110°W	10	65
48°N	80°W	30	350	42°N	94°W	32	61 ± 9
37°N	91°W	5.6	320 ± 80	29°N	99°W	2.4	40
39°N	83°W	6.4	320	55°N	63°W	28	38 ± 4
50°N	73°W	4	300	46°N	80°W	8.5	37 ± 2
37°N	92°W	6	300	75°N	89°W	20	21.5 ± 1.2
40°N	87°W	13	300	61°N	73°W	3.2	5
36°N	83°W	6	300	35°N	111°W	1.2	0.05
56°N	74°W	22	290 ± 20	37°N	99°W	0.011	?
56°N	104°W	5	250	31°N	102°W	0.168	?
51°N	98°W	23	225 ± 40	38°N	109°W	5	?
51°N	68°W	100	212 ± 2				

—Source: This data was collected from Terrestrial Impact Craters, a Hypercard® stack created by Jim Vedda and Chuck Wood, Department of Space Studies, University of North Dakota. This stack was based on data in R.A.F Grieve, et al., "Astronaut's Guide to Terrestrial Impacts Craters," LPI Technical Report 88-03, 1988. An expanded survey of impact craters on Earth is provided by Richard Grieve, "Terrestrial Impact: The Record in the Rocks," Meteoritics, 1991, volume 26, pp. 175-194.

PROCEDURE

1. Obtain a blank map of North America (Figure 3). The lines on the map indicate longitude (vertical lines) and latitude (horizontal). Latitude is given in degrees north from the equator. Longitude is given in degrees west of the prime meridian, located at an observatory in Greenwich, England.

2. Data Table 1 lists 39 known and likely impact sites on North America, arranged by the estimated date of impact. Approximate crater diameter also is provided for comparison. Read this chart as follows: Barringer Crater in Arizona has the coordinates 35°N 111°W, is 1.2 kilometers in diameter, and was formed approximately 0.05 million (50,000) years ago. Draw a data point on your map for each of the impact sites provided in Data Table 1.

3. After everyone in your group has completed plotting the data points, discuss how best to interpret your maps.

DATA TABLE 2	
CRATER DIAMETER (KM)	**NUMBER OBSERVED**
under 2.0	_____
2.0–3.9	_____
4.0–7.9	_____
8.0–15.9	_____
16.0–31.9	_____
32.0–63.9	_____
64.0 and over	_____

QUESTIONS/CONCLUSIONS

1. Are there more crater sites on your map than you expected? Are there patterns to the distribution of crater sites in North America or does this distribution seem to be random? Is this distribution other than what you had expected?

2. How might you explain this distribution?

3. Investigate the size distribution of the craters listed in Data Table 1. Summarize the size distribution in Data Table 2. Is the size distribution different from what you expected? What explanation can you offer to explain the difference?

FIGURE 3

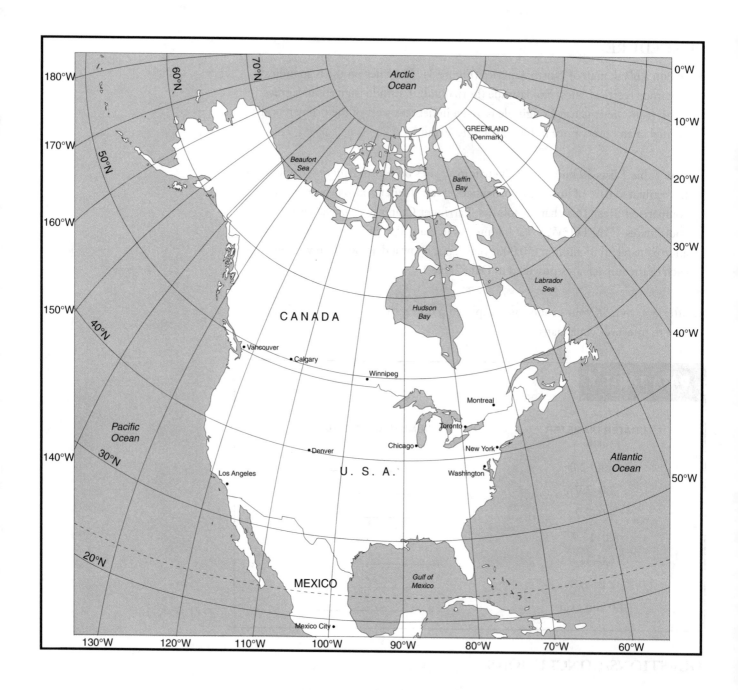

THERE'S NO PLACE LIKE HOME, OR IS THERE?

WHAT IS HAPPENING?

Before this lesson, activities in this book have emphasized cratering on the Moon and other planetary bodies. However, little has been said about cratering on Earth. Has Earth's surface received as many impacts as other surfaces? The present activity explores this question.

After quick examination, students will see that Earth's surface looks quite different from the Moon's. What explains this contrast? Has Earth received fewer impacts? As a matter of fact, on the basis of many studies, astronomers believe Earth receives 20 times the number of impacts as does the Moon. However, the impact rate per square kilometer is nearly the same. (Earth is a bigger target in terms of its surface area and its gravitational pull.) This being the case, if few craters can be found on Earth, the question becomes: where is the evidence of impacts?

Earth is a dynamic planet. Weather alters its surface through wind, water, heating, and cooling. Tectonic activity creates, alters, and destroys surfaces. It also covers and otherwise obliterates surface features—as can glaciers and changes in sea level, among other things. Such geological processes remove evidence of impacts. The age of a surface also is important to the study of cratering. The longer a surface is exposed, the more likely it is to have evidence of impacts. The Moon's heavily cratered surface is at least 2 billion years old and probably records 3 to 4 billion years of impacts. Most of Earth's surface is *considerably* younger than this. Most surface features, such as mountains and plains, are 50 to 500 million years old. No wonder Earth has fewer craters!

IMPORTANT POINTS FOR STUDENTS TO UNDERSTAND

- When it comes to impacts, Earth is *not* unique. Many bolides have collided with our planet over its 4.6 billion year history. Impact sites are known on all seven continents.

- Geological processes—like erosion, weathering and plate tectonics—have obscured and destroy evidence of many impacts on Earth's surface. Similar processes do not occur on the Moon.

- The number of impacts on a surface depends mostly on the amount of time that surface is exposed. Surfaces exposed for longer periods usually show evidence of more impacts.

MATERIALS

Part I

Work in small groups. Each student will need

- at least one topographic or geologic map of an area on Earth
- one sample image of the Moon's surface

Part II

Work in small groups. Each student will need

- blank map of North America (Figure 4)

DATA TABLE 3

A sample of Earth's largest impact sites

SIZE (KM)	AGE (MILLION YEARS AGO)	LOCATION
140	1,840	Sudbury, Ontario, Canada
140	1,970	Vredefort, South Africa
100	40	Popigai, Siberia, Russia
80	183	Puchezh-Katunki, Russia
70	210	Manicouagan, Quebec, Canada
50	57	Kara, Russia
52	365	Slijan, Sweden
46	360	Charlevoix, Canada
40	<250	Araguainha Dome, Brazil

Source: Grieve, 1982, "The Geological Record of Impacts," in L.T. Silver and P.H. Schultz, "Geological Implications of Large Asteroids and Comets on the Earth," GSA Special Paper 190.

PREPARATION

When selecting maps, your choice of geographical region is not as important as the map's scale. You want the maps to show enough detail that craters can be identified. Scales no smaller than 1 centimeter equals 10 to 20 kilometers should be used. Tourist maps and road atlases are barely adequate because they identify almost no craters except Arizona's Barringer Crater. Try topographic or geologic maps. Photographs of Earth taken by satellites are another option. Available from NASA, these photos can reveal that craters are hard to find on Earth.

CD-ROM

Many types of maps—topographic and otherwise—can be obtained from the U.S. Geological Survey. For images of the Moon, use images supplied in Activity 2 (which also are available on *Craters!-CD)*. Because students need only make qualitative comparisons, these can just be posted. If you want quantitative comparisons, copy images for each student.

Your choice of region can coincide with other geographical projects on which students are working. Good results can be obtained by focusing on eastern Canada, western Australia, and western China. Locations of particularly large craters are given in Data Table 3. Major crater sites in North America are listed in Data Table 1. To keep student interest, be sure to use maps on which craters are easy to find. However, because impacts are relatively rare on Earth, be sure most students obtain negative results. Learning why craters are relatively rare on Earth is the goal of this activity.

Part II of this activity examines impact sites in North America. Be sure to make the point that craters are known on all seven continents. The Resources List provides sources for surveys of impacts on other continents.

SUGGESTIONS FOR FURTHER STUDY

This activity provides a convenient launching point to discuss many geological processes—e.g., erosion, weathering, volcanism, and plate tectonics. Students can experiment with the effects of weathering, for example, on crater shape by placing a crater model outside for an extended period of time. They could also make a model crater and subject it to "rain" and other types of weathering.

This activity intentionally skips over questions about the relative *rate* of impacts over time. Some astronomers believe many more impacts occurred during the Solar System's earliest times. As the amount of debris was reduced, impact rates dropped dramatically. (Compare, for instance, high crater densities on 4 billion-year-old, highly cratered lunar surfaces with low crater densities on 3.5 billion-year-old lunar lava plains. See Activity 6.) Other astronomers believe impact rates fluctuate periodically, with planetary bodies sometimes exposed to high impact rates and other times exposed to low impact rates. Students can investigate these different interpretations, the evidence for them, and how each interpretation affects our understanding of Earth's history of impacts. A recent article by G. Jeffrey Taylor in *Scientific American* (see Resources List) provides an excellent starting point. That article also raises questions about the origin of the Moon. The theory currently most widely accepted indicates that the Moon formed from debris blown into space by an enormous impact on a very young Earth.

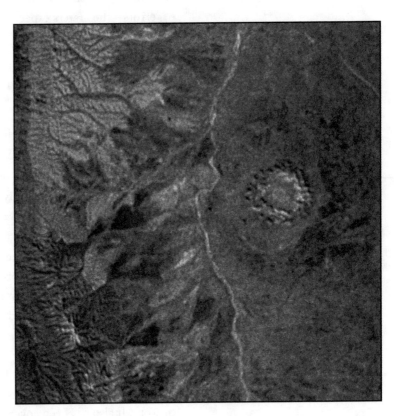

Gosses Bluff, in the arid Missionary Plain in the Northern Territories, Australia, is a highly eroded impact site, with a rim diameter of 22 km. Gosses Bluff is approximately 142.5 million years old (+/- 0.5 million years). On Craters!-CD this is file Earth122.tif

CONNECTIONS

Students can compare crater distributions on geologically active planetary bodies (e.g., Earth and Venus) with geologically inactive ones (e.g., the Moon and Mars).

To investigate the early history of observations of meteors and meteorites, see the paper by Ursula Marvin in the Resources List.

ANSWERS TO QUESTIONS FOR STUDENTS

Part I

1. Regardless of which Moon photographs you use, students should conclude that craters are much less frequent on Earth than on the Moon. Encourage quantitative comparisons.

2. Answers will vary but encourage ideas that can be realistically tested. Popular answers include

   ◆ Crater frequency is different between Earth and the Moon because of sampling errors—the craters expected to be on Earth simply exist in places where students have not looked. Test this by changing the sample.

   ◆ Earth's surface is mostly water, so that's where impacts occur. Test this be studying crater distribution on other planetary bodies. Compare patterns of distribution.

   ◆ Impact rates are not the same on the two planetary bodies. Test this with a survey of impact frequencies for many planetary bodies.

   ◆ Impact rates are the same, but many craters on Earth disappear after they are formed. Test this by identifying eroded or obliterated craters. Also study how geological processes remove evidence of impacts.

3. Much of Earth's surface is covered with water. It also is exposed to weathering and erosion processes. Furthermore, geological activity creates new surfaces and destroys others. Earth also has an atmosphere which provides enough friction to burn up smaller incoming meteors.

4. Barringer Crater is in northern Arizona; Clearwater Lakes are in Quebec, Canada. At nearly 300 million years old, Clearwater Lakes craters are perhaps 60 times as old as Barringer Crater. Quebec has more severe weathering and erosion processes at work. It also has been covered with glaciers at different times after the craters were formed. Arizona provides a more stable environment.

5. Weathering in more severe climates. Erosion from environments that are wetter. These clues help explain why craters disappear faster on Earth compared to the Moon.

DATA TABLE 2 - KEY

CRATER DIAMETER (KM)	NUMBER OBSERVED
under 2.0	3
2.0–3.9	6
4.0–7.9	9
8.0–15.9	9
16.0–31.9	6
32.0–63.9	3
64.0 and over	3

6. Students are investigating *crater* frequency. If impact rates on Earth were much lower than on the Moon, then the explanation for sentence (a) is relatively simple: crater frequency depends only on impact rate. But what if impacts occur on Earth at about the same frequency as they do on the Moon? The question needing explanation becomes what happens to the craters to make them relatively rare here compared to the Moon?

Part II

1. Answers will vary. Usually students are surprised to find so many craters.

2. Answers will vary.

3. The size distribution is shown in Data Table 2–Key. Many craters smaller than 7.9 km diameter have probably been lost by erosion—hence the "normal" size distribution found on the Moon or asteroids is not preserved. Craters larger than 8 km diameter are large enough that traces of most remain.

If students performed activities in Activities 6 and 7 on crater size distribution, they should have expected many more small fragments and a more nearly logarithmic pattern. More very large craters are found than expected because the smallest craters are more easily obliterated than larger ones. Thus, larger craters persist for unusually long periods of time. This distorts the results.

FIGURE 4 - KEY

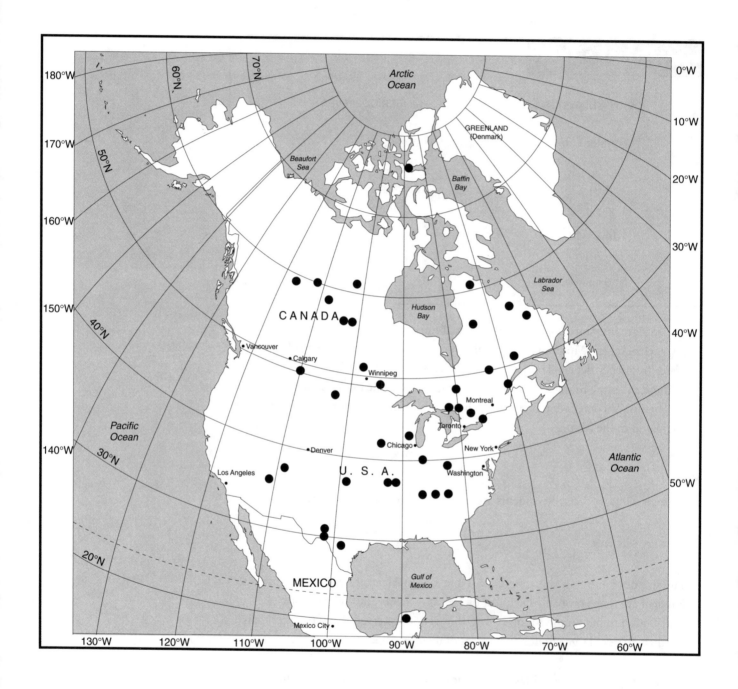

THAT'S LIFE

OBJECTIVE

In this activity, students investigate general patterns in the history of life, especially mass extinctions, in preparation for more detailed work on the final extinction of dinosaurs at the end of the Cretaceous.

WHAT IS HAPPENING?

Biology and historical geology courses devote weeks—sometimes months—to studying life's history and its patterns. Still, the results can be incomplete. Rather than expecting students to digest the entirety of this record in a short time, this activity uses focused research projects, where students collect, analyze, and present information on a single topic. If coordinated by the teacher, the cumulative product of these many separate investigations can be a comprehensive study of life's history. The presentation of this collective effort can be a learning experience for everyone involved.

Geologists divide Earth's history into three major sections, called eons: Archean (from 4.6 to 2.5 billion years ago), Proterozoic (from 2.5 to 0.6 billion years ago), and Phanerozoic (from 600 million years ago until today). Although the Phanerozoic covers less than 15 percent of Earth's history, it includes the whole history of complex life on our planet—from the Cambrian Period to today (Figure 1). Geologists know relatively little about the Archean and Proterozoic eons (sometimes collectively called the "Precambrian"). One reason for this is that less than 20 percent of Earth's surface rocks are Precambrian in age. (The surface rock of Canada north and east of Manitoba is mostly of Precambrian age. This helps explain why so many impact craters have been found in this region of North America. See Activity 12.) This activity offers several strategies for launching student investigations into the Phanerozoic.

MATERIALS

◆ instructions for student research

There is no student section for this activity.

Fiddler Crab.

Stegosaurus, dinosaur from the Upper Jurassic.

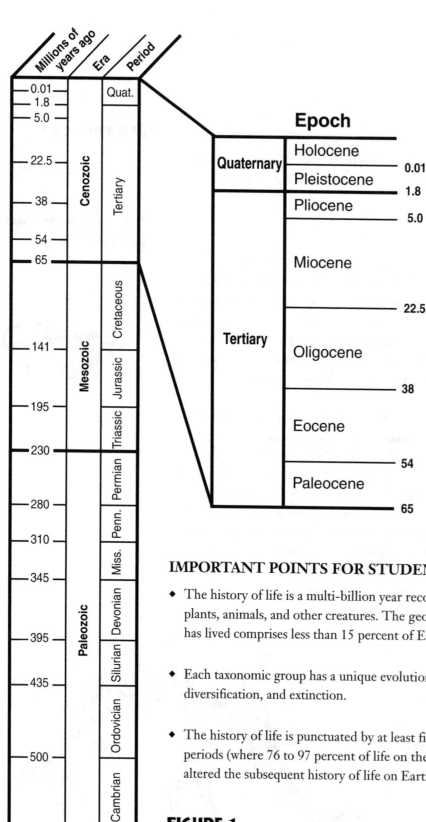

IMPORTANT POINTS FOR STUDENTS TO UNDERSTAND

♦ The history of life is a multi-billion year record filled with a fascinating range of plants, animals, and other creatures. The geological eon in which all complex life has lived comprises less than 15 percent of Earth's total history.

♦ Each taxonomic group has a unique evolutionary history that involves origins, diversification, and extinction.

♦ The history of life is punctuated by at least five periods of mass extinction. These periods (where 76 to 97 percent of life on the planet became extinct) profoundly altered the subsequent history of life on Earth.

FIGURE 1

Geological time scale of the Phanerozoic.

◆ Many scientists believe there is strong evidence that at least one of these extinctions was caused by an asteroid impact. Causes for others are still unknown.

PREPARATION

The basic design of this activity involves subdividing the history of life into segments for which individual students or student teams can research and create presentations. Each student or team investigation should culminate in a poster board panel. These panels can be hung in sequence along a wall; the collective product provides a backbone for further discussion and elaboration. Four approaches to panel creation are suggested here. Each accomplishes the learning objectives for this activity.

Research can be divided by geological period or epoch (Figure 1). Students can be assigned particular periods—from the Cambrian to the Quaternary—and asked to describe life's history in that period: major first appearances and extinctions, global geology, typical environments, and so on. If the number of teams is large, subdivide each period or epoch into marine and terrestrial environments. If you want to keep the number of teams small, emphasize periods in the Mesozoic and Cenozoic eras—this is where later activities focus.

Another approach is to assign certain taxonomic groups to student teams. Each team can investigate the evolutionary history, basic anatomy, ecological niche, taxonomy, distribution, and extinction of their assigned groups. You will find that student interest—and accessible resources—tend toward some groups (e.g., dinosaurs and mammals) and away from others (e.g., echinoderms and algae). In such cases, concentrate on vertebrates and include invertebrates of special interest. Alternatively, concentrate on groups with representatives found in nearby paleontological deposits. Contact your state's geological survey or a nearby natural history museum for expert advice.

Ornitholestes, a Triassic dinosaur.

If students focus on taxonomic groups, vary the size of the group according to the level of student interest. The kingdom of prokaryotes, for example, can be studied by one team, whereas several teams can investigate different subdivisions of more popular groups. Instead of asking one group to examine the entire

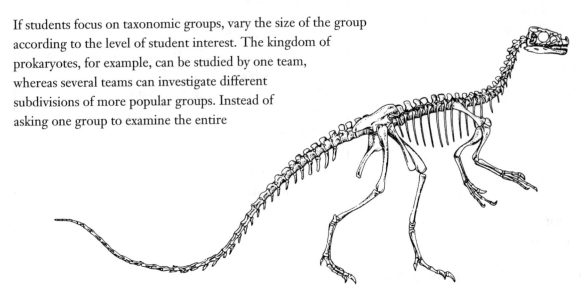

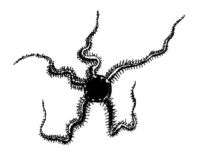

Brittle star.

class of reptiles, assign the subclasses—including turtles (anapsids), lizards and crocodiles (diapsids), dinosaurs, and mammal-like reptiles (synapsids). Mammals can be similarly subdivided. Table 1 provides a sample list of groups (divided on several levels of specificity) you could assign.

As a third approach, assignments can focus on major extinctions in the fossil record. The well-documented, "big five" mass extinctions in the fossil record are listed in Table 2. Student research on extinctions can explore what fauna and flora existed before and after the extinction interval, provide data on the extent and selectivity of the extinction, and examine possible causes for that particular extinction. Another extinction event that can be studied occurred during the Quaternary period. Humans may have played a role in the mass extinction of large animals at that time.

TABLE 1

Sample list of taxonomic groups for assignment

Prokaryotes
Protists (algae, foraminifera, and radiolarians)
Plants
  Gymnosperms (ferns, ginkgos, and conifers)
  Angiosperms (flowering plants)
Animals
  Anthozoans (corals)
  Brachiopods
  Molluscs
    gastropods (snails) and bivalves
      (clams, mussels and oysters)
    cephalopods (squids, octopi,
      nautiloids, and ammonoids)
  Annelids (worms)
  Echinoderms
  Arthropods
    trilobites
    crustaceans
    insects
  Fishes
    placoderms (armored jawed fishes)
    chondrichthyes (sharks)

Osteichthyes (bony fishes)
    actinopteryians (ray-finned fishes,
      most living fishes)
    sarcopterygians (fleshy fins and air breathing)
Amphibians
Reptiles
    anapsids (stem reptiles and turtles)
    euryapsids (ichthyosaurs, placodonts,
     and plesiosaurs)
    diapsids (lizards, crocodiles, and pterosaurs)
    dinosaurs
      saurichians (carnivores and sauropods)
      ornithischians (herbivores)
    synapsids (mammal-like reptiles)
Birds
Mammals
    Mesozoic mammals
    marsupials
    placentals

Note: This compilation does not include all taxonomic groups and combines some simply for convenience.

A final approach combines elements of each of the other three into a comprehensive understanding of life during one geological period or the changes that occurred from one period to the next. In a project titled, "Life in the Jurassic," for example, ask different student teams to report on the history of particular groups during that period only. Other teams could examine important geological events and environmental features. In another project titled, "Life from the Cretaceous to the Tertiary," ask each team to report on the differences in life from one period to the next. Such a project will raise questions that are directly related to issues of mass extinction. The advantage of this fourth approach is that it creates an integrated and detailed study of one geological interval and provides a more ecological perspective. This approach is ideal preparation for investigations of the extinction at the end of the Cretaceous (see Activities 15 and 17).

Ichthyornis, an Upper Cretaceous bird.

Before launching this activity, survey local resources for student research. Identify materials in your school and local libraries. On-line services, reference works, and CD-ROM encyclopedias also provide starting points. Be aware of the quality of sources used by students. Sometimes simple treatments mislead; worse are sources that are grossly out-of-date. Also be aware of the balance students must achieve between uncovering detail and generating a broad picture of their topic. Mere catalogs of information are not as useful as well-formed syntheses of knowledge. As a starting point, consult college-level textbooks on historical geology, paleontology, and Earth science. These usually have chapter-by-chapter discussions of subjects likely to be assigned to students.

Also review research techniques with your students. Tell them what kinds of materials you expect them to locate, where they might find them, and what form their final reports or panels should take. To make assignments, ask students to pick topics from a hat. Of course, if students have particular interests, you can assign these accordingly.

INTEGRATION AND ASSESSMENT

If students create posters to present their research questions, post these on walls around the classroom. Panels can be evaluated on the basis of quality of research, depth of analysis, and thoughtfulness in presentation. To encourage integration of content, create a scavenger hunt. After hanging the panels, collect information from the different presentations and create a questionnaire that incorporates information from many panels. Allow a class period (or a portion) for students to study the different panels and complete the questionnaires.

TABLE 2

Primary mass extinctions in the fossil record and their probable causes

EXTINCTION	AGE (MILLION YEARS)	GENERA EXTINCT (%)	SPECIES EXTINCT (%)	PROBABLE CAUSE *
"Big Five" Mass Extinctions				
End of Cretaceous	65	47	76 (±5)	Bolide impact producing global environmental disturbances
End of Triassic	208	47	76 (±5)	Possibly related to increased rainfall and drop in sea level or to impact that created 100-km Manicouagau (Canada) crater
End of Permian	245	84	96 (±2)	Long period of freezing and the widespread drop in sea level that caused huge loss of warm, shallow seas; massive volcanism in Siberia extending global cooling
End of Devonian	367	55	82 (±3.5)	Global cooling and reduced oxygen in seas
End of Ordovician	439	61	85 (±3)	Major sea level drop related to growth of ice sheets
Other Possible Mass Extinctions				
End of Pleistocene	0.01			Climatic warming combined with hunting by humans
End of Eocene	38			Possible bolide impact combined with severe cooling and glaciation resulting from changes in ocean circulation
End of Cambrian	500			Sharp rise in sea level
End of Precambrian	570			Major sea level drop combined with reduced oxygen in oceans and increased ecological stress

* - None of these explanations is certain. Encourage students to examine evidence for and against particular explanations or combinations of explanations. The results may surprise them! Be sure to emphasize that the same cause need not explain every mass extinction. Some extinctions, for instance, seem to be unrelated to bolide impacts (e.g., at the end of the Permian), whereas others almost certainly are related to a major impact (e.g., at the end of the Cretaceous). Nevertheless, ask them to look for evidence of major bolide impacts on Earth around the times of each extinction. See the Resources List for places to start.

—Source: S.K. Donovan, Mass Extinctions: Processes and Evidence (New York: Columbia University Press, 1989), p. xii. Numerical data derived from David Jablonski, "Extinctions: A Paleontological Perspective," Science, 16 Aug. 1991, volume 253, pp. 754–757. Other useful materials are noted in the Resources List. See also The History of Earth, W.K. Hartmann, 1991, (New York: Wolkman Publishing) for discussion of these boundaries.

As an alternative, ask students to make presentations on their particular research topics. (If students turn in a written report prior to their presentations, the scavenger hunt technique can still be used.) Encourage teams to personify their topic—e.g., "I am a trilobite. My body is divided into three parts...."—or make diagrams and illustrations as needed. Rather than presenting collages of mere facts, encourage teams to look for patterns and general themes in their studies.

SUGGESTIONS FOR FURTHER STUDY

Most natural history museums have exhibits on the history of life. Highlights vary, depending on what collections each museum possesses. Exceptional exhibits can be found at major museums across the country, such as the American Museum of Natural History (New York City), the National Museum of Natural History (Washington, DC), the Field Museum of Natural History (Chicago), and Museum of Vertebrate Zoology (Berkeley). Most major and local museums and planetariums offer guided tours by arrangement, and curators often are willing to make presentations if contacted in advance. In-class presentations also can be arranged.

CONNECTIONS

Encourage students to examine the study of extinction as it occurs today. How does the rate of extinction today—say in tropical rain forests—compare with extinction rates in the fossil record? Are we currently in a period of extinction on the same scale as the "big five" mass extinctions?

Brine Shrimp.

It is likely that fossils can be found in your region, and students may have opportunities to do some collecting for class. Contact your state's geological survey or ask your reference librarian for specific information. Before students do any collecting, however, be sure to learn techniques for proper collecting and check for local restrictions.

Archeologists and anthropologists have found considerable evidence that the first human populations in North America (around 10–12,000 years ago) hunted some big game animals to extinction. The mammoth is a good example. Ask students to investigate this case. It should remind them that human-caused extinctions are not restricted just to this century.

LAYER BY LAYER

MATERIALS

- pencil
- ruler
- protractor
- colored pencils (optional)

OBJECTIVE

This activity will introduce you to stratigraphy—the study of rock layers.

BACKGROUND

Researchers must sample Earth's interior to determine what is underneath its surface (Figure 1). Bore holes and road cuts are two common kinds of samples that geologists use. Bore holes are made by drilling below the surface and removing a sample core. By studying these cores, geologists can derive considerable information about rock layers underground. After the core is removed, special cameras and other instruments can be lowered into the hole, giving geologists a direct look at other processes—such as sedimentation rates, faulting, and joint patterns in their true orientation. Road cuts or river cuts also reveal rock layers, but these are usually much shallower than bore holes.

Drilling bore holes is expensive and cannot be done everywhere. So geologists have developed techniques for correlating results from different areas to fill in the space in between the wells. You will use data from bore holes in this activity to create a cross section drawing of the rocks under a particular area. Here, you are going to locate the boundary between Cretaceous and Tertiary periods—the time when all dinosaurs finally became extinct.

In this activity, you're a geologist at (the imaginary) Greggston State University doing research on mass extinctions. You're trying to locate the boundary separating the Cretaceous and Tertiary periods around the university and have convinced an oil and gas exploration company to share their data from bore holes they recently drilled nearby. From these data, you're sure you can locate that boundary.

FIGURE 1

Schematic view of rock layers in the Grand Canyon, Arizona.

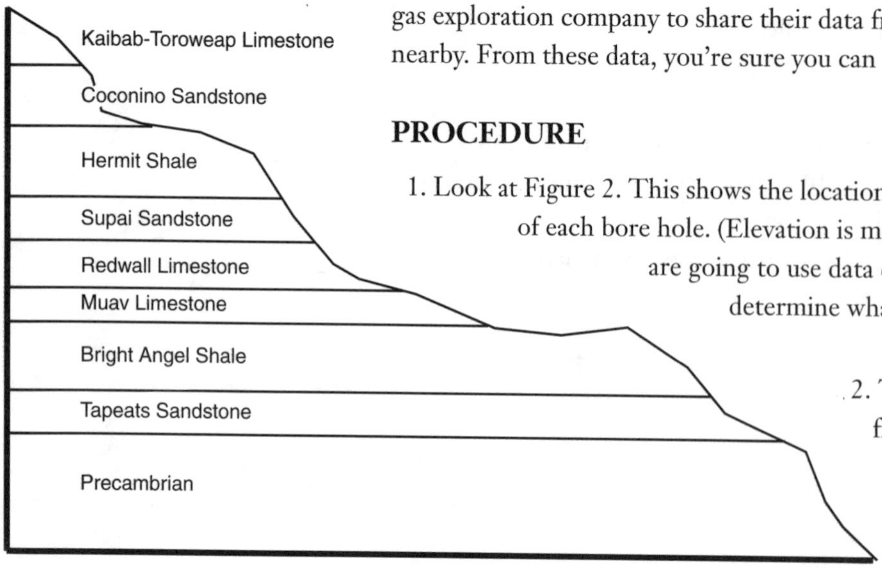

Kaibab-Toroweap Limestone

Coconino Sandstone

Hermit Shale

Supai Sandstone

Redwall Limestone

Muav Limestone

Bright Angel Shale

Tapeats Sandstone

Precambrian

PROCEDURE

1. Look at Figure 2. This shows the location of the three drilling sites and the depth of each bore hole. (Elevation is measured as height above sea level.) You are going to use data derived from bore hole studies to determine what rock layers are underneath the surface.

2. Table 1 provides data from bore holes from samples in nearby Wattstown, Cain County, and Eugeni. While the holes were being drilled, each time the drill

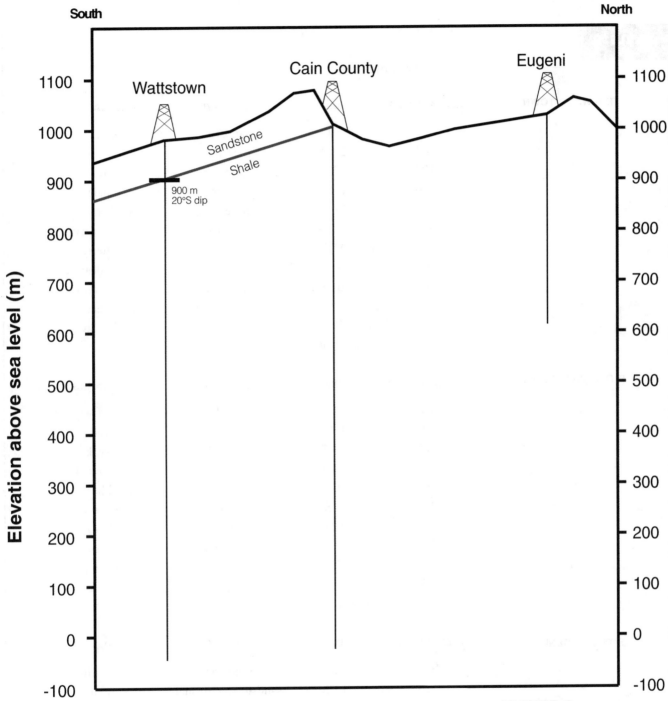

South   North

FIGURE 2

Cross section of the geology around Greggston State University. In this activity, you will determine the layering of rocks underneath the surface.

entered a new rock type the depth and angle of the layer's orientation (its dip) were recorded. By connecting the contact points from the three drill sites, you can create a cross section of the local area.

3. Look at the data in Table 1 for the Wattstown site. On your cross section, mark the elevation where each transition in rock type occurred and mark the dip. Below that mark, write the name of the rock type found underneath that elevation. *The first one is done for you.* Continue down the entire column.

TABLE 1

Bore hole data

SITE 1–WATTSTOWN	ELEVATION (M)	DIP	ROCK TYPE	REMARKS
	970	0	sandstone	surface
	900	20° S	shale	weak
	790	17° S	sandstone	red
	700	15° S	sandstone	shaley
	625	13° S	limestone	pink, blocky
	525	10° S	limestone	fossil bearing
	405	8° S	clay	cherty
	390	8° S	limestone	fossil bearing
	260	6° S	limestone	high strength
	110	5° S	limestone	cherty
	5	2° S	limestone	blocky
	-50	bottom of hole		

SITE 2–CAIN COUNTY	ELEVATION (M)	DIP	ROCK TYPE	REMARKS
	1010	0	shale	surface
	900	17°S	sandstone	red
	800	15°S	sandstone with shale	weak
	715	14°S	limestone	pink, blocky
	595	10°S	limestone	fossil bearing
	455	9°S	clay	cherty
	440	9°S	limestone	fossil bearing
	300	6°S	limestone	high strength
	150	5°S	limestone	cherty
	25	3°S	limestone	blocky
	-25	bottom of hole		

SITE 3: EUGENI	ELEVATION (M)	DIP	ROCK TYPE	REMARKS
	1025	0	sandstone	red, surface
	925	15°S	sandstone with shale	weak
	820	13°S	limestone	pink, blocky
	680	10°S	limestone	fossil bearing
	610	bottom of hole		

4. Repeat Step 3 for the bore holes from Cain County and Eugeni. When you have finished, connect the marks on each drilling site for points separating the same pair of rock types. In doing this, you are creating a geological column.

TABLE 2					
ERA	PERIOD	EPOCH	SAMPLE AGE (MILLION YEARS)	FIELD DATA	DESCRIPTION
			20		Wilson Creek Sandstone: yellow, high-strength, dune deposits
			24		Cat Creek Shale: weak, carboniferous, shallow swampy deposit
			36		Poison Creek Sandstone: red, high-strength, near shore dunes
			50		Rattler Gulch Sandstone: dark with shale, inter-tidal deposits
			56		Limestone: pink and blocky
			62		Fossil Butte Limestone: fossil bearing, corals and brachiopods
			65		Cedar City Claystone: gray with chert nodules
			68		Green Creek Limestone: fossil bearing, abundant corals and ammonoids
			91		Canyon Limestone: high-strength gray, foraminifera present
			110		Wilson Ridge Limestone: cherty
			138		Rimecreek Limestone: blocky, some foraminifera

5. Drilling at the Eugeni site was stopped at about the 600 m elevation. But with the data collected from other drill sites you can predict the rock structure below 600 meters. What rock strata would probably have been encountered if the drilling was continued to sea level? Fill in your predictions in the cross section, using dotted lines to show predicted features. When you have completed your cross section, label the layers A through K from the surface to the bottom of the core holes.

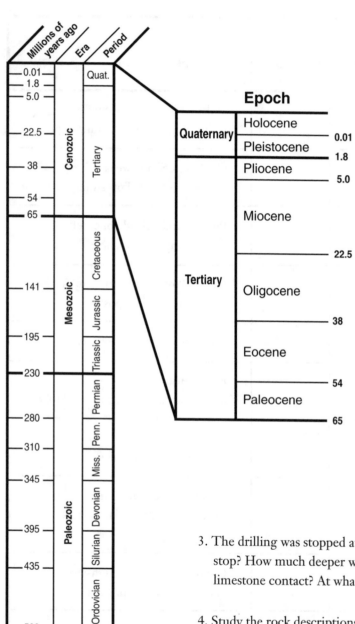

FIGURE 3

Geological time scale with a view of Cenozoic epochs.

6. Your team at the university has analyzed the core samples, looking for fossils and determining the ages of each layer. Their results have been summarized in Table 2. Match the layers you've identified in the cross section (A–K) with the rocks (named after local features but extending for hundreds of miles) described for that layer in the field data column of Table 2.

7. Using the geologic time scale (Figure 3) as a reference, fill in the appropriate eras, periods, and epochs for Table 2.

QUESTIONS/CONCLUSIONS

1. Use a protractor to measure the angles of the strata on your cross section. How closely do the dip values on your cross section agree with the dip values from the bore hole data? What could explain the differences between the two measurements?

2. In what layer is the Cretaceous/Tertiary boundary found? Which drill site had the deepest occurrence of the Cretaceous/Tertiary boundary? What is the elevation at the top of that rock layer?

3. The drilling was stopped at the Eugeni site. In what type of rock did the drilling stop? How much deeper would the hole need to be to reach the Limecreek limestone contact? At what depth would the Limecreek limestone be found?

4. Study the rock descriptions on both sides of the Cretaceous/Tertiary boundary on Table 2. Besides geologic age, what other clues indicate a mass extinction?

5. What types of rock are found at the top of the ridges? Can you explain why this rock type is at the top of the ridges?

6. When you connect the data points for the different drilling sites, what assumptions are you making about the rocks in between? How can you test those assumptions?

LAYER BY LAYER

WHAT IS HAPPENING?

By studying sequences of rock layers and observing the character of rocks in each layer, this activity introduces basic concepts of stratigraphy. Two simple principles are applied here. First, in an undisturbed sequence, younger rocks are to be found on top of older rocks. This is the principle of superposition. Second, as a rock layer is being formed, it is laid down without breaks over a particular area. This is the principle of lateral continuity. It explains why in this case the layering is the same in each of the three sampling sites—they are all part of continuous deposition environment. Geologists in the 1800s discovered the concept of continuous strata and named the layers according to the specific groups of fossil animals and plants in each layer.

Deposition occurs in many places on Earth, although the rate of accumulation varies widely. A slow moving river, like the Mississippi or Nile, deposits sediments in a delta at a more or less regular rate over many years. In contrast, volcanoes erupt sporadically, but one eruption can deposit ash many meters thick over a wide area. Torrential rains might wash large quantities of soil from a hillside, followed by years of gentler rainfall with relatively little erosion. These different geological processes may be happening at the same time in different places around the world. The resulting rocks will be the same age, but they will vary in type. In this activity, the three locations studied had been part of the same deposition environment; this explains why the sequence of layers is the same for each. Other cases can be far more complicated.

Earth is an active place. The sediment being deposited in any one location is determined by what geological processes are active in that place. One layer of rock, representing the material laid down in one deposition area, is called a bed. Rock beds usually extend over limited areas, such as over the floor of an ocean or river delta. For example, rock is being formed at the bottom of the Gulf of Mexico from sediment coming out of the Mississippi River. Rock is also being formed in the Mediterranean Sea from Nile River sediment. When geologists in the future examine these two locations, they will discover rocks of the same age but of different composition. The different composition results from variations in the sediments carried in the two rivers.

When a large enough bolide strikes Earth or when a major volcano erupts, dust and ash are ejected into the atmosphere, forming huge clouds of debris. These clouds carry debris over the globe. As debris settles from these clouds, it forms a distinct rock

MATERIALS

- pencil
- ruler
- protractor
- colored pencils (optional)

layer, entering the geological record on top of whatever local event is underway. Traces of ash from the explosion of Mount Mazama about 6,800 years ago—which left the crater that is now Crater Lake in Oregon—can be found worldwide. Rocks from the very end of the Cretaceous period show a distinct layer that is related to some kind of worldwide event. This layer will be examined in Activity 16.

IMPORTANT POINTS FOR STUDENTS TO UNDERSTAND

♦ Deposition is always taking place over much of the Earth's surface.

♦ Deposition rates vary.

♦ The character of rocks formed through deposition varies. It is determined by the kind of material found in its source.

♦ Usually deposition occurs in a limited area, such as on the floor of an ocean or river bed.

♦ Major events—such as volcanic eruptions or bolide impacts—can create worldwide marker layers as the result of material settling out from enormous debris clouds.

PREPARATION

You might want to review the principles of superposition and lateral continuity prior to launching this activity. As an alternative, before handing out the worksheets, have a pre-activity discussion using the following kinds of questions:

♦ Where are sediment deposits being formed on our planet today? (Students probably will say "lakes and oceans." Answers also may include beach areas, stream beds, and areas around active volcanoes, sand dunes, and deserts. Just about anywhere will be a correct answer if students can describe how material is deposited there.) Make a list of these locations on the board or overhead transparency. Be sure to point out that deposition is an ongoing process.

♦ Where does the material that is deposited come from? (Depending on the sediment discussed, answers can include eroded areas, volcanic eruptions, and ejecta from bolide impacts.) Be sure to emphasize that what gets deposited in one place was taken away (eroded, erupted, or ejected) from another.

In a post-activity discussion, develop the principles of stratigraphy from the information students have just collected.

SUGGESTIONS FOR FURTHER STUDY

This activity focuses on direct sampling of rock types by drilling. Geologists also use energy waves—natural ones such as earthquakes or ones generated by explosives—to study rock units. Much of what is now known of Earth's deep layers was generated by seismic sounding. Ask students to investigate the development of seismic sounding and report to your class on the discovery of Earth's internal structure.

How long does it take for one centimeter of stalagmite to form? What is the rate of deposition on the sea floor? What is the deposition rate of the Mississippi or Amazon or Nile deltas? What is the deposition rate behind a dam? Research of these questions will give students a better understanding of various deposition rates.

Compare types of deposition in the Mississippi delta with the Sahara desert, the Antarctic, or Hawaii. This will give students a better understanding of where rock types come from and the forces controlling deposition rates.

CONNECTIONS

Another technique geologists use for dating rocks makes use of the fossils found therein. Called biostratigraphy, this approach compares the species found in different samples and correlates rocks according to how similar and different the faunas and floras are. Most introductory texts in historical geology have activities to teach students these techniques. These activities also introduce students to the problem of temporal resolution: what is the narrowest interval of time that can be distinguished in a stratigraphic sequence? Accurately reading events in the fossil record depends heavily on the degree of temporal resolution in stratigraphic sequences.

ANSWERS TO QUESTIONS FOR STUDENTS

1. Answers will vary. Encourage students to consider where sources of error can creep into an investigation. Also encourage them to consider ways of reducing these sources.

2. The Cretaceous/Tertiary boundary is found in the G layer—the Cedar City claystone. The Cretaceous/Tertiary boundary layer is deepest at the Wattstown site, about 400 meters at the top of the rock.

3. The drilling was stopped at the Eugeni site in Fossil Butte limestone. To reach the Limecreek limestone, the drill hole would need to be extended about 120–130 meters. The Limecreek limestone is found at 0 meters, or sea level.

4. The types of fossils below the Cretaceous/Tertiary boundary are abruptly different from fossils above the boundary.

FIGURE 4

Answer key for Figure 2 in the student section.

5. Sandstone is the type of rock found at the top of the ridges. Students might know from previous experience that sandstone is resistant to erosion. (This answer is not developed in this activity.)

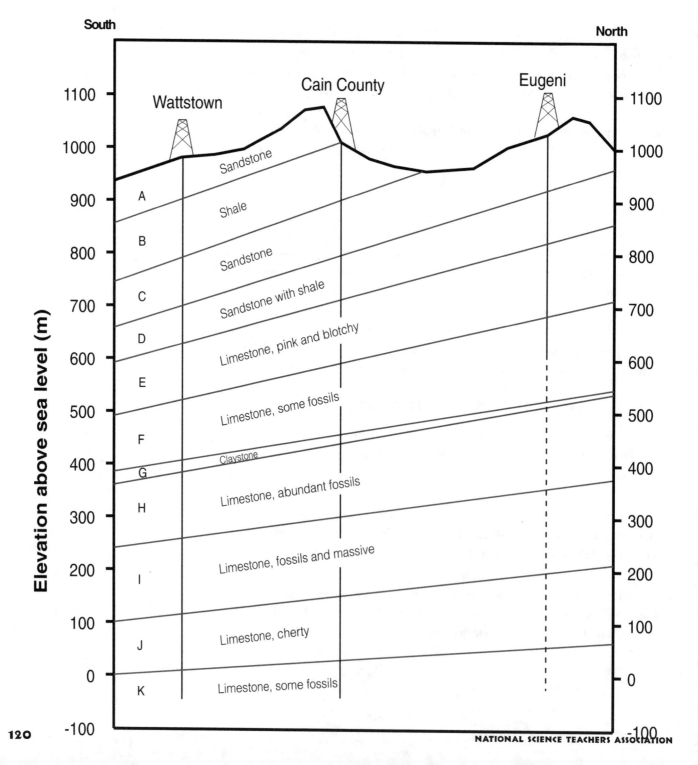

6. In connecting the sites, you assume the rocks in between were created as part of the
   same deposition process. This is the principle of lateral continuity. It can be tested
   by additional drilling.

| TABLE 3 | | Key to Table 2 from Student Section | | | |
ERA	PERIOD	EPOCH	SAMPLE AGE (MILLION YEARS)	FIELD DATA	DESCRIPTION
Cenozoic	Tertiary	Miocene	20	A	Wilson Creek Sandstone: yellow, high-strength, dune deposits
		Miocene	24	B	Cat Creek Shale: weak, carboniferous, shallow swampy deposit
		Oligocene	36	C	Poison Creek Sandstone: red, high-strength, near shore dunes
		Eocene	50	D	Rattler Gulch Sandstone: dark with shale, inter-tidal deposits
		Paleocene	56	E	Limestone: pink and blocky
		Paleocene	62	F	Fossil Butte Limestone: fossil bearing, corals and brachiopods
K/T boundary layer			65	G	Cedar City Claystone: gray with chert nodules
Mesozoic	Cretaceous	(no epochs)	68	H	Green Creek Limestone: fossil bearing, abundant corals and ammonoids
			91	I	Canyon Limestone: high-strength gray, foraminifera present
			110	J	Wilson Ridge Limestone: cherty
			138	K	Rimecreek Limestone: blocky, some foraminifera

DISCOVERING DINOSAUR DIVERSITY

MATERIALS

Each pair of students will need

- Dino Data Sheet

- blank Species Lifetime charts (1 per student)

- blank higher-level Diversity Diagrams (4 or 5 per student)

- colored pencil or marker

- scissors

OBJECTIVE

In this activity you will examine the scale of dinosaur extinction at the end of the Cretaceous and learn when else, if ever, mass extinctions of dinosaurs occurred.

BACKGROUND

Everybody knows something about dinosaurs—those "terrible lizards" (that's what the word "dinosaur" means) that lived long ago. You've seen them in books and movies, on television documentaries, and in museums. Dinosaurs came in many shapes and sizes. Some ate plants; others ate meat. No matter what else you know about dinosaurs, you know they're now extinct. But how many types of dinosaurs were there? When did they flourish? When did they

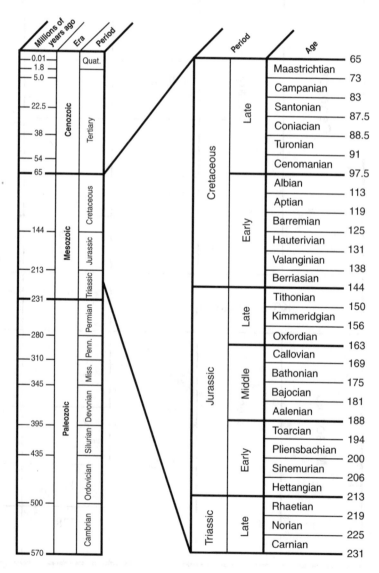

FIGURE 1
Geologic time scale.

become extinct? In this activity, you will explore these questions. In later activities you will investigate theories to explain their disappearance.

Perhaps you already know that dinosaurs evolved from early reptiles in the Late Triassic period and flourished during the Jurassic and Cretaceous periods (Figure 1). At the very end of the Cretaceous, the last of the dinosaurs went extinct. But this is the barest of pictures. Paleontologists know an enormous amount about dinosaurs; enough to provide a detailed record of dinosaur diversity. Studying this diversity—with different periods of abundance and extinction—will put the last mass extinction of dinosaurs into clearer perspective.

To look at the record of dinosaur evolution, you're going to construct a kind of graph called a *diversity diagram* (Figure 2). In these diagrams, time is the vertical axis, with the oldest at the bottom and youngest at the top. The horizontal axis measures a group's diversity—e.g., number of species or number of families in a larger group. The more numerous a group is, the wider the horizontal line is for that particular time. (To improve readability, each level is centered.) If the line contracts rapidly—e.g., between levels 7 and 8, or 14 and 15 in Figure 2—a large-scale extinction is indicated. An expansion—e.g., between levels 11 and 13 in Figure 2—represents expansion and diversification of a group. When many groups show extinctions at the same time, paleontologists have evidence for a mass extinction.

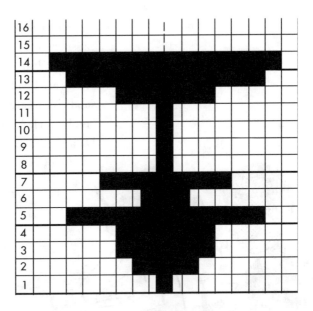

FIGURE 2

Sample diversity diagram showing occasional large-scale extinctions and diversifications. Each square represents one species known to be alive at that geological level. To make the diagram easy to read, the blocks are centered on the dotted line.

Diversity diagrams offer a convenient way to summarize large amounts of data on the evolution of a group. As shown in Figure 2, over its entire history, a group may experience several large-scale extinctions and diversifications prior to its final disappearance. In your study of dinosaur diversity, you'll see considerable change in the number of dinosaur groups. Whether you know a little or a lot about dinosaurs, you're sure to find a few surprises, too.

PROCEDURE

1. Obtain the Dino Data Sheet from your teacher and look over it. For the groups listed, this data sheet shows *every dinosaur species* known at the time the table was created. It is divided into three columns:

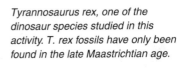

Tyrannosaurus rex, one of the dinosaur species studied in this activity. T. rex fossils have only been found in the late Maastrichtian age.

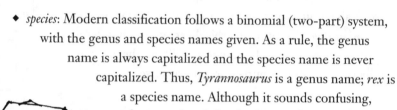

- *higher taxonomic group*: Taxonomists divide living forms into an outline-like classification of finer and finer groupings: kingdom, phylum, class, order, family, genus, and species. As in any outline, there are subdivisions too—for example, orders are divided into suborders, families are divided into subfamilies. These subdivisions are represented in this column; the one you will focus on is the family level. All names with the suffix *-idae* are family-level names. In the Dino Data Sheet, families are numbered with lower case roman numerals: i, ii, iii, iv, etc.

- *species*: Modern classification follows a binomial (two-part) system, with the genus and species names given. As a rule, the genus name is always capitalized and the species name is never capitalized. Thus, *Tyrannosaurus* is a genus name; *rex* is a species name. Although it sounds confusing, when people ask for the "species" name, they usually are asking for the binomial (genus-species) name, *Tyrannosaurus rex*. Sometimes full names are abbreviated, as in *T. rex*. (Can you see that there are actually two species of *Tyrannosaurus*?)

- *age:* Paleontologists date fossils according to the age of the rocks where fossils were found. *Tyrannosaurus rex* fossils have been found only in rocks of late Maastrichtian age (about 66 million years), for example. The other *Tyrannosaurus* species has been found only in the Campanian age (about 80 million years ago). Therefore, *T. rex* is the younger of the two species. The last age in the Cretaceous period is the Maastrichtian. Just above the Maastrichtian age is the Cretaceous/Tertiary boundary. (Paleontologists have never found convincing evidence of dinosaurs above the Cretaceous/Tertiary boundary.)

2. If you don't understand what these three columns represent, ask your partner and then your teacher for additional explanation. Once you feel comfortable reading the Dino Data Table, you are ready to study dinosaur diversity.

Creating a Species Lifetime Chart

3. The first step in your investigation will be to create a diversity diagram for the species in a particular dinosaur group. Your teacher will assign a dinosaur group to your group. Locate this group on the Dino Data Table. Also, posted in your classroom will be an Outline of Dinosaur Classification. Write your and your partner's name next to the group(s) you were assigned.

4. Plot the age of each species on your Species Lifetime Chart, draw a vertical line through the ages noted in the data set, then fill in one box for each of the ages this species existed. You might encounter several trouble spots:

a. If the Dino Data Sheet lists only part of an *age* (e.g., late Aptian), fill in only part of the box.

b. If it lists only part of a *period* (e.g., Late Jurassic), fill in all the boxes for that portion of the period.

c. If it lists an uncertain date (shown by a "?"), place an "x" in those age boxes instead of filling them in.

d. Use one column for each of the dinosaur species in the group you were assigned. (Each partner should make her or his own diagram with the shared results.)

5. When you have finished charting your group of species, take a minute to look for patterns in this graph. Answer questions 1–6 in the Questions/Conclusions section below.

Creating a Family-Level Diversity Diagram

6. Working with species-level data can be confusing—with so many jumbled data points together, sometimes it's hard to generalize. Condense your results for a larger investigation by creating a graph to represent ages for the taxonomic *family* you are studying (families have the suffix *-idae*). Use your species lifetime chart as a starting point. For each age level, count the number of species present. Then, on a blank Diversity Diagram, fill in one block at that age level for each species in that count. For convenience or for clarity, group these blocks around the center line, as in Figure 2. (Each partner should make her or his own diagram.)

Camarosaurus, a dinosaur from the Upper Jurassic.

7. Your family-level Diversity Diagram provides a measure of diversity for your group over time: the wider the bar, the more diverse that group was at that particular time. To analyze your data, answer questions 7–10 in the Questions/Conclusions section below. When you have finished these questions, cut out your diagram, write your two names on the back, and post it as directed by your teacher.

Creating Higher-Level Diversity Diagrams

8. Diversity diagrams work for any taxonomic level. When you have finished your analysis at the family level, locate your group on the posted Outline of Dinosaur Classification. Move up one level in the outline (e.g., from i., ii., iii., etc. to a., b., c., etc.). Write the name of this higher category on another blank Diversity Diagram. Look on the Outline for the names of your classmates working with other families in this group.

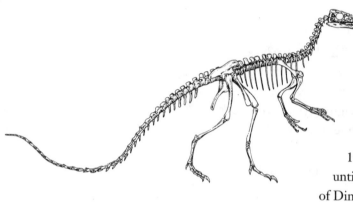

9. Working with these other teams, combine together results from all the families in this higher group and create a higher-level Diversity Diagram, just as you created the family-level one from your species data: add up the number of species present at each age, then block out that number of squares for these ages.

10. Repeat steps 8 and 9 with successively higher groups until you reach the most inclusive level, shown in the Outline of Dinosaur Classification (Your teacher has this) with Roman numerals: I., II., III., etc. Each student should make her or his own diagrams for the shared results.

Ornitholestes, a dinosaur genus from the Kimmeridgian through the Tithonian ages.

11. To analyze this data, answer questions 11–14 in the Questions/Conclusions section below. When you have finished these questions, cut out one set of diagrams for the complete sequence of levels and post them as directed by your teacher.

QUESTIONS/CONCLUSIONS

Species Lifetime Chart

1. What group(s) are you investigating?

2. How many species does this group have?

3. What is the average lifetime (in number of ages) for species in this group?

4. In what age are species most abundant?

5. Do you observe any places in your species-level diagram that might show large-scale extinctions?

6. Report anything else you find interesting about this graph.

Higher-Level Diagrams

7. What is the duration (in number of ages) of the families in your graph?

8. When do the members of these families become completely extinct? Do families live longer than the average species? Use your answer to Question 3.

9. As you read the Family Diversity Diagram vertically, ages where widening occurs represent periods of diversification. Ages where thinning occurs represent extinctions. Describe the record of diversification and extinction for the families under study. Do you observe any places in your family-level analysis to suggest large-scale extinctions?

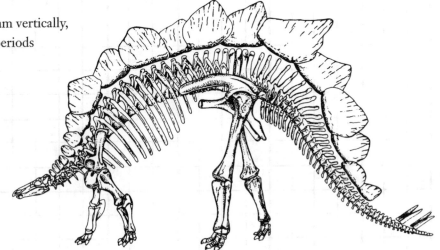

10. When do the members of this family ultimately become extinct?

Stegosaurus, a dinosaur from the Upper Jurassic period.

Overall Interpretation

11. At the most general level, saurischians and ornithischians form the two major groups of dinosaurs. Describe the record of diversification and extinctions in groups at this most general level. When was each most abundant? When did they experience large-scale extinctions and diversifications? When was your group's final extinction? If you can, compare these to patterns found for other major groups.

12. Some people have the impression that *all* dinosaur species appeared in the late Triassic, lived through the entire Mesozoic era, and went extinct at the Cretaceous/Tertiary boundary. Is this what you observed in your study of dinosaur diversity? If you found something else, describe how it differs from this common impression. Is it true for higher levels?

13. In this activity, you've varied the level of analysis—from species to families to higher taxonomic groups. Do you see a pattern at the higher-level that does not appear at the family-level? Does a pattern disappear?

14. How does changing your level of analysis affect the patterns you observe? Which level is most appropriate for studying extinction?

Triassic			Jurassic											Cretaceous											Group:
Late			Early				Middle				Late			Early						Late						Species Diversity
Carnian	Norian	Rhaetian	Hettangian	Sinemurian	Pliensbachian	Toarcian	Aalenian	Bajocian	Bathonian	Callovian	Oxfordian	Kimmeridgian	Tithonian	Berriasian	Valanginian	Hauterivian	Barremian	Aptian	Albian	Cenomanian	Turonian	Coniacian	Santonian	Campanian	Maastrichtian	

Triassic			Jurassic											Cretaceous											Higher-Level Diversity
Late			Early				Middle				Late			Early						Late						
Carnian	Norian	Rhaetian	Hettangian	Sinemurian	Pliensbachian	Toarcian	Aalenian	Bajocian	Bathonian	Callovian	Oxfordian	Kimmeridgian	Tithonian	Berriasian	Valanginian	Hauterivian	Barremian	Aptian	Albian	Cenomanian	Turonian	Coniacian	Santonian	Campanian	Maastrichtian	

Group

Source: David Weishampel, et al., *The Dinosauria*
(Berkeley: University of California Press, 1984).

Higher Taxonomic Group	Species	Age

I. Saurischia

A. Theropoda

   1. Ceratosauria

	Species	Age
	• *Ceratosaurus nasicornis*	Kimmeridgian–Tithonian
	• *Sarcosaurus woodi*	Early Jurassic (?Sinemurian)
	• *Segisaurus halli*	Early Jurassic (?Sinemurian–Pliensbachian)
	• *Dilophosaurus wetherilli*	Early Jurassic (?Sinemurian–Pliensbachian)
	• *Liliensternus lilliensterni*	Late Norian
	• *Coelophysis bauri*	Late Carnian–Early Norian
	• *Syntarus rhodesiensis*	Early Jurassic (?Hettangian–Sinemurian)
	• *Syntarus kayentakatae*	Early Jurassic (?Sinemurian–Pliensbachian)

   2. Tetanurae

     a. Carnosauria

       i. Allosauridae

	Species	Age
	• *Acrocanthosaurus atokensis*	late Aptian–early Albian
	• *Allosaurus fragilis*	Kimmeridgian–Tithonian
	• *?Allosaurus tendagurensis*	Kimmeridgian
	• *Chilantaisaurus maortuensis*	Albian
	• *Chilantaisaurus tashuikouensis*	Aptian–Albian
	• *?Chilantaisaurus sibiricus*	Berriasian–Hauterivian
	• *Piatnitzkysaurus floresi*	Callovian
	• *Szechuanosaurus campi*	Oxfordian–Tithonian

       ii. Tyrannosauridae

	Species	Age
	• *Albertosaurus libratus*	late Campanian–Maastrichtian
	• *Albertosaurus sarcophagus*	late Campanian–early Maastrichtian
	• *Alectrosaurus olseni*	Late Cretaceous (?Cenomanian, ?Maastrichtian)
	• *Alioramus remotus*	early Maastrichtian
	• *Chingkankousaurus fragilis*	Campanian–early Maastrichtian
	• *Daspletosaurus torosus*	late Campanian
	• *Nanotyrannus lancensis*	late Maastrichtian
	• *Tarbosaurus bataar*	?late Campanian or early Maastrichtian
	• *Tyrannosaurus rex*	late Maastrichtian
	• *Tyrannosaurus luanchuanensis*	Campanian
	• *"Ornithomimus" grandis*	early Campanian
	• *"Gorgosaurus" novojilovi*	?late Campanian or early Maastrichtian

       iii. Carnosauria incertae sedis

	Species	Age
	• *Bahariasaurus ingens*	?late Albian or ?early Cenomanian
	• *Carcharodontosaurus saharicus*	late Aptian–early Cenomanian
	• *Aublysodon mirandus*	late Campanian–Maastrichtian
	• *Compsosuchus solus*	middle–late Maastrichtian
	• *Eustreptospondylus oxoniensis*	Callovian
	• *Gasosaurus constructus*	Bathonian–Callovian
	• *Iliosuchus incognitus*	middle Bathonian
	• *Kaijiangosaurus lini*	Bathonian–Callovian
	• *Kelmayisaurus petrolicus*	?Valanginian–Albian
	• *Labocania anomala*	?Campanian
	• *"Laelaps" gallicus*	?Jurassic

Source: David Weishampel, et al., *The Dinosauria*
(Berkeley: University of California Press, 1984).

Higher Taxonomic Group	Species	Age
	• *Magnosaurus nethercombensis*	Aalenian–Bajocian
	• *Megalosaurus bucklandii*	Bathonian, ?Oxfordian
	• *Megalosaurus hesperis*	Aalenian–Bajocian
	• *?Megalosaurus cambrensis*	Rhaetian
	• *Piveteausaurus divesensis*	late Callovian
	• *Spinosaurus aegyptiacus*	?early Cenomanian
	• *Stokesosaurus clevelandi*	Kimmeridgian–Tithonian
	• *Torvosaurus tanneri*	Kimmeridgian–Tithonian
	• *Yangchuanosaurus shangyouensis*	Late Jurassic
	• *Yangchuanosaurus magnus*	Late Jurassic

3. Coelurosauria

   a. Ornithomimosauria

      i. Harpymimidae

	• *Harpymimus okladnikovi*	Aptian–Albian

      ii. Garudimimidae

	• *Garudimimus brevipes*	Cenomanian–Turonian

      iii. Ornithomimidae

	• *Ornithomimus velox*	late Maastrichtian
	• *Ornithomimus edmontonensis*	late Campanian–early Maastrichtian
	• *Struthiomimus altus*	late Campanian–early Maastrichtian
	• *Dromiceiomimus brevitertius*	early Maastrichtian
	• *Dromiceiomimus samueli*	late Campanian
	• *Archaeornithomimus asiaticus*	Late Cretaceous (?Cenomanian, ?Maastrichtian)
	• *Gallimimus bullatus*	?late Campanian or early Maastrichtian
	• *Anserimimus planinychus*	?late Campanian or early Maastrichtian

      iv.Ornithomimosauria incertae sedis

	• *Elaphrosaurus bambergi*	Kimmeridgian

   b. Maniraptora

      i. Elmisauridae

	• *Chirostenotes pergracilis*	middle Campanian–early Maastrichtian
	• *Elmisaurus rarus*	?late Campanian or early Maastrichtian
	• *Elmisaurus elegans*	middle Campanian

   c. Oviraptorosauria

      i. Oviraptoridae

         a. Oviraptorinae

	• *Oviraptor philoceratops*	?late Santonian or early Campanian
	• *Oviraptor mongoliensis*	?late Campanian or early Maastrichtian
	• *Conchoraptor gracilis*	middle Campanian

         b. Ingeniinae

	• *Ingenia yanshini*	middle–Campanian–early Maastrichtian

      ii. Caenagnathidae

	• *Caenagnathus collinsi*	late Campanian
	• *Caenagnathus sternbergi*	late Campanian

      iii. Troodontidae

	• *Troodon formosus*	late Campanian–early Maastrichtian
	• *Sauronithoides mongoliensis*	late Santonian or early Campanian
	• *Sauronithoides junior*	?late Campanian or early Maastrichtian
	• *Borogovia gracilicrus*	?late Campanian or early Maastrichtian

Source: David Weishampel, et al., *The Dinosauria*
(Berkeley: University of California Press, 1984).

Higher Taxonomic Group	Species	Age
iv. Dromaeosauridae		
	• *Adasaurus mongoliensis*	?late Campanian or early Maastrichtian
	• *Deinonychus antirrhopus*	Aptian–Albian
	• *Dromaeosaurus albertensis*	late Campanian
	• *Hulsanpes perlei*	middle Campanian
	• *Saurornitholestes langstoni*	late Campanian
	• *Velociraptor mongoliensis*	?late Santonian or early Campanian
v. ?Dromaeosauridae		
	• *Chirostenotes pergracilis*	late Campanian
B. Problematic Theropoda: "Coelurosaurs"		
	• *Avimimus portentosus*	?late Santonian or ?early Campanian
	• *Coelurus fragilis*	Kimmeridgian–Tithonian
	• *Compsognathus longipes*	Kimmeridgan
	• *Deinocheirus mirificus*	?late Campanian or early Maastrichtian
	• *Ornitholestes hermanni*	Kimmeridgian–Tithonian
	• *Therizinosaurus cheloniformis*	?late Campanian or early Maastrichtian
	• *Avisaurus archibaldi*	late Maastrichtian
	• *"Halticosaurus" orbitoangulatus*	middle Norian
	• *Kakuru kujani*	Aptian
	• *Lukousaurus yini*	Rhaetian–Pliensbachian
	• *Microvenator celer*	Aptian–Albian
	• *Noasaurus leali*	?late Campanian–Maastrichtian
	• *Podokesaurus holyokensis*	?Pliensbachian–Toarcian
	• *Walkeria maleriensis*	Carnian–middle Norian
C. Problematic Theropoda: "Carnosaurs"		
	• *Abelisaurus comahuensis*	early Maastrichtian
	• *Altispinax dunkeri*	Barremian
	• *Baryonyx walkeri*	Barremian
	• *Carnotaurus sastrei*	Albian–Cenomanian
	• *Dryptosaurus aquilunguis*	Maastrichtian
	• *Erectopus sauvagei*	Albian
	• *Erectopus superbus*	Albian
	• *Frenguellisaurus ischigualastensis*	Carnian
	• *Genyodectes serus*	Late Cretaceous
	• *Indosaurus matleyi*	middle–late Maastrichtian
	• *Indosuchus raptorius*	middle–late Maastrichtian
	• *Itemirus medullaris*	late Turonian
	• *Majungasaurus crenatissimus*	Campanian
	• *Marshosaurus bicentesimus*	Kimmeridgian–Tithonian
	• *Metriacanthosaurus parkeri*	early–middle Oxfordian
	• *Poekilopleuron bucklandii*	early Bathonian
	• *Proceratosaurus bradleyi*	Bathonian
	• *Rapator ornitholestoides*	Albian
	• *Shanshanosaurus huoyanshanensis*	?Campanian–Maastrichtian
	• *Unquillosaurus ceibalii*	?Campanian
	• *Xenotarsosaurus bonapartei*	?Campanian
	• *Xuanhanosaurus qilixiaensis*	Bathonian–Callovian

DISCOVERING DINOSAUR DIVERSITY

WHAT IS HAPPENING?

The final extinction of dinosaurs is probably the most discussed issue concerning the history of life. Dinosaurs have captured popular imagination since their appearance in museums early in the 19th century. The last twenty years has seen an explosion of interest in these creatures, with fascinating new discoveries, radical reinterpretations, powerful new research techniques, and a sharp growth in the sheer scale of investigation. Today, well over a hundred vertebrate paleontologists are working full-time on dinosaur studies—that's about 25 times the number forty years ago.

However, as much as people talk about dinosaurs, relatively little information is passed along. Everybody knows *Tyrannosaurus*, *Triceratops*, and the huge sauropods. But for most people, this superficial level is where the knowledge ends. Dinosaur extinctions are a typical example. Dinosaurs went extinct at the end of the Cretaceous, right? The answer is more complicated. This activity is designed to introduce students to the topic of dinosaur extinctions in a more sophisticated way, using real data to study precisely which dinosaurs went extinct and when. In addition, it makes a difference to this study how certain questions are framed. To that end, this activity also introduces students to questions regarding appropriate levels of analysis.

THE CRETACEOUS/TERTIARY MASS EXTINCTION

The last dinosaur groups became extinct at the end of the Cretaceous. They weren't the only ones. *All* land vertebrates with a body weight greater than 25 kg became extinct. In North America, that meant not only dinosaurs, but also most marsupials. Some groups of non-dinosaur reptiles (pterosaurs, ichthyosaurs, plesiosaurs, mosasaurs) also met their final extinction at the end of the Cretaceous—although ichthyosaurs had almost completely disappeared by early Late Cretaceous and these other groups had dwindled in numbers by the start of the Maastrichtian age. Table 1 (on the next page) lists the major vertebrate groups and their extinction rates.

Marine invertebrates suffered considerably at the end of the Cretaceous. Ammonites, already on the decline, became extinct, as did most microplankton (two-thirds of the species became extinct) and planktonic foraminifera (which decreased from 36 to 1 species at the boundary). In general, planktonic and sessile benthic species were far more affected than mobile benthic ones. Groups in the tropics were more affected than those outside the tropics. In addition, species with narrow geographic ranges were more affected than those with widespread range.

MATERIALS

Each pair of students will need

- Dino Data Sheet
- blank Species Lifetime charts (1 per student)
- blank higher-level Diversity Diagrams (4 or 5 per student)
- colored pencil or marker
- scissors

At the same time, many groups were either little affected by or benefited from events at the end of the Cretaceous period. Placental mammals underwent an extensive diversification, as did birds. Turtles lost only 16 percent of their diversity across the Cretaceous/Tertiary boundary, and the extinction rate of lower vertebrates remained the same as at other times—although marine fishes and lizards suffered moderate extinctions. In the oceans, bryzoans, brachiopods, bivalves, gastropods, echinoderms, crustaceans, and benthic foraminifera were little affected. Encourage students to appreciate the complexities of the important changes in life's diversity around the Cretaceous/Tertiary boundary. Species extinction occurred on a massive scale, but the story of what happened at the end of the Cretaceous is more complicated.

How you gauge the extent of extinction at the end of the Cretaceous period depends largely on the level of analysis. Taxonomists use families as a measure of overall diversity within a kingdom. At the family level, 85 percent of marine families and 86 percent of non-marine families *continued* into the Tertiary. This means that the overall diversity of animals was only mildly altered. However, at a more-detailed level of analysis—genera or species—the end-Cretaceous was more catastrophic. Overall, the number of genera declined 47 percent, and the number of species declined 76±5 percent. Which level is more important is a matter of debate. The point to emphasize is that what happened to the diversity of life at the Cretaceous/Tertiary transition was a collage of events as fascinating as they were complicated. Students wanting to know more about taxonomy and paleontology should be encouraged to pursue this further.

TABLE 1		

Magnitude of vertebrate extinctions during the Cretaceous/Tertiary transition

TAXON	GENERA EXTINCT	FAMILIES EXTINCT
Freshwater food chains		
Osteichthyans	13	10
Amphibia	13	10
Chelonia	18	4
Eosuchia	1	1
Crocodilia	4	1
Total	49	26
Terrestrial Food Chains		
Eolacertilia	1	1
Lacertilia	15	7
Serpentes	2	1
Ornithischia	14	8
Saurischia	8	5
Multituberculata	11	8
Marsupialia	4	3
Placentalia	9	4
Total	64	37

—data derived from article by Clemens in Elliott's (1986) Dynamics of Evolution.

In this activity, students only examine the effect that using different taxonomic levels has on conclusions. For example, at the end of the Jurassic many species went extinct but many higher taxonomic groups continued.

Part of the problem with studying mass extinctions involves deciding what counts as a mass extinction in the first place. Most paleontologists raise three issues when counting mass extinctions: duration, magnitude, and breadth. Mass extinctions must be geologically sudden or short lived—this raises the issue of how well geologists and paleontologists can define stratigraphic layers. Gauging the timing of events at the Cretaceous/Tertiary boundary around the world (especially in areas where dinosaurs fossils are found) usually is no more precise than about a hundred thousand or a million years. This means that processes or events that occur over tens of thousands of years cannot be distinguished from events that occur over the periods of a month, year, or decade. (Should we call an event a "catastrophe" if it lasts for 10,000 years?) During mass extinctions, there also is a substantial increase in extinction rates over so-called normal and background levels. The magnitude of this rise provides a measure of the severity of the mass extinction. Finally, mass extinction events must be broad in effect, involving a wide variety of organisms from many different environments. (The level of analysis changes in different studies of mass extinctions. Researchers interested in extinction *magnitude* count species percentages; those interested in extinction *breadth* count family percentages.)

What caused the Cretaceous/Tertiary mass extinction? From data described in Activity 16, it is nearly certain that a major bolide impact occurred on Earth around this time. Activity 17 asks students to consider ways of testing the theory that connects this impact to the mass extinctions at the Cretaceous/Tertiary transition. In that second activity, students explore how an impact might trigger geological and ecological circumstances that created unusually high rates of extinction. But do your students have to decide on what *one thing* occurred that caused mass extinctions? Certainly not. A bolide impact need not be the only cause of events that took place at the Cretaceous/Tertiary transition.

Whether or not a major bolide impact occurred, the Maastrichtian age was a time of considerable ecological and geological change. It was a time of significant climate change. Moving across the Cretaceous/Tertiary transition, global temperatures declined. One result of this change was increased freezing at the poles. That caused a 100–150 meter (!) drop in sea level during the Maastrichtian age. One result was the disappearance of the great inland sea that had covered most of central North America. It also caused the draining of flood plains and intertidal zones. (Imagine the extent of this habitat change.) In addition, there were large scale changes in water temperature, water oxygen content, and ocean circulation patterns. Moreover, there appears to have been considerable volcanic activity in the Maastrichtian. The evidence is clear that the late Maastrichtian was a time of significant environmental change, and extinction rates were accelerated as a result. If on top of these changes, a major bolide impact occurred—and it is nearly certain that one did—then the effect would have been to push the extinction rate still further. Encourage students to consider combinations of causes for the Cretaceous/Tertiary extinction by exploring these additional factors in more detail.

IMPORTANT POINTS FOR STUDENTS TO UNDERSTAND

◆ Dinosaurs were a diverse group, ranging from the Late Triassic period to the end of the Cretaceous period.

◆ Species extinction is commonplace in every geological age. Mass extinctions are periods, short in duration, where extinction is high in magnitude and wide in breadth.

◆ On average, dinosaur species existed only one or two ages before becoming extinct.

◆ Although dinosaurs as a group met their final end at the close of the Cretaceous, their overall history is a more detailed series of diversifications and extinctions.

◆ Changing your level of analysis can lead to different—often more interesting—results.

PREPARATION

Some preparation is necessary prior to beginning this activity. For the Dino Data Sheet, students can use the three-page data sheet printed in this activity. This covers one major dinosaur group, the saurischians (most carnivores and some herbivores). As an alternative, a complete list of dinosaur species exists as a file on *Craters!-CD* in the directory DINODATA. You have the option of substituting this comprehensive list for the Dino Data Sheet provided here. Students should receive all pages of the data sheet that include members of at least one major group (e.g., every group under the heading I. Saurischia). The outline of dinosaur classification is provided as Table 2. It should be reproduced as a transparency and projected—or copied onto a large sheet of paper and posted—during this activity.

CD-ROM

For the species-level diagrams, each student team (one pair) should work with about ten species. To assign species groups to these teams, place family or subfamily names (grouped if need be) on separate pieces of paper and draw them from a hat. This avoids initial confusion on the part of the students.

You might choose to review basic taxonomy prior to launching this activity, and you should have around your classroom images of representative dinosaurs from most of the major groups. (As an extension, students can locate those images for you.) Connecting names on the Dino Data Sheet to pictures of dinosaur reconstructions gives a reality to this activity that it otherwise may not have. (See the Resources List for useful printed resources; many images are posted on the Internet's World Wide Web—search using the key word "dinosaurs.")

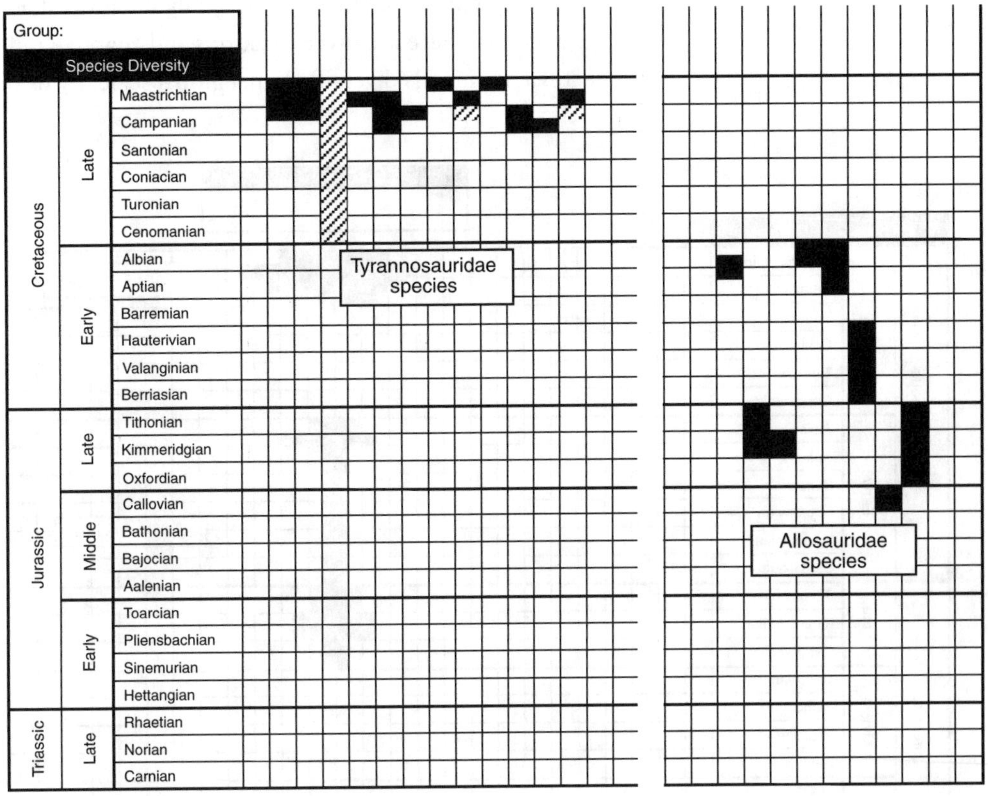

Creating the family and higher-level diversity diagrams can be confusing at the start. You might choose to walk through a sample group before asking students to complete their own. (Sample solutions are included here—Figures 3 and 4; be sure to choose samples *not* used by student teams.) Have plenty of copies of the blank diversity diagrams available. While posting them on the wall, keep all family-level diagrams in one row, and repeat this for successively higher categories in rows above the family-level diagrams. Patterns will develop if this order is used. Also, if the sequence across the row follows the order provided in Table 2, evolutionary relationships will be preserved, with groups closest together being most closely related. You might also have diversity diagrams for other groups available as transparencies for display and discussion after student teams have completed work on dinosaur groups. (See the Resources List, especially Valentine's *Phanerozoic Diversity Patterns*.)

SUGGESTIONS FOR FURTHER STUDY

Some points about the end-Cretaceous mass extinction cannot be stressed strongly enough. First, not every dinosaur that ever lived died at the end of the Cretaceous. Second, the end-Cretaceous extinctions involved more than the dinosaurs; indeed, some of the most extensive extinctions took place in other groups. Third, while extinction was common in end-Cretaceous times, not everything became extinct; indeed, some groups benefited from the extinctions of other groups. Fourth, the fossil record is our primary source of evidence for what occurred in the past. Encouraging further study into the history of life will reinforce these basic points.

Figure chart labels:

Group:
Species Diversity

Cretaceous — Late: Maastrichtian, Campanian, Santonian, Coniacian, Turonian, Cenomanian
Cretaceous — Early: Albian, Aptian, Barremian, Hauterivian, Valanginian, Berriasian
Jurassic — Late: Tithonian, Kimmeridgian, Oxfordian
Jurassic — Middle: Callovian, Bathonian, Bajocian, Aalenian
Jurassic — Early: Toarcian, Pliensbachian, Sinemurian, Hettangian
Triassic — Late: Rhaetian, Norian, Carnian

Tyrannosauridae species

Allosauridae species

FIGURE 3

Sample of Species Lifetime Chart. The groups shown here are families within the Carnosauria (I.2.a. in the Dino Data Sheet).

In the big picture, extinctions are really one side of a two-sided coin. Following extinctions, there are diversifications and adaptive radiations. When dinosaurs became extinct, mammals diversified on a global scale. Birds did too. Why? Paleontologists believe that mass extinctions remove groups that generally are not at risk during times of background extinctions. They break the hold well-adapted groups have ecologically, thereby permitting the expansion of groups that previously had been minor elements in the ecosystem. In a sense, they take up the vacant environmental niches. Mammals provide a good example. Mammals evolved from mammal-like reptiles in the Late Triassic— about the same time dinosaurs first appeared—but remained a relatively small part of terrestrial faunas until dinosaurs declined. When dinosaurs disappeared, mammals underwent a huge diversification. Ask students to investigate the two sides of this and other extinction periods (see the Resources List).

Encourage students to reflect on what should count as a "mass" extinction. (See the paper by Karl Flessa in the Resources List for a discussion of this point.) How many species or families must go extinct to count as a *mass* extinction? How quickly must these extinctions occur to count as a unit?

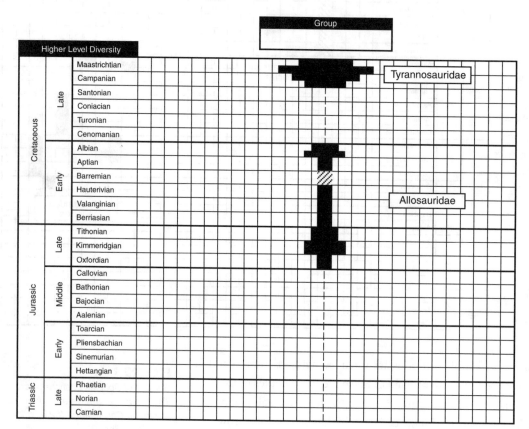

FIGURE 4

Sample of higher-level Diversity Diagram. The groups shown here are families within the Carnosauria (I.2.a. in the Dino Data Sheet). Paleontologists believe the Tyrannosauride evolved from the Allosauridae.

CONNECTIONS

In a recent survey of the problem, two vertebrate paleontologists wrote, "The problem of dinosaur extinction has a lengthy history of idiosyncratic explanations, the majority of which have been sterile, neither convincing in themselves nor stimulating further research." Ask students to investigate these explanations—some will seem to be truly preposterous—but encourage students to learn why ideas that seem silly to us are proposed by serious researchers.

What is the current extinction rate and how does it compare to periods of mass extinction? Students can study global or regional extinction rates, for example, due to habitat destruction. Estimates of current species loss vary, but the subject has provoked much debate about the value of biodiversity to life on Earth. Comparisons can be made using materials drawn from readily available environmental atlases and almanacs (also see the Resources List, especially Wilson's *Biodiversity*). Students also might investigate extinctions at other times in the fossil record.

Are dinosaurs *really* extinct? Dinosaurs consisted of three major groups: theropods, sauropodomorphs, and ornithischians. The second two left no descendants following the Cretaceous/Tertiary boundary, but theropods include animals that were the direct ancestors to birds. Some taxonomists and paleontologists classify birds as a subgroup of dinosaurs. Encourage students to examine the evolutionary transition from dinosaurs to true birds, especially the species *Archaeopteryx*. Drawing the line between dinosaurs and birds is always arbitrary; encourage students to see the transition as an evolutionary whole.

Ask students to investigate how species get their names. Who gets to name a species or other taxonomic group? Each name has its own history. Moreover, classification is a dynamic specialty in science: with the arrival of new information, old groups are reorganized, new groups are added, and relationships are reassessed. The species list provided for this activity has had modifications since its first publication in 1990. Encourage students to investigate those changes. Taxonomists follow certain customs to accommodate changes in classification. What are these customs? Who decides what changes are acceptable?

ANSWERS TO QUESTIONS FOR STUDENTS

1. Answers will vary.

2. Answers will vary.

TABLE 2

Outline of known dinosaur species

I. SAURISCHIA

A. Theropoda
  1. Ceratosauria
  2. Tetanurae
    a. Carnosauria
      i. Allosauridae
      ii. Tyrannosauridae
      iii. Carnosauria incertae sedis
  3. Coelurosauria
    a. Ornithomimosauria
      i. Harpymimidae
      ii. Garudimimidae
      iii. Ornithomimidae
      iv. Ornithomimosauria incertae sedis
    b. Maniraptora
      i. Elmisauridae
    c. Oviraptorosauria
      i. Oviraptoridae
        a. Oviraptorinae
        b. Ingeniinae
      ii. Caenagnathidae
      iii. Troodontidae
      iv. Dromaeosauridae
      v. ?Dromaeosauridae
B. Problematic Theropoda:" Coelurosaurs"
C. Problematic Theropoda: "Carnosaurs"

II. SAUROPODOMORPHA

A. Prosauropoda
      i. Thecodontosauridae
      ii. Anchisauridae
      iii. Massospondylidae
      iv. Yunnanosauridae
      v. Plateosauridae
      vi. Melanorosauridae
      vii. Blikanasauridae
B. Sauropoda
      i. Vulcanodontidae
      ii. Cetiosauridae
        a. Cetiosaurinae
        b. Shunosaurinae
      iii. Cetiosauridae incertae sedis
      iv. Brachiosauridae
      v. Brachiosauridae incertae sedis
      vi. Camarasauridae
        a. Camarasaurinae
        b. Opisthocoelicaudiinae
      vii. Diplodocidae
        a. Diplodocinae
        b. Dircaeosaurinae
        c. Mamenchisaurinae
      viii. Titanosauridae
      ix. Titanosauridae incertae sedis
C. Sauropoda incertae sedis

III. SEGNOSAURIA

      i. Segnosauridae

IV. ORNITHISCHIA

A. Genasauria
  1. Thyreophora
  2. ?Thyreophora incertae sedis
    a. Stegosauria
      i. Huayangosauridae
      ii. Stegosauridae
    b. Ankylosauria
      i. Ankylosauridae
      ii. Nodosauridae
B. Cerapoda
  1. Ornithopoda
      i. Heterodontosauridae
      ii. Hypsilophodontidae
    a. Iguanodontia
      i. Dryosauridae
      ii. Camptosauridae
      iii. Iguanodontidae
        a. ?Probactrosaurus
      iv. Iguanodontidae incertae sedis
      v. Hadrosauridae
        a. Hadrosaurinae
          1. "Gryposaurs"
          2. "Brachylophosaurs"
          3. "Edmontosaurs"
        b. Lambeosaurinae
        c. Lambeosaurinae incertae sedis
      vi. Hadrosauridae incertae sedis
    b. Marginocephalia
    c. Pachycephalosauria
      i. Homalocephalidae
      ii. Pachycephalosauridae
    d. Pachycephalosauria incertae sedis
    d. Ceratopsia
      i. Psittacosauridae
    e. Neoceratopsia
      i. Protoceratopsidae
      ii. Ceratopsidae
        a. Centrosaurinae
        b. Chasmosaurinae
(undetermined taxa)
      i. Herrerasauridae

V. DINOSAURIA INCERTAE SEDIS

—Source: David Weishampel, et al., *The Dinosauria* (Berkeley: University of California Press, 1984).

3. Answers will vary. Few dinosaur genera lived for more than one age before going extinct. Overall, the average duration of a dinosaur species is 2–3 million years; for genera, 5–6 million years. Ask students if they are surprised to learn that the average species duration usually is relatively short.

4. Answers will vary.

5. Answers will vary; however, major losses in dinosaur diversity can be easily identified at the end of the Jurassic and Cretaceous periods. But students might select other times as well. Each time, encourage them to consider what criteria they use to *count* mass extinctions.

6. Answers will vary.

7. Answers will vary.

8. Answers will vary. Families tend to have longer duration than species. They also tend to have a lower extinction rate, when measured as the number of extinctions per age.

9. Answers will vary.

10. Answers will vary.

11. Answers will vary. For diversity diagrams of other groups, see Valentine's *Phanerozoic Diversity Patterns* (in Resources List).

12. Students should *not* find that all dinosaur species evolved in the Late Triassic and went extinct at the end of the Cretaceous. Otherwise, their analysis will vary.

13. Extinction is the rule at the species level, but it is less frequent (when measured as number of extinctions per age) at family or higher levels. To say dinosaurs went extinct at the Cretaceous/Tertiary boundary is an oversimplification because it passes over the complex history of diversification and extinction throughout dinosaur history. It is better to say that dinosaurs experienced their *final* extinction at the end of the Cretaceous.

14. Answers will vary. There is no best level of analysis for all extinction studies. What the most appropriate level of analysis is for a study depends on the kinds of questions you ask.

ON THE PATH OF DISCOVERY

MATERIALS

♦ 2 sheets of graph paper

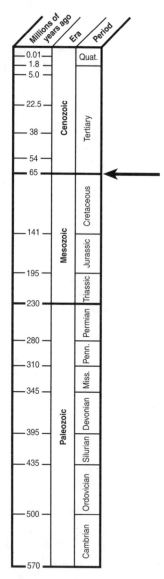

FIGURE 1
Geologic time scale. Arrow marks the K/T boundary. Geologists use the symbol K as an abbreviation for the Cretaceous Period and T for the Tertiary Period.

OBJECTIVE

This activity introduces you to the discovery of anomalies in the iridium abundance at the boundary that separates the Cretaceous and Tertiary periods.

BACKGROUND

Making a new discovery is one of the most exciting aspects of scientific research. Sometimes discoveries are small and relatively minor—a new species, a new star, a new chemical reaction. Sometimes discoveries are huge and make the discoverers world famous. Galileo became famous when he discovered craters on the Moon and determined that other planets had moons, too. Marie and Pierre Curie discovered radium and its use for making x-rays; for this, they won the Nobel prize. Edmond Halley discovered that some interplanetary bodies followed elliptical orbits. Halley's comet, which reappears near Earth every 76 years, was named in his honor. Discoveries can happen anywhere, and they can be made by anyone.

In 1980, a team lead by physicist Luis Alvarez and his son, geologist Walter Alvarez, announced a discovery that has made them famous. This team reported an abnormally high abundance of rare chemical elements in a thin layer of clay positioned exactly on the boundary between the Cretaceous and Tertiary periods (Figure 1). Finding this superabundance was unusual because it also was found in other locations around the world and it was found precisely at the K/T boundary regardless of the kinds of geologic formations on either side.

In this activity, you are going to examine the methods used by the Alvarez team and learn more about what they found. Their discovery has important implications for explaining the final extinction of dinosaurs and other groups at the end of the Cretaceous.

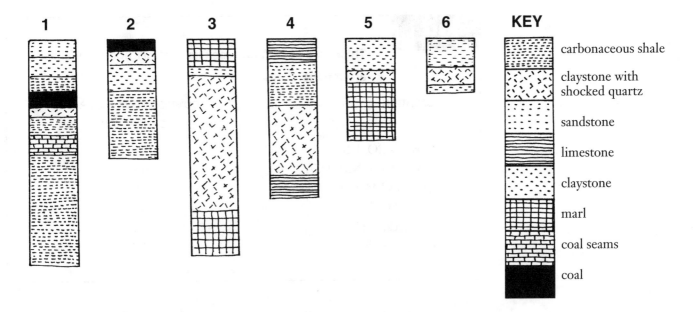

1 2 3 4 5 6 KEY

carbonaceous shale

claystone with
shocked quartz

sandstone

limestone

claystone

marl

coal seams

coal

PROCEDURE

1. The Alvarez team took a sample core of the rock layers at a site in Gubbio, Italy. When they compared it with sample cores taken from K/T boundary sites around the world, they found one layer common to all the samples. Figure 2 shows the rock types from six of these sample cores. The locations where these samples were taken are shown on Figure 3. Study the six columns and identify the one rock type that is common to all six locations.

2. Identify each of the sample sites shown in Figure 2, based on the thickness of the common layer, using the data from Table 1 (on the next page). Which area has the thickest deposit of the rock layer common to all samples?

FIGURE 2
Six stratigraphic cores from K/T boundary sites around the world.

FIGURE 3
Locations of the sites where K/T sample cores were taken. (Numbers correspond to cores shown in Figure 2.)

TABLE 1	
Thickness of common rock layer at K/T boundary sites around the world	
LOCATION	COMMON ROCK LAYER THICKNESS (CM)
Carmel, CO, USA	8.0
Raton Basin, NM, USA	0.8
Arroyo El Mimbral, Mexico	100
Beloc, Haiti	50
Caravaca, Spain	0.1
Gubbio, Italy	1.0

3. The Alvarez team examined their sample core from Gubbio using a special microscope that helped them see the mineral structure in fine detail. When they did this, something surprising was discovered. In the samples located exactly on the K/T boundary, the quartz grains showed clear shock lines (Figure 4). This is unusual because producing shock lines in quartz requires extremely high pressures, like the kinds that occur during a nuclear explosion and a major bolide impact. Describe the difference between shocked and regular quartz.

FIGURE 4

Compare these two sets of quartz grains. On the left is "shocked" quartz from a site near the Clearwater lakes, Quebec. On the right is "unshocked" quartz from near Barringer Crater, Arizona. Note the differences in magnification.

4. The Alvarez team also had geochemists analyze the chemical composition of the common rock layer. In that analysis, they discovered that rare elements such as iridium occurred at the K/T boundary layer in sharply higher concentrations than normal. Table 2 shows the relative abundance of the rare chemical element, iridium

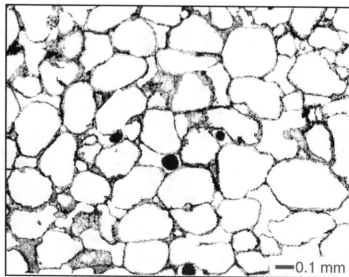

Relative abundance of iridium in Carlsbad, New Mexico, sample

DEPTH BELOW SURFACE (M)	IR ABUNDANCE (PPB)
0	0.00
50	0.00
100	0.00
111	0.50
113	1.00
115	0.50
119	13.5
120	0.50
122	0.25
128	0.25
132	0.25
135	0.00

(Ir), in a core sample taken in Carlsbad, New Mexico. Note that at the 113 meter depth the iridium abundance is 1 ppb (parts per billion), or 1 gram in 1 billion grams of material. What is the depth of the layer where it is most abundant? How many grams of iridium will be found in a kilogram of sample taken from that level? At what depth would you expect to find the K/T boundary?

Relative abundance of iridium in Gubbio, Italy, sample

SAMPLE	IR ABUNDANCE (PPB)
2.7 meters above boundary	<0.3
1.2 meters above boundary	<0.3
0.7 meters above boundary	0.36 ± 0.06
at K/T boundary	41.6 ± 1.8
0.5 meters below boundary	0.73 ± 0.08
2.2 meters below boundary	0.25 ± 0.08
5.4 meters below boundary	0.30 ± 0.16

—data from Table 1 in the Alvarez team's original 1980 paper.

TABLE 4

Chemical character of anomaly at K/T boundary sites

LOCATION	MASS (G)	VOLUME (CM³)	DENSITY (G/CM³)
Carmel, Colorado	0.500	0.0220	_____
Raton Basin, New Mexico	0.750	0.0330	_____
Arroyo El Mimbral, Mexico	0.901	0.0397	_____
Beloc, Haiti	0.802	0.0360	_____
Caravaca, Spain	0.200	0.0089	_____
Gubbio, Italy	0.401	0.180	_____
		total	_____
		average	_____

5. Graph the data from Table 2, with "Ir abundance" on the vertical axis and "depth below surface" on the horizontal axis. Describe the shape of the line on your graph. What does your graph show you about the relative abundance of iridium over the period of time represented in these rocks?

6. When the Alvarez team measured the iridium abundances in the layers of their Gubbio samples, they produced the data in Table 3. Graph the data in this table as you did in Question 5. How do these two data sets compare?

7. Because the Alvarez team found such strange results—they called it the iridium anomaly—they had the Gubbio samples tested and retested to make sure their analysis was correct. You can double-check their data, too, using density as an indicator. In Table 4, mass and volume data are provided for the six sites shown in Figure 2. Calculate the density of iridium from these samples (do the division to three decimal places and round off to two) and complete Table 4. Density is calculated as the ratio of mass to volume (grams per cubic centimeters). What is the average density of these samples?

8. Compare the average density of your samples with the density of chemical elements listed in Table 5. (Density of selected elements). Can you confirm the presence of iridium in the sites listed in Table 4? How confident can you be about the iridium sample from Gubbio?

TABLE 5

Density of selected elements

ELEMENT	SYMBOL	DENSITY	ELEMENT	SYMBOL	DENSITY
Aluminum	Al	2.70	Carbon	C	3.5
Cerium	Ce	6.70	Copper	Cu	8.92
Erbium	Er	4.77	Gold	Au	19.30
Iodine	I	4.93	Iridium	Ir	22.42
Iron	Fe	7.86	Lead	Pb	11.30
Magnesium	Mg	1.74	Nickel	Ni	8.90
Mercury	Hg	13.60	Platinum	Pt	21.45
Silver	Ag	10.50	Sodium	Na	0.97
Tin	Sn	7.30	Titanium	Ti	4.50

9. Where does the superabundance of iridium come from? Use Table 6 to suggest a source.

10. Describe a way to test your suggestion. What other features of the K/T boundary samples could help in your test?

TABLE 6

Relative abundance of iridium in various geological materials

LOCATION	IR ABUNDANCE (PPB)
K/T boundary layer, typical values	5–50
Earth's surface, typical rock types	0.02–0.2
Earth's core (estimated)	1,000
Martian rocks (estimated)	0.2
Lunar rocks (average)	0.1
Metallic meteorites (average)	1,000
Metal-rich asteroids (estimated)	500–1,000

ON THE PATH OF DISCOVERY

MATERIALS

◆ 2 sheets of graph paper

WHAT IS HAPPENING?

The Alvarez team's discovery was one of the most famous in geology in the last fifty years. As the team described, iridium at the Gubbio K/T boundary "increases by a factor of about 30...whereas none of the other elements as much as doubles..." What was important in the discovery, ultimately, was not the iridium increase *per se*, but rather the implication that the iridium increase came from a large asteroid impact. Following up on this implication has occupied the attention of many Earth and space scientists ever since.

In this activity, students examine original data—as reported in scientific research papers—for iridium abundances around the K/T boundary. (Some comes from the Alvarez team's original 1980 paper, which students can examine for themselves—see the Resources List. Some comes from elsewhere.) The purpose is to have your students appreciate the *magnitude* of the iridium spike found in the K/T boundary superabundance. Make no mistake, these results are *truly* unusual and require an explanation. In Activity 17, students will have an opportunity to explain these results.

IMPORTANT POINTS FOR STUDENTS TO UNDERSTAND

◆ Iridium is present in superabundance at the K/T boundary.

◆ Iridium is present but rare in other rocks, but is abundant in meteoroids and asteroids.

◆ The iridium superabundance occurs in locations around the world precisely at the K/T boundary, although it varies in magnitude at different sites.

◆ New discoveries are at the core of the scientific process. They can happen anywhere and anytime. They can be made by anyone.

PREPARATION

This activity uses graph-making and data analysis skills. You might want to review these skills prior to beginning this activity. All values in the data tables represent averages calculated from multiple samples. Table 3 includes values as an average ± one standard deviation, which provides an opportunity to discuss statistical measurements and how to represent them in graphs.

To answer likely questions from students, you might choose to read the Alvarez team's original paper in advance of this activity. The citation is in the Resources List. Prepare a transparency of the paper's Figure 5 (simplified here as Figure 5), which summarizes the data in Table 3, and compare the style of graph making with graphs produced by your students.

To help students understand the significance of the iridium superabundance, you might want to discuss its nature in more detail. In rock samples from the Cretaceous period taken around the world, the natural—or background—level of iridium is around 0.25–0.30 ppb. Ask students to consider what might explain the iridium superabundance at the K/T boundary. Also, what would explain its wide distribution around the globe?

SUGGESTIONS FOR FURTHER STUDY

Iridium superabundance is one remarkable feature of rocks found at the K/T boundary. Another is the presence of shocked quartz. When quartz is subjected to sudden, intense pressures—as in a nuclear explosion—shock lines appear in the quartz grains. Bolide impacts create pressures so intense that shocked quartz is commonly found near impact craters. Indeed, geologists use the presence of shocked quartz as an indicator of bolide impacts. This activity provides an opportunity to discuss the features of shocked quartz. Shocked quartz has been found in the K/T boundary layers listed in Figure 2 as well as at other K/T boundary locations. Students can search for data on shocked quartz as an extension to this activity.

Students now have several pieces of the puzzle. Table 6 shows that metallic meteorites and their parent bodies, metal-rich asteroids, have roughly 10 to 100 times the iridium concentration of the K/T boundary layer. If we had some way to dilute and distribute such material in the form of dust, we could create the observed boundary layer all over Earth. Students learned in Activity 3 that craters can blast ejecta over a large area. Ejected material is a mixture of one part exploded meteorite and as much as 100 parts soil from the impact site. Thus, a large enough meteorite impact could blast out a mixture of diluted meteorite plus surface rocks that could match the iridium content of the K/T boundary layer! That's the reasoning the Alvarez group used to arrive at their hypothesis. A small group of geologists still believes the mantle is the source of the iridium superabundance at the K/T boundary, suggesting that a period of intense volcanic activity occurred at the end of the Cretaceous. Students can explore this alternative (see volcanism readings in the Resources List), but remind them that they

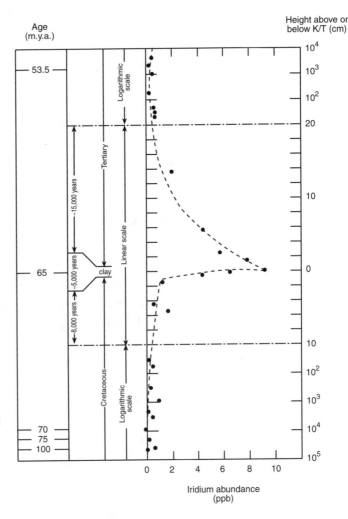

FIGURE 5

Iridium spike at the K/T boundary from the Alvarez, et al. team's site in Gubbio, Italy. This is a redrawn and simplified version of Figure 5 that appears in their original 1980 paper.

also need to explain the presence of the shocked quartz in K/T boundary layers. Also, the patterns of concentrations for other rare elements follow that for iridium, though to a lesser degree. Students can investigate these patterns, which are reported in the original Alvarez team's paper, and compare them to what volcanoes might produce.

Students can explore reports of iridium abundances at K/T boundary localities around the world. Create a class project, posting a globe or map and compiling these data. Students can be assigned particular geographic regions to survey. This map could then be used in Activity 17, where students consider the Alvarez team's own explanation for the iridium superabundance.

CONNECTIONS

Explaining the origins of the K/T boundary's iridium superabundance offers an opportunity to introduce the topic of geological *differentiation*. The concept of differentiation helps explain why iridium is abundant in some types of geologic material and not in others (see Table 6); it also helps to explain why the iridium superabundance at the K/T boundary is so unusual.

Differentiation is a term used to identify processes that separate or concentrate chemical elements or compounds in nature. Differentiation occurs on a planetary scale during the melting of planetary interiors. When a planet's interior is melted, heavy metallic elements tend to sink to the center and lighter, silica-rich materials tend to float to the surface. Iridium is a dense metal. Chemically, it has an affinity for iron and other metals. During the melting of planetary bodies in the early history of our solar system, iridium became concentrated in the cores and depleted in the surface rocks of those bodies. This explains why Earth's surface rocks have little iridium while its mantle rocks have so much. Metallic meteorites, which are fragments from the iron cores of asteroids, have high iridium levels too (see Table 6). Thus, when iridium occurs in superabundance in surface rocks, two of the most likely places to look for the iridium source are volcanoes and meteorites.

Differentiation also explains why planetary surface rocks have less iridium than primitive asteroids that have never been melted. Primitive asteroids have moderately high iridium levels. Planets formed from such materials during a process known as accretion. In the resulting melting, differentiation processes caused iridium to concentrate in Earth's mantle.

ANSWERS TO QUESTIONS FOR STUDENTS

1. The common rock layer is claystone with shocked quartz.

2. The thickest deposit is found in Arroyo El Mimbral, Mexico.

3. The shocked quartz has parallel lines in it.

4. The layer is 119 meters deep, and the iridium abundance is 13.5 ppb.

5. Answers will vary, but should point out a "spike" in abundance.

6. Answers will vary, but should show a similar spike.

7. The key to Table 4 is presented in Table 4–Key.

8. The given density value for iridium (in Table 5) is 22.42 and the calculated average of the samples is 22.53. This confirms (within the range of experimental error) the presence of iridium in the K/T boundary samples.

9. Answers will vary. This question will be the subject of investigation for Activity 17. Encourage hypotheses that are global. The Gubbio data could be a fluke, an anomaly. But the chances are small that such a fluke might appear in *three* sites (and others have found it in many more locations) at the same geological horizon.

10. Answers will vary.

TABLE 4 - KEY

Chemical character of anomaly at K/T boundary sites

LOCATION	MASS (G)	VOLUME (CM³)	DENSITY (G/CM³)
Carmel, Colorado	0.500	0.0220	22.73
Raton Basin, New Mexico	0.750	0.0330	22.73
Arroyo El Mimbral, Mexico	0.901	0.0397	22.70
Beloc, Haiti	0.802	0.0360	22.28
Caravaca, Spain	0.200	0.0089	22.47
Gubbio, Italy	0.401	0.180	22.28
		total	135.19
		average	22.53

PUTTING IT TO THE TEST

MATERIALS

♦ no special materials are needed for this activity

OBJECTIVE

In this activity you will examine one scenario for the impact theory of the K/T extinction. You also will develop ways to test this theory.

BACKGROUND

Testing is another activity at the center of what scientists do. For a theory to qualify as a *scientific* one, it must be testable. The easiest way to test a theory is to create a series of predictions based on that theory and see if those predictions hold up during tests. If testing confirms these predictions, then the theory gains support; if testing does not confirm these predictions, the theory loses support and may deserve rejection.

In this activity, you are going to examine the impact theory for the K/T extinction and consider how it can be tested. To help you better understand the impact theory, it's best to have some background. In 1980, a team including Nobel-prize winning physicist Luis Alvarez published what has become a famous paper. In it, they reported an abnormally high abundance of the chemical element iridium (abbreviated Ir) in the thin rock layer on the boundary between the Cretaceous (K) and Tertiary (T) periods. In this and subsequent reports, superabundances of iridium were described in K/T boundary rocks around the globe.

Did a large bolide collide with Earth to end the Cretaceous Period and cause a period of mass extinction? In this Activity, you will put that theory to the test.

In their 1980 paper, the Alvarez team considered several sources for the iridium anomaly. It could not have come from the oceans, they said, because there simply isn't enough iridium in ocean water (less than 0.007 ppb, parts per billion) to account for the concentrations found at the K/T boundary layer (Figure 1). It might have come from lava flows rising out of Earth's mantle (iridium's abundance in the upper mantle is about 20 ppb), but at some locations the K/T boundary showed iridium levels double this. Furthermore, the K/T boundary material is not volcanic.

The most likely source for iridium in the necessary quantities, the team argued, was metal-rich meteorite material. An asteroid would contain enough iridium to account for the superabundances if it were 10 ± 4 km in diameter. "In brief," they reported, "our hypothesis suggests that an asteroid struck [Earth], formed an impact crater, and some of the dust-sized material ejected from the crater reached the stratosphere and was spread around the globe." (Alvarez, et al., 1980, p. 1105) The dust cloud would contain the vaporized asteroid, including its iridium. When the contents of that cloud were deposited, they would form the K/T boundary layer.

The Alvarez team knew the K/T boundary marked a major transition in the history of life, including the final extinction of dinosaurs. This transition and the hypothesized impact were not coincidences, the team concluded. In fact, a 10 ± 4 km asteroid striking Earth would produce effects that could easily have caused the extinctions of the magnitude seen at the K/T boundary. The theory they presented to explain that connection is discussed in this activity. Imagine you are a scientist reading this theory for the first time. How would you go about testing it? How would you evaluate the evidence for and against it? That is what you'll be asked to do here. You'll develop a series of predictions based on Alvarez's theory and consider ways to put them to the test.

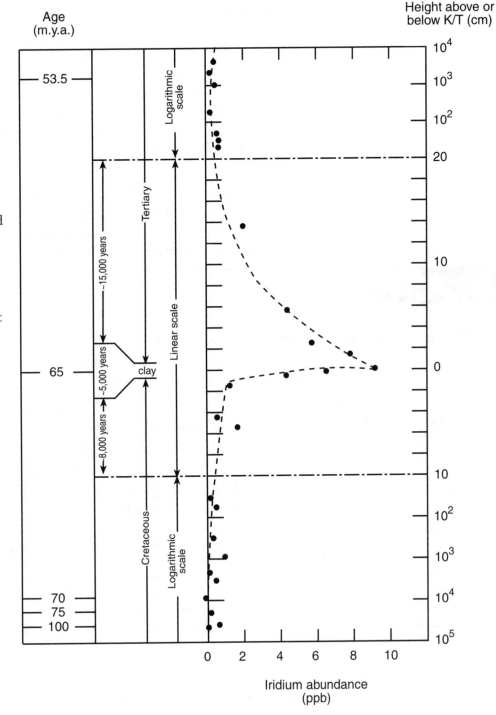

FIGURE 1

Iridium levels in samples taken from different elevations at the Gubbio site. (Adapted from the original in Alvarez, et al., 1980)

PROCEDURE

After nearly a decade of study by the scientific community, the impact hypothesis for the K/T extinction was evaluated by co-founder Luis Alvarez in 1987. In that evaluation, Alvarez updated the impact theory and provided a detailed scenario to explain how the impact that caused the iridium anomaly also created circumstances that produced the mass extinction at the K/T transition. That scenario is described in Theory Box 1. (You can read Alvarez's discussion yourself. It appears in *Physics Today*, July 1987, volume 40, pages 24–33.)

1. Read Alvarez's scenario. Read it several times carefully so you have a good overall picture of the scenario and a good appreciation for the details. Working with your team, list the steps in sequence that Alvarez suggests connect the impact to the mass extinction. Write these steps in Table 1.

THEORY BOX 1

The Alvarez team's impact theory for the K/T extinction

"[In developing the original impact theory,] I tried the idea that a bolide 10 kilometers in diameter struck the Earth and enveloped it in an opaque blanket of dust. While the dust fell for some months onto the ground and into the ocean, it cut out the sunlight, thereby stopping photosynthesis, so most of the missing animal life on Earth [the ones that went extinct] died of starvation.* We now see the fallen dust as the worldwide K/T boundary layer."

"Detailed computer modeling of the atmosphere has shown that it would have been extremely cold during the period of darkness, that it would have been as though all the animals had been transported to present-day Antarctica....[If the impact had occurred in the ocean] the temperature would first go way down but then would increase as a result of a greenhouse effect, and that heating could be a major contributor to the killing."

"Perhaps one of the most important killing mechanisms would derive from the shock-heating of the atmosphere by the expanding fireball: The impact would have released an energy equivalent to the detonation of 100,000,000 megatons of TNT. It would give rise to the production of huge amounts of nitrogen oxides in the atmosphere, leading to highly acidic rain and surface ocean waters with pHs low enough to dissolve the calcium carbonate shells of marine invertebrates....Robert Prinn of the MIT [Massachusetts Institute of Technology] group said recently, 'Essentially pure nitric acid would be pouring over about 10 percent of the global surface in the first few months.'"

* - In their 1980 paper, the Alvarez team described why this starvation would have occurred: "A temporary absence of sunlight would effectively shut off photosynthesis and thus attack food chains at their origins."

—*Source: Luis Alvarez, et al., "Mass Extinctions Caused by Large Bolide Impacts," Physics Today, July 1987, volume 40, pages 24–33.*

2. A theory this complicated is really a collection of hypotheses and assumptions. For example, Alvarez says, "We now see the fallen dust as the worldwide K/T boundary layer." Other scientists turn this into a prediction—that a layer of dust should exist around the world at the K/T boundary—and subject it to testing. Geologists have examined K/T boundary layers in many parts of the world, looking for a dust layer and an iridium superabundance like that found in the sites the Alvarez team studied. In doing this, they are testing part of Alvarez's theory.

3. Based on your understanding of Alvarez's theory, list in Table 2 *at least five* predictions contained for this scenario. For each, identify how it is drawn from the scenario. Try to think of other effects that might have been created in the K/T boundary layer if a large asteroid made a crater in those days. Use your knowledge of impact craters.

TABLE 1

Steps connecting impact to K/T extinction

Step 1 _____

_____

Step 2 _____

_____

Step 3 _____

_____

Step 4 _____

_____

Step 5 _____

_____

Step 6 _____

_____

Step 7 _____

_____

Step 8 _____

_____

(Extend this chart on another page if necessary.)

---

4. Predictions have no value unless they can be tested by experiments or checked against existing evidence. Select for testing two hypotheses or predictions—the ones you think are most important—from Table 2. Write a report describing imaginary experiments or research projects in which you subject these predictions to scientific testing. What kinds of evidence would you look for and where would you expect to find them?

Please note: Your discussion should take the form of 2 one-page reports. State the prediction at the top of the page, then describe the research you would perform as part of the test. Include whatever sketches, maps, or diagrams you think will help describe your test. Although you don't have to do the research yourself, be sure the work is *possible*—for example, you can't recreate the event or travel back in time.

TABLE 2

Most important predictions of Alvarez's scenario

PREDICTION	CONNECTION TO SCENARIO
1. _____	_____
_____	_____
2. _____	_____
_____	_____
3. _____	_____
_____	_____
4. _____	_____
_____	_____
5. _____	_____
_____	_____
6. _____	_____
_____	_____

5. Many additional discoveries have been made in recent years to support the hypothesis of a large impact 65 million years ago. Try to find reports of some of these discoveries and observations. Has an actual impact site been found? If so, where is it?

QUESTIONS/CONCLUSIONS

1. For any particular theory, a large number of predictions can be created. How many predictions did you create for the Alvarez scenario?

2. Given all the predictions *possible* for a theory, some are more crucial than others. What two predictions did you choose to design tests for? Why do they seem to be more crucial than other ones?

3. When a test is done and results do *not match* the predictions, what options does a scientist have?

4. With the two predictions you chose to design research for, suppose the tests give results that were not predicted.

   a. Suppose further that you are a critic of Alvarez's theory. What would you conclude?

   b. Suppose instead that you are a supporter. How would you explain the results?

PUTTING IT TO THE TEST

MATERIALS

◆ no special materials are needed for this activity

WHAT IS HAPPENING?

Since the mid 19th century, the K/T mass extinction has been a focus of study and debate within the scientific community. Over that time, a number of theories to explain this mass extinction have gained and lost popularity. Although not the only mass extinction in the fossil record, and certainly not the most devastating (see Activity 13), what happened near the K/T boundary captures wide attention largely because it involved the final extinction of the dinosaurs.

The strongest current candidate to explain the K/T mass extinction is the impact hypothesis, proposed in its modern form by the Alvarez team in 1980. The original team's hypothesis was that the impact ejected enough debris into the atmosphere to block out sunlight for a period long enough to affect primary production (photosynthesis). At the same time the light was blocked out, temperatures changed sharply, strong acid rain fell, and other environmental stresses occurred. The effect of this series of events was a collapse of food chains all over the planet. The ensuing mass extinction reduced the number of species on Earth by about 75 percent.

In this activity, students examine the impact theory as an exercise in prediction and theory testing. When the Alvarez team proposed this interpretation, scientists in every discipline and around the globe put their conclusions to the test. If an impact occurred the way they described, then iridium, shocked quartz, and debris should be scattered over Earth in predictable ways. This evidence was searched for, and these searches formed part of the scientific debate over the impact theory. In other fields, ecologists developed models of ecosystem collapse to see if the collapse of primary production would bring down whole food chains, paleontologists studied patterns of extinction to see what went extinct and what did not, and Earth scientists searched for the crater that fit the hypothesized 10 ± 4 km asteroid. Students should be encouraged to investigate the details of these results, but the point of this activity is to develop an awareness for how other scientists go about putting theories to tests. Once this skill is acquired, students will not only be able to understand the results of scientific research, but they will also understand why scientists choose to undertake research in the first place and how that research functions as a theory test.

IMPORTANT POINTS FOR STUDENTS TO UNDERSTAND

◆ As originally proposed, the impact theory for the K/T mass extinction hypothesized the impact of a 10 ± 4 kilometer asteroid on Earth. This impact produced a collapse of ecosystems around the planet.

- The impact theory currently is the most widely accepted explanation for the K/T mass extinction. However, there are alternatives.

- Testing predictions is an important part of scientific research. Making accurate predictions is one measure for the quality of a scientific theory. Theories whose predictions do not match the evidence run the risk of rejection.

PREPARATION

The activity presumes you have worked through other activities in this lesson, especially Activities 15 and 16. Students should already know about the iridium anomaly at the K/T boundary. They also should know that dinosaurs were not the only group that met their final extinction at the end of the Cretaceous. Students should work in teams of 3–4.

You might launch this activity with a discussion about testing hypotheses and how to formulate tests. Ask students, for example, how they would test the claim "water heats in a microwave oven." Then ask how they would test the claims "water heats faster in higher power microwave ovens," and "water heats at a linear rate (same increase in temperature per unit time) in microwave ovens." Being able to create tests from hypotheses is an acquired skill. It requires background knowledge in the discipline, but it also involves creativity and ingenuity. Try working though the student section yourself prior to assigning this activity. This way, you'll learn which elements are easiest and most difficult to make predictions about and create tests for.

SUGGESTIONS FOR FURTHER STUDY

In this activity, students design thought experiments and imaginary research to test predictions from the impact theory. Encourage them to look for results from real studies that have tested their ideas. Also encourage them to perform simple elements of their tests. For example, the impact theory claims that dust clouds obscured light for several months; this stopped photosynthesis and caused primary producers to die. A possible test of this hypothesis is to see if plants can survive without light for this time period. In designing this test, students can deprive plants of light for different periods of time to see the consequences. Variants of this experiment could investigate different intensities of light (e.g., from 10 percent reduced to 100 percent reduced), different species of plants (e.g., alfalfa versus clover versus bluegrass). Multiple variables can be added. For example, a temperature or pH change can be added to a change in light intensity. Exactly what is needed to halt photosynthesis? Then students can research what evidence exists to suggest these conditions actually occurred.

Since the impact theory's proposal in 1980, many researchers have contributed additions, modifications, and alterations. Students can follow this discussion in the scientific literature (see Resources List). They can compare how scientists in different disciplines (planetary scientists versus paleontologists, for example) have responded to the impact theory, and whether impacts have been invoked to explain other mass extinctions.

Students can search among recent magazines for continuing articles and evidence on this subject. Recent discoveries about the K/T impact theory include

♦ The iridium anomaly continues to be found all over Earth wherever scientists find exposures of the K/T boundary layer.

♦ Not only iridium, but other elements concentrated in metal-rich meteorites are concentrated in the K/T boundary layer, supporting the idea that it contains meteorite debris.

♦ As already mentioned, shocked quartz grains indicate the K/T debris was ejected from a huge explosion, larger than known volcanic explosions. Other shocked crystals, such as zircons, have also been found.

♦ Scientists Wendy Wolbach, Roy Lewis, and Edward Anders, from the University of Chicago, discovered the K/T layer also contains a huge concentration of soot, apparently from fires. To get this much soot all over the world, you would have to burn the majority of forests and grasslands present at the end of the Cretaceous Period. These scientists believe these fires started when ejected debris from the explosion shot above the atmosphere and fell back into the atmosphere around the world. The debris heated on re-entry. The rain of glowing meteors in the hours after the impact lit up the sky and crated a large radiant heat pulse that ignited fires. Certain regions that happened to be under intense rainstorms or snowstorms could have survived this effect without fire.

♦ Scientists calculate that the soot and debris from the impact would settle in the high atmosphere and take months to settle out, blocking or dimming sunlight during that time. This would kill many plants and disrupt the food chain, demonstrating that extinction patterns are complex.

♦ Jumbled deposits from tsunamis (popularly but incorrectly called tidal waves) have been found in the K/T boundary layer in some regions, especially around the Gulf of Mexico coast. This indicated a huge tsunami wave at the time of the K/T catastrophe and also suggested that the event was centered in that region.

♦ Most convincing of all, many scientists believe the crater itself has finally been located. The crater isn't visible on the surface; it straddles the north coast of Mexico's Yucatan peninsula and extends into the Gulf of Mexico. This impact site is buried by 300 to 1,100 meters of sediments. Drilling, gravity surveys, and other techniques indicate it has a multiple ring concentric structure, like similar-sized craters mapped on our similar-sized neighboring planet, Venus. Depending on the ring that represents the original rim, it is about 180–300 km in diameter, which is the right size to have caused the effects described by the Alvarez team. The crater itself is named Chicxulub, a Mayan place name and has been dated to be about 65 million years old, which matches the time of the K/T extinctions.

The impact hypothesis is not the only explanation for the iridium boundary or the K/T mass extinction. Some scientists believe a major impact explains only part of the mass extinction and that additional factors—such as unrelated global cooling and a drop in sea-level—must be included in a complete account of the period. A few even reject the suggestion that an impact event occurred at the K/T boundary, suggesting instead that the end-Cretaceous was a period of massive volcanic activity. Material cited in the Resources List provides starting points for launching into these issues.

CONNECTIONS

The scientific discussion of the K/T mass extinction and the impact theory intertwines with accounts in the popular press. Students can study how the press portrays this scientific debate: does it take sides, what points does it emphasize or ignore, how does it treat the presence of "controversy" in science?

As scientists debated and evaluated the impact theory in the 1980s, they carried on a parallel discussion over the global effects of nuclear war. Ask students to compare those two discussions and how they were related.

ANSWERS TO QUESTIONS FOR STUDENTS

1. Answers will vary. Encourage students to be creative in looking for predictions. The most telling ones usually are not the most obvious.

2. Answers will vary. Encourage students to think about what constitutes a *crucial* text.

3. In response to failed predictions, the hypothesis can be revised, the test can be redone or reevaluated, or the prediction can be reassessed.

4. a. Critics use failed predictions to argue for rejecting a theory.

   b. Supporters usually argue that failed predictions require further study and do not require rejecting a theory.

5. Answers will vary. Some possibilities are listed in Suggestions for Further Study.

WHAT ARE THE CHANCES?

MATERIALS

◆ no special materials are
needed for this activity

OBJECTIVE

In this activity, you will explore the likelihood of future bolide impacts on Earth.

BACKGROUND

You know bolides—i.e. asteroids and comets—crash into our planet and that this has happened throughout Earth's history. If you completed Activity 12, you'll remember Figure 1, which shows major impact sites on North America. If impacts have happened throughout the past, how likely are they in the future? What are the chances that large bolide impacts will happen in the next hundred years? Can we expect a mass extinction-causing impact any time soon? In this activity, you will investigate these questions.

Asteroids and comets travel in elliptical paths around the sun. Each has its own, unique orbit. Some have orbits that pass near Earth's orbit. Others have orbits that *cross* Earth's path (Figure 2). At the end of 1992, 163 asteroids with Earth-crossing orbits had been identified. A sampling of these asteroids is provided in Table 1; additional ones are discovered every year.

FIGURE 1

Major impact sites in North America.

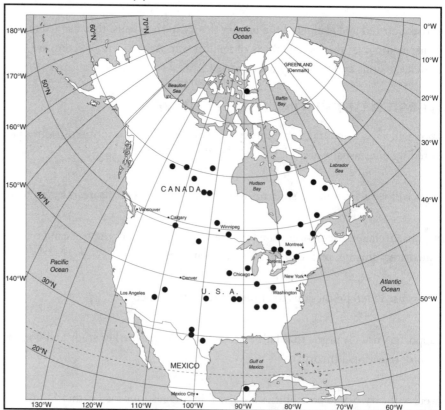

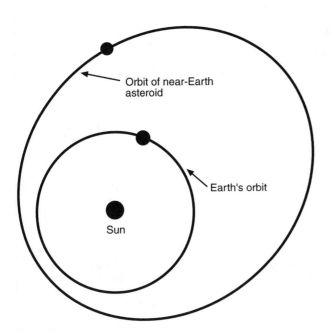

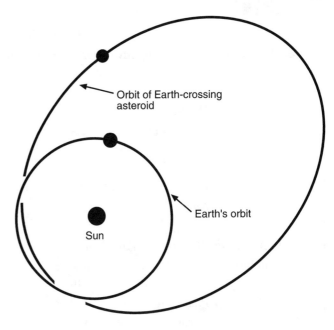

Part I
PROCEDURE

1. Table 1 presents a sample of Earth-crossing asteroids whose orbits have been precisely determined. For each asteroid, you are given

- *number/name*: The discoverer of a planetary body has the right to name it. Astronomers assign an identifier number to asteroids after their orbits have been precisely determined.

- P_s is the probability that this asteroid will collide with Earth, as calculated by asteroid expert Eugene Shoemaker and his colleagues. Probabilities are given as the number of occurrences expected per billion years.

- P_o is the probability that this asteroid will collide with Earth, as calculated by asteroid expert Ernst Julius Öpik. Probabilities are given as the number of occurrences expected per billion years. (The differences in calculating P_s and P_o involve technical assumptions about how best to determine these probabilities. Notice that in most cases the two calculations agree once you round them off to one significant digit.)

- v is the estimated velocity (kilometers per second) the asteroid is expected to have at the time of its projected collision with Earth.

- throughout Table 1 uncertain values are given in parentheses; undetermined values are listed as "nc" (not calculated).

TABLE 1

Earth-crossing asteroids

Aten Asteroids (These are slightly closer to the Sun than to Earth's orbit.)

number	name	diameter (km)	Impact chance per billion years P_s	P_o	velocity (km/s)
2340	Hathor	(0.2)	14	14	16.3
2100	Ra-Shalom	2.4	6.3	6.7	17.9
3753	1986 TO	~3	nc	(3)	(22)
3362	Khufu	0.7	5.3	6.2	19.8
2062	Aten	0.9	7.1	6.5	16.0
3554	Amun	2.0	5.4	5.0	17.4

Apollo Asteroids (These cross Earth's orbit.)

number	name	diameter (km)	Impact chance per billion years P_s	P_o	velocity (km/s)
3200	Phaethon	6.9	nc	(1.4)	(35)
1566	Icarus	0.9	1.8	2.2	30.6
2212	Haphaistos	~5	0.44	1.2	34.6
1864	Daedalus	(3.1)	1.0	1.6	26
3838	1986 WA	~3	nc	(1)	(29)
2201	Oljato	1.4	2.3	6.1	26.4
2101	Adonis	~1	2.8	6.2	25.4
1865	Cerberus	1.0	2.5	3.1	20.9
3752	1985 PA	~2	nc	(1)	(27)
4034	1986 PA	~1	4.5	5.3	18.0
3360	1981 VA	1.8	0.66	1.6	26.6
1981	Midas	~1	3.8	0.7	30.7
1862	Apollo	1.4	2.8	4.3	20.3
4183	1959 LM	~4	1.3	2.2	21.3
1685	Toro	5.2	(4)	(4.2)	17.2
2329	Orthos	~3	1.8	2.2	23.3
2063	Bacchus	~1	6.5	7.2	15.8
2135	Aristaeus	~1	(2.0)	(1.5)	20.8
1620	Geographos	2.0	3.8	3.9	16.7
4197	1982 TA	1.8	nc	(1)	(27)
2102	Tantalus	~2	2.5	1.5	34.8
4257	1987 QA	~2	nc	nc	nc
3361	Orpheus	~0.3	nc	(21)	14
4179	1989 AC	~4	32	15	14.4
4015	1979 VA	~5	nc	1.0	15
1863	Antinous	1.8	nc	0.54	19.7
3103	1982 BB	1.5	nc	3.8	17.3
3671	Dionysius	~1	nc	(1.5)	(16)

TABLE 1

Amor Asteroids (These have orbits that closely approach Earth's orbit, but are further from the Sun than Earth.)

number	name	diameter (km)	Impact chance per billion years P_s	P_o	velocity (km/s)
2608	Seneca	0.9	nc	nc	nc
3122	1981 ET3	~4	nc	3.2	16.9
3757	1982 XB	0.5	nc	2.5	13.4
3908	1980 PA	~1	nc	4.0	14.7
2061	Anza	(2.7)	nc	1.3	14.2
1915	Quetzalcoatl	0.3	nc	nc	nc
1917	Cuyo	~3	nc	1.3	17.8
1943	Anteros	1.8	nc	1.1	13.4
3988	1986 LA	~1	nc	nc	nc
3551	1983 RD	0.9	nc	nc	nc
1221	Amor	~1	nc	1.6	15.4
3288	Seleucus	2.8	nc	1.4	20.8
1580	Betulia	7.4	0.5	1.7	30.6
2202	Pele	~2	nc	0.1	14.6
1627	Ivar	8.1	nc	1.8	13.9
887	Alinda	4.2	nc	nc	nc

—*Source: These selected data points were taken from Eugene Shoemaker, et al., "Asteroid and Comet Flux in the Neighborhood of Earth," in Virgil Sharpton and Peter Ward, Global Catastrophes in Earth History: An Interdisciplinary Conference on Impacts, Volcanism, and Mass Mortality (Boulder, CO: Geological Society of America, 1990), pp. 155–170, Table 1.*

2. Notice that in general the smallest asteroids in Table 1 are most likely to hit Earth soonest. Because they are small, these asteroids had to be close to Earth in the first place to be bright enough to be discovered. This is an example of a bias in the statistics.

QUESTIONS/CONCLUSIONS

1. Use Table 1 to answer the following questions.

a. Identify the Earth-crossing asteroid from this sample that has the *largest* diameter.

b. Identify the Earth-crossing asteroid from this sample that has the *smallest* diameter.

c. Identify the Earth-crossing asteroid from this sample with the *largest* estimated collision velocity.

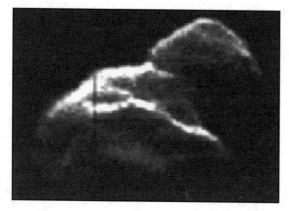

FIGURES 3 (ABOVE) AND 4 (BELOW)

Two images of Asteroid 4179 Toutatis, a "contact binary" asteroid (so-called because this asteroid is composed of two pieces of 4 and 2.5 kilometers respectively). These are not photographs, but images created by radar when this asteroid passed close to Earth in 1992.

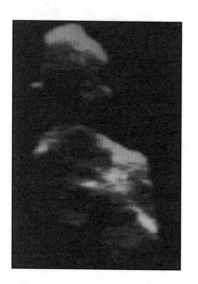

d. Which asteroid, following the Shoemaker calculation, is *most likely* to collide with Earth? What is the probability of this impact occurring next year? Does Öpik's calculation agree?

e. Which, following Öpik's calculations, is the *least likely* to collide with Earth? What is the probability of this occurring next year? Does Shoemaker's calculation agree?

2. Estimates vary, but astronomers believe major global effects can be produced by a bolide larger than 0.5–5 kilometers in diameter. Assume the smallest size bolide that can cause profound global effects is 2.5 kilometers in diameter. Which Earth-crossing asteroids in this sample pose such danger?

3. The sample provided in Table 1 is biased towards larger objects because it is easier for astronomers to discover larger objects than smaller ones. Using statistical models, they estimate a sample like this is only about five percent complete for objects one kilometer in size and less than 0.1 percent complete for objects 0.1 kilometers in size. Some experts want NASA to undertake a complete survey of Earth-crossing asteroids. If such a study were done, how many more one kilometer-sized asteroids (use the interval 0.9–1.1 km just to be safe) would you expect a sample like this to include? Show your calculations.

4. On December 8, 1992, the 6.4 kilometer wide, Earth-crossing asteroid Toutatis came within 3.5 million kilometers of our planet. This is a "near miss" by solar system standards.

a. The distance between Earth and Moon averages about 382,000 kilometers. How many Earth-Moon radii away was Toutatis in this "near miss"?

b. On this near miss, NASA astronomers used radar to map Toutatis (Figures 3 and 4) and found it to be a dumbbell-shaped asteroid roughly 2.6 and 4 kilometers in diameter. If either part were to strike Earth, would it produce effects on a global scale?

5. The closest recorded approach of an asteroid was reported in 1993, when Object 93KA2 passed within 144,000 kilometers of Earth's surface. How many Earth-Moon radii away was Object 93KA2 at its closest point?

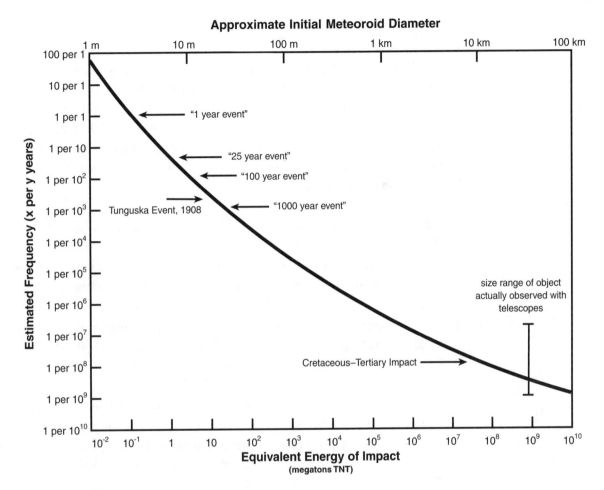

Approximate Initial Meteoroid Diameter

Part II: Probabilities of Asteroid Impacts

BACKGROUND

In Part I, you studied *known* asteroids and examined the probabilities of each colliding with Earth. While Table 1 lists many of the asteroids that might eventually collide with our planet, this table has one important limitation. It does not include all the asteroids that have yet to be identified. An enormous number of small asteroids, for example, are not listed because they are too small for astronomers to see. Using complicated statistical techniques, astronomers estimate that an enormous number of small asteroids are on potential collision courses with Earth.

The possibility that many asteroids remain undetected raises important questions about future impacts on Earth. What is the overall impact rate on Earth? How likely are small impacts compared with large impacts? How frequently can we expect catastrophic impacts to occur? How long might it be before another impact causes widespread damage on our planet? In this part of the activity, you will explore some of these questions.

FIGURE 5
Estimates of future asteroid threats.

PROCEDURE

Examine Figure 5 closely. This graph was created to estimate the probability of future impacts for bolides of different sizes. It is based on statistics of asteroids and also on the cratering rate measured on the Moon from data brought back by Apollo astronauts and Soviet sample-return probes. Note that there are two scales for the X-axis. This gives you two ways to talk about future impacts, either in terms of the bolide size or in terms of the energy released in the future impact. The predicted frequency of future impacts is represented on the Y-axis. You should also note that the scales are not linear, but increase in factors of ten.

1. In Figure 5, locate the approximate point on the curve for the Tunguska Event. This "event" was the explosion of an asteroid just above Earth's surface. It happened in Siberia in 1908. Estimate the energy released in that explosion and the size of that asteroid. How often can we expect explosions such as this?

2. Locate the approximate point on the curve for the likely impact at the Cretaceous/ Tertiary boundary. Estimate the energy released in that explosion and the size of that asteroid. How often can we expect explosions such as this?

3. Find the largest object listed in Table 1 and locate where it fits on the curve in Figure 5. What is the largest object in Table 1? What would be your estimate for the energy released if that object collided with Earth? What is your estimate for the frequency of such impacts? How would this impact compare with the Cretaceous/ Tertiary impact or the Tunguska explosion?

4. The asteroid Toutatis (Figures 3 and 4) had parts approximately 4 and 2.5 km in size. Estimate the energy released if they collided with Earth. What is your estimate for the frequency of such impacts? How would these compare with the Cretaceous/ Tertiary impact and the Tunguska explosion?

5. "Shooting stars" are small asteroids that pass through Earth's atmosphere. They can be seen on most nights; sometimes they are extremely common. Larger bolides, causing a bright, fiery flash across the sky, are called fireballs. Fireballs can be caused by meteoroids about 10 cm–1 meter in diameter. Using Figure 5, estimate how common asteroids 1 meter in size are.

6. Describe the relationship between the size and frequency of interplanetary debris impacts with Earth.

WHAT ARE THE CHANCES?

WHAT IS HAPPENING?

Studying impacts and cratering on planetary bodies raises important questions for Earth's future. Students know that impacts of many sizes have already occurred on our planet. What are the chances that more impacts will happen in the future?

Space scientists know that future impacts are inevitable. The more important questions to ask are when and what size will they be? Small impacts are relatively common. Large impacts are relatively rare. (This can be inferred from Activity 6.) To determine the likelihood of future impacts, astronomers use two techniques. Both are introduced in this activity.

Based on direct observations of Earth-approaching and Earth-crossing asteroids, planetary scientists can determine their orbits and project their orbits far into the future. Using sophisticated models that take into account the orbits and gravitational attraction of other planetary bodies, these scientists can estimate the likelihood that particular asteroids might come dangerously close to Earth. This likelihood forms the basis of probability estimates given in Table 1.

Historical records of impacts also give planetary scientists information about what kinds of impacts have *actually* occurred in the past. A simple technique for this kind of research was given in Activity 6 for the Moon. Similar work on Earth could be done with data provided in Activity 12. Combined with further estimates, these historical records provide the basis of Figure 5 in Part II of this activity.

IMPORTANT POINTS FOR STUDENTS TO UNDERSTAND

◆ Our solar system contains a population of asteroids and comets with Earth-crossing orbits. Thus, interplanetary space is not totally empty.

◆ Comets and asteroids of all sizes will continue to collide with Earth in the future. The only questions are when and what size will they be.

◆ No known large asteroid or comet is now on a collision course with Earth; however, our knowledge of Earth-crossing planetary bodies is grossly incomplete.

MATERIALS

◆ no special materials are needed for this activity

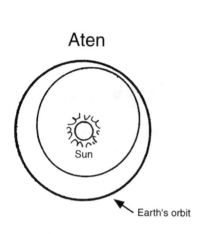

Aten

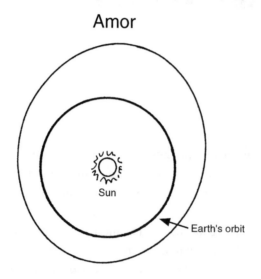

Amor

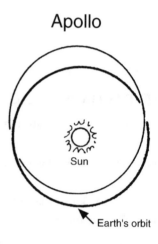

Apollo

FIGURE 6

The difference in orbits between Aten, Amor and Apollo asteroids identified in Table 1.

PREPARATION

This activity assumes students understand fundamental concepts in probability—e.g., what does it mean to say there is a 1 in 20 chance of an event occurring? Students might benefit from probability activities prior to launching this investigation (see Activity 20.)

SUGGESTIONS FOR FURTHER STUDY

Students can investigate the differences between the three types of asteroids listed in Table 1: Aten, Apollo, and Amor. In short, Aten asteroids are close to Earth on the sunward side of its orbit; Apollo asteroids cross Earth's orbit; and Amor asteroids are toward Mars outside Earth's orbit. Atens and Amors have a good chance of being deflected across Earth's orbit—and therefore a chance of hitting Earth—because of the gravity of Earth and other planets (Figure 6).

Two events in the 20th century have focused attention on bolide collisions: the Tunguska explosion in 1908 and the Shoemaker-Levy 9 impact on Jupiter in 1994. The latter is discussed in Appendix 2. Earth and space scientists believe the Tunguska explosion occurred when a large stony meteorite broke up and exploded high in the atmosphere over a remote forest region in Siberia. The actual explosion leveled 2,000 square kilometers of forest and created widespread fires. Its shock wave was detected by seismometers as far away as North America. It also affected the atmosphere. A few nights later, it was possible for a Londoner to read a newspaper well after sunset thanks to sunlight reflected over the horizon by sunlit "noctilucent" clouds 50 kilometers high. An eyewitness to the Tunguska explosion later recalled,

When I sat down to have my breakfast beside my plow, I heard sudden bangs, as if from gunfire. My horse fell to its knees. From the north side above the forest a flame shot up. Then I saw that the fir forest had been bent over by the wind, and I thought of a hurricane. I seized hold of my plow with both hands so that it would not be carried away. The wind was so strong it carried soil from the surface of the ground, and then the hurricane drove a wall of water up the Angora [River]. [quoted in "The Threat from Space," *The Economist*, September 11, 1993, pp. 13–14.]

This "wind" was the blast wave from the meteoroid explosion.

Spy satellites and national defense early warning systems tell us about bolide collisions with Earth, too. The U.S. Department of Defense has reported that these networks have recorded at least 136 large, high-altitude explosions thought to be caused by incoming bolides. Ranging in size from 500–15,000 tons of TNT, these explosions occurred between 27 and 32 kilometers high in the atmosphere. Ask students to investigate these reports. How are they made? What has been reported? Over what parts of the world have these explosions occurred? Is there a danger of these explosions being confused with bomb explosions? See the Resources List, especially the *Sky and Telescope* report.

CONNECTIONS

Ask students to learn how planetary bodies receive their names. Who names them? What are the rules for naming them? How does someone go about officially naming something? At the same time, you can ask them to learn the derivations of various chosen names. (The same can be done for craters in other activities.)

On December 8, 1992, the 6.4 kilometer wide, Earth-crossing asteroid Toutatis came within 3.5 million kilometers of our planet (Figures 3 and 4). Students can investigate what space scientists learned from studying this asteroid. It was mapped with radar using facilities at NASA's Goldstone Deep Space Communication Complex in the Mojave Desert. Asteroids Gaspra and Ida were photographed at close range when the Galileo Space probe flew past them, and they remain the only three asteroids studied in detail by space scientists. Surprises came quickly. Toutatis turned out to have the form of two potato-shaped rocky bodies stuck together end to end. Ida turned out to have a small moon-shaped asteroid orbiting around it. Scientists believe both types of pairings may have originated during collisions that shattered larger "parent asteroids" into thousands of pieces, and adjacent pieces became associated with each other— falling together into a compound body or orbiting each other. This can explain occasional pairs of impact craters such as Clearwater Lakes in Canada, shown in Activities 11 and 12.

ANSWERS TO QUESTIONS FOR STUDENTS

Part I

1. (a.) 1627 Ivar, which is 8.1 kilometers in diameter, is the largest in the sample.

   (b.) Students should answer that both 3361 Orpheus, which is approximately 0.3 kilometers in diameter, and 1915 Quetzalcoatl, which is 0.3 kilometers in diameter, are the smallest. Students might also answer 2340 Hathor, but they must have noted that the diameter of this asteroid is uncertain.

   (c.) Students could answer 2102 Tantalus, which should impact at a velocity of 34.8 km/s, or 3200 Phaeton, which should impact at a velocity of approximately 35 km/s. For the second, they must note that this determination is approximate.

   (d.) From the Shoemaker calculation, the most likely asteroid collision will involve 2340 Hathor, whose P_s is 14×10^{-9} years or roughly one in 71.4 million years. Therefore, the probability of it occurring next year is roughly one in 71.4 million. The two calculations produced the same probability.

   (e.) From the Öpik calculations, 2202 Pele, whose P_o is 0.1×10^{-9} years, is the least likely to strike Earth. The probability of a collision with Earth occurring next year is 1 in 10 billion. Probabilities using the Shoemaker calculation are not performed for many of the asteroids listed in Table 1. Of those provided, 2212 Haphaistos is the least likely collision, with a P_s is 0.44×10^{-9} years or roughly one in 2.27 billion years.

2. Which Earth-crossing asteroids pose such danger?

number	name	diameter (km)
3200	Phaethon	6.9
4183	1959 LM	~4
1685	Toro	5.2
2329	Orthos	~3
4179	1989 AC	~4
4015	1979 VA	~5
3122	1981 ET3	~4
2061	Anza	(2.7)
1917	Cuyo	~3
3288	Seleucus	2.8
1580	Betulia	7.4
1627	Ivar	8.1
887	Alinda	4.2

3. The number of asteroids between 0.9 and 1.1 kilometers in diameter is 14, which is five percent of 280. Therefore, this sample would show about 280 1-kilometer asteroids if none were missed. The correct answer is 266 (280 minus 14) more.

4. (a.) Toutatis was between 9.1 and 9.2 Earth-Moon radii. Be sure students pay attention to significant digits.

   (b.) Students should reply with uncertainty, as Earth scientists are unsure precisely where the threshold is. Both diameters fall within the uncertain range of 0.5–5 km. However, even if they did not cause global effects, the impact of either asteroid would produce dramatic regional effects.

5. Object 93KA2 passed within 0.38 Earth-Moon radii of Earth's surface. (Object 93KA2 was 6 meters across and traveled at a speed of 21.3 km/s. It probably would have exploded in Earth's upper atmosphere had it been on a collision course.)

Part II

1. The energy released from the Tunguska explosion was approximately 10 megatons TNT; the estimated asteroid size was 30 meters. The expected frequency for such an impact is once every 500 years.

2. The energy released in the Cretaceous/Tertiary impact is estimated to have been just less than 50 million megatons TNT. Earth can expect such an impact slightly more than once every 100 million years.

3. The largest object in Table 1 is asteroid 1627 Ivar at 8.1 km. The estimated energy would be more like the Cretaceous/Tertiary impact, with an anticipated energy release of about 10 million megatons and an anticipated frequency also just over once every 100 million years.

4. Like Ivar and the Cretaceous/Tertiary impact, if Toutatis impacts on Earth, the energy release will be more than a hundred thousand megatons TNT, but the frequency is between once every million and 10 million years.

5. Asteroids that are 1 meter in size occur at a frequency just under 100 per year, or once every 3 or 4 days.

6. Answers will vary. Be sure students note the logarithmic features of the graph.

RIGHT ON TARGET

MATERIALS

♦ No special materials are needed for this project.

OBJECTIVE

This activity emphasizes public policy. You will develop a plan to protect Earth's citizens against a future major bolide collision.

BACKGROUND

Today reminds you why you got that promotion last month. In the morning staff meeting, the division director thanked you for a "job well done" for your work with the last space shuttle crew. Over lunch, you held a video-conference with groups from four different countries about how best to analyze their recent findings on the asteroid belt. And now, the head of your department just told you about a major, agency-wide project to which you're being assigned. She says it's big—really BIG!—and you need to start on it right away. The first briefing about this project is just starting. Grab your notebook and head off to the conference room.

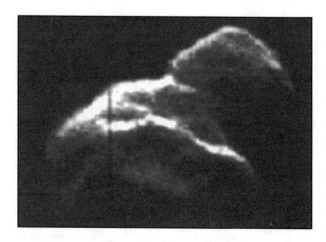

Earth-crossing and near-Earth asteroids pose a potentially serious threat to life on our planet. Toutatis (shown in this radar image) is one such asteroid. Toutatis is composed of two pieces, 4 and 2.5 km respectively.

THE BRIEFING

As part of a routine survey, astronomers working at the Keck Observatory in Hawaii—the largest optical telescope in the world—discovered Justus, a 12 kilometer wide asteroid moving in an elliptical orbit through the solar system at 23.6 kilometers per second. From studies of the asteroid's path, astronomers at the Keck observatory believe it was pulled out of the asteroid belt by the combined gravitational forces of Jupiter and the Sun. Apparently the three bodies were aligned in an unusual configuration, one that hasn't happened in 500 million years. The Keck team also plotted the asteroid's future course, and this is where there's big news.

Justus is an Earth-crossing asteroid. Projecting its motion through several future orbits around the Sun, the Keck team has determined that Justus will come dangerously close to Earth after the next three orbits (roughly six years from now). Due to uncertainties in determining its orbit, Justus might even collide with Earth (Figure 1).

After a technical presentation about Justus by the Keck team, the director for the agency describes the assignment you've just been made a part of. "Do something about this," you are told. "It's top priority. The President is going to hold a press conference in two days to make Justus public. The White House needs to have a plan that'll take care of this problem in time for that announcement." You and the people around you are now a team charged with that task. Develop a plan for ending the threat that Justus poses. "Do it the best way you know how. Just make sure it works. Work on the plan today. Give us a presentation tomorrow. And remember, I'm counting on you. The President is counting on you. The entire population of the world is counting on you."

As the director leaves the room and your group gathers together, there's a mixture of panic and relief in your head. You're confident that this problem is solvable.

PROCEDURE

1. Gather your group. Identify the problem that needs to be solved. What must be done to end the threat Justus poses? Make whatever sketches you need.

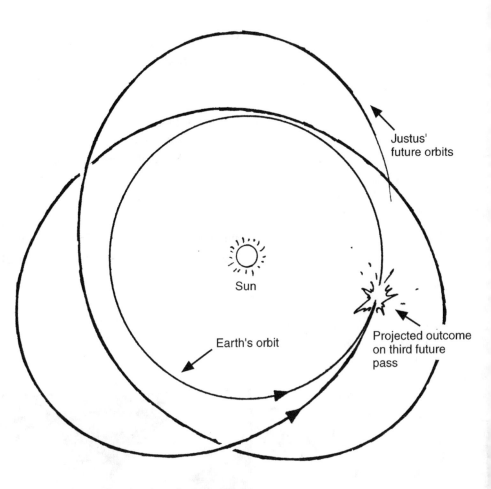

FIGURE 1
The next three orbits projected for asteroid Justus.

2. In order to tackle this problem successfully, you will need to divide tasks among yourselves. Decide who will handle the following roles (there may be other roles):

   a. recorder for the brainstorming session
   b. artist for any diagrams you may need
   c. summary plan writer
   d. presenter of the final plan

3. Begin a five to ten minute brainstorming session on possible solutions to the problems identified in Question 1. At first, don't worry about finding the "right" solution. Just collect ideas. Have someone in your group record the ideas that are presented.

4. Look over the results of your brainstorming session. What are potential problems with each of your plans? (Hint: Some limitations are technical ability, cost, laws of physics.) What information will you need to determine whether each plan will work? As a group, make a list of the pros and cons of each plan.

5. With your group, choose and develop a plan to end the Justus threat. Because you don't want anything to go wrong, build into your plan a backup solution, just in case. Also include a schedule for when equipment and procedures need to be ready.

6. Once your plan is complete, create a presentation to give tomorrow at the director's meeting. You'll have five minutes to present your plan. Make whatever diagrams you need. You'll also need to prepare a one-page written summary of your plan for the director.

7. Your proposal is going to be judged as to whether or not it is a workable plan with minimal side effects. You're not the only team working on options, but all the workable plans will be sent to the President. Remember how important this is. Good luck!

RIGHT ON TARGET

WHAT IS HAPPENING?

The pattern is simple. Bolides of many sizes have struck Earth innumerable times in the past. This process continues today and it will continue for the foreseeable future. We also know that bolides larger that one kilometer can have global environmental effects. In Activity 18, students examined the likelihood of impacts of different magnitudes in the future. They should know that, while there is now no known threat of a catastrophic impact, chances are high that large bolides will again collide with our planet. The only questions are when and what kinds of effects will it produce.

In this activity, students are presented with a scenario in which a large asteroid travels on a collision course with Earth. Although simply a fictitious scenario—be sure to stress this at the activity's end—it provides students with the opportunity to combine creative thinking and fresh understanding of the subjects in this book and to apply them towards positive goals. They are going to save Earth!

IMPORTANT POINTS FOR STUDENTS TO UNDERSTAND

◆ None of the known Earth-crossing asteroids and comets are on collision courses with Earth.

◆ A civilization-threatening impact is possible but not probable (on purely statistical grounds) in the next few centuries. Such an impact becomes probable over time scales of 10 thousand years or so.

◆ However, astronomers have identified only a small fraction of the likely Earth-crossing asteroids and comets.

◆ Deciding what to do about Earth-crossing asteroids is a public policy issue about which your students' opinions matter.

PREPARATION

No specific preparation is required for this activity. Have students work in groups of 4 or 5. You may want to have additional asteroid images on hand so that students can focus on a specific object—it may affect their choice of solutions. Several images on *Craters!-CD* will be useful for this.

A variety of issues can be raised to direct the teams' solutions. What are the pros and cons of each solution? What if even the backup plan fails? Who should pay for this:

MATERIALS

◆ No special materials are needed for this project.

Sample solution for solving problems posed by asteroid Justus.

the United States, the United Nations, the richest countries, or someone else? Should the people working on the problem be Americans or should this be an international effort? Should it be a public or private effort? What kind of schedule should be set?

Encourage your teams to think their solutions through. Exploding Justus might scatter fragments in unpredictable directions, and this swarm of fragments can still threaten Earth. Some scientists argue that trying to blow up an asteroid is therefore one of the worst solutions. Timing might be important too. Pushing an asteroid away at one point of its orbit may be more effective than at other points. Likewise, a slight change in direction far away will have large effects as Justus approaches, whereas a large change when the asteroid is nearby may not. Challenge students to engage such complications. Students will have varying understanding of Newton's laws; this is a good time for review.

On the day presentations are made, begin the class by allowing the teams a few minutes for preparation. Then, explain the procedure. You are the agency director and you want two things today: expert advice and a list of workable options to take to the President. After each presentation, you'll allow a short discussion and question period. Then the class as a whole—as a group of consulting experts—will be asked to evaluate the plan on a thumbs-up/thumbs-down basis. Is it a workable plan? Should it be one of the options presented to the President? Point out that there may be several solutions that are sound and that solve the problem well. Ask the class to evaluate each plan on its own merits.

If you have several classes doing this assignment at the same time, post the plans approved for presentation to the President so that students can compare their ideas. Perhaps you can hold a vote for the most viable three solutions.

At the conclusion of this activity, remind students that this is an imaginary scenario. None of the known Earth-crossing asteroids are on a collision course with our planet.

SUGGESTIONS FOR FURTHER STUDY

This scenario raises a public policy question of ongoing interest to astronomers. Should the federal government create a program to look for Earth-crossing comets and asteroids? Astronomers estimate that only a small fraction of such asteroids have been identified. Many scientists thus agree that the best first step is to complete the discovery and cataloging of all Earth-approaching asteroids that might pose a threat. In a 1992 report called *The Spaceguard Survey*, an expert panel recommended a program to create a complete census of Earth-crossing objects. Six ground-based telescopes will be built around the world for the survey, costing $50 million, plus about $10 million a year to operate (see the Resources List).

Arguments for and against such a survey have been made in both the popular and scientific media. Ask students to examine these opinions, pro and con. What are the issues? What arguments do the different sides make? How has this debate progressed and what is its likely outcome? Has this been raised in other countries too? This study—ask them to prepare for a debate—can begin with a search through the Reader's Guide to Periodical Literature, other reference sources, or on-line databases. Long articles on this subject have appeared in *The New York Times*, for example (see Resources List). Contact NASA's public information offices for more information. If the issue is one of active Congressional interest, encourage your students to express their views in letters or e-mail messages to their representatives.

Sample solution for solving problems posed by asteroid Justus.

CONNECTIONS

Once students begin considering public policy issues, a wide range of questions can be raised. When discussing such issues be sure to point out how complicated the decision-making process usually is. Real decision making involves choosing between alternatives—and most alternatives have pros and cons. Policy makers are forced to balance competing interests and make trade-offs that will advance some concerns while stifling others. These more complicated decisions mix economic, technical, social, political, and moral dimensions. They are rarely easy to make. Students should develop an understanding of the complexity of public policy decisions, and realize that they have roles to play in debates over public policy.

For example, policy makers concerned with future planetary and space exploration debate whether new missions into space should be made by robot probes or by astronauts. Each side has strong technical, scientific, and economic arguments in favor of its position. They disagree about whether or not robots can do what people can as explorers and whether it is worth risking human lives to do things that might be done by machines. On top of this is the contrast between those who link space exploration to the expansion of human civilization and those whose priorities are focused towards more tangible projects. You can encourage students to discuss and debate particular public policy issues: what should we, as a nation, seek in space? (Historically-minded students can explore the soul searching that took place in the United States following the *Challenger* explosion in 1986.)

Ask your students to imagine they have been elected to Congress or appointed science advisor to the President. Working in groups, your students can discuss (or debate) public policy issues relating to space. Possible issues to explore include

♦ Should the United States continue to develop a new, improved space station? Should we work with other countries on such a project? What kinds of research should it emphasize? (Note: This is a good case to show how complex policy issues can be. The program to develop a space station has, at times, consumed most of the science and technical research portions of NASA's budget. As a result, other research areas were reduced. Where should NASA's priority be?)

♦ What should a space station do? Should it be involved in experiments on manufacturing and other commercial processes? Should the federal government play a role in helping industry? Should it help only American industries or multi-national ones? What about technological "spin-offs"? Do these justify the expense or is having a space station justification in itself? Should the space station have military applications?

♦ Should NASA pursue ways to create an economic value for asteroids and the Moon or should this be left to industry? Should other planetary bodies be mined for their natural resources? Is it worth the cost? Are there alternatives—e.g., should we recycle more and depend less on mining? Who owns material in space? Should it be property of the international community, should it be something people can't own, or should it be available on a finders-keepers basis? (Compare this situation with similar resources on Earth—e.g., Antarctica, sea bed mining, or fishing in international waters.) If anyone can own asteroids, then how should we regulate who can go into space?

♦ Should there be international regulations for what can go into space? Should weapons be banned from space? Should we consider disposing of radioactivity or toxic wastes in space?

♦ Should governments be the only organizations allowed in space? Should privately financed companies be allowed or permitted or encouraged to work in space without federal support or regulation?

♦ Should we spend money restarting the search for extraterrestrial life? What efforts have already been taken to locate or contact extraterrestrial life? What sort of priority should this project take?

ONE IN A MILLION

OBJECTIVE

In this activity, you will explore the meaning of probability statements such as "once every 100 million years."

BACKGROUND

When you flip a coin, chances are 1 in 2 that it will fall with the head side up. Flip it twice and chances are 1 in 4 that heads will come up.

 A statement such as "chances are 1 in 2" is a claim about probability. You talked in similar language in Activities 18 and 19 about possible asteroid collisions with Earth. Impact probabilities in those activities were given in terms of how many impacts can be expected per thousand, million, or billion years. But what do probability statements such as these really mean? What do they tell us about the likelihood of future events? How can we gauge the seriousness of the problems that asteroid collisions pose for us in the future?

MATERIALS

Students work in pairs. Each pair will need

◆ pencil

◆ deck of cards

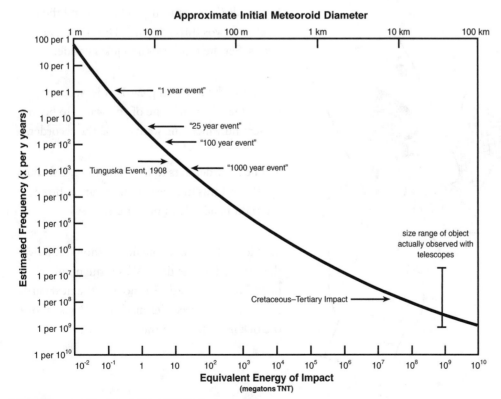

FIGURE 1
Estimates of future asteroid threats.

PROCEDURE

Making a Prediction

1. Look at Figure 1 (it's the same one you examined—or will examine—in Activity 18). Be sure you understand the scales used for both axes. The bolide that struck Earth at the K/T boundary, evidence suggests, was approximately 10 kilometers in diameter. What is the frequency of impacts of that size? Write your answer in Data Box 1.

2. Given this frequency estimate, when would be the most likely time the next impact of this size would occur? Discuss possible answers with your partner, and when you come to an agreement write your estimate in Data Box 1.

DATA BOX 1

Frequency of bolide at K/T boundary?   once every _____ years

Hypothesis for next occurrence?   _____

Testing Your Prediction

3. You and your partner can easily test your hypothesis. Sort the deck of cards into two piles: face cards (kings, queens, and jacks) and the rest (aces and twos through tens). Don't use the jokers. Set the face cards and jokers aside.

4. Shuffle the remaining cards at least seven times. Decide which one of you wants to be the dealer and which one wants to be the recorder.

5. The recorder gets to pick a number, 1 through 10. Record this number in Observation Box 1, at the right hand side of tick line 1.

6. One card at a time, the dealer should flip over the top card on the deck. Was it the number picked by the recorder? If no, flip the next card. If yes, have the recorder mark an "X" just above the tick mark for 1 on the line.

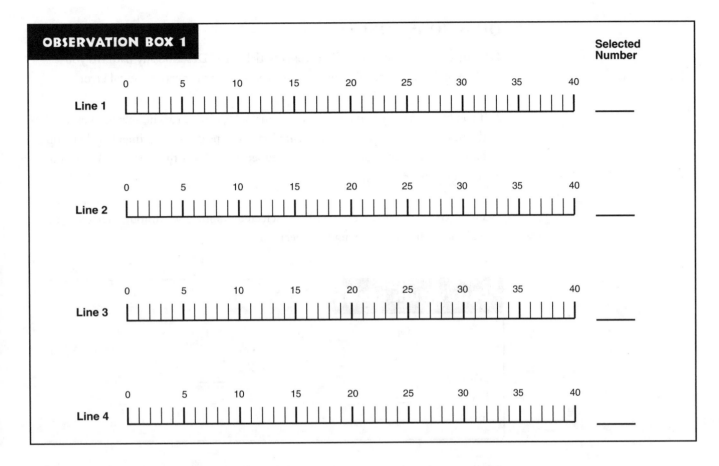

7. Repeat step 6 for all the cards in the deck. If, for example, the eighth, seventeenth, twenty-second, and twenty-third cards are the number selected, you should have an "X" above each of these tick marks.

8. When you have worked through the entire deck, repeat this exercise (steps 4 through 7) a total of four times, using each of the tick lines in Observation Box 1 and alternating who deals and who records. After the four trials, answer questions 1 through 7 below.

More About Probability

9. Summarize your data from the previous section in Observation Box 2. For each line, record the place in the sequence where the selected number appeared. Your teacher has created a master table for recording the results for each group. Add your data to that table.

10. You're going to explore how the occurrence of selected numbers is distributed over many trials. When everyone has contributed their results to the master table, create a histogram, plotting the position in the sequence (1 through 40) as the X-axis and frequency of appearance as the Y-axis. Answer questions 8 and 9 below.

QUESTIONS/CONCLUSIONS

1. Study the distribution of "X"s across the tick lines. Describe any patterns you observe. Is there a regular interval, even accounting for experimental error?

2. If you know that an X appeared on tick mark 10, can you accurately predict when the next X will appear? Make a prediction and repeat the experiment. When you have the first occurrence, count the number of cards for the next one. Were you right (±1 card)?

3. This activity uses 40 cards: 4 with the selected number, 36 without. What are the odds of the first card having the selected number?

<table>
<tr><td colspan="5">OBSERVATION BOX 2</td></tr>
<tr><td></td><td>1st</td><td>2nd</td><td>3rd</td><td>4th</td></tr>
<tr><td>line 1</td><td>____</td><td>____</td><td>____</td><td>____</td></tr>
<tr><td>line 2</td><td>____</td><td>____</td><td>____</td><td>____</td></tr>
<tr><td>line 3</td><td>____</td><td>____</td><td>____</td><td>____</td></tr>
<tr><td>line 4</td><td>____</td><td>____</td><td>____</td><td>____</td></tr>
</table>

4. What are the odds of the *second* card having the selected number? Explain your reasoning.

5. To create a *simulated* history of Earth impacts, go back to Observation Box 1. Replace the sequence numbers (1 through 40) with hypothetical ages. Start from the right and work to the left. Label the tick marks from -300 to +100 million years in 10 million year intervals. (On this line, 0 is the present, positive numbers are the future, and negative numbers are the past.) Would you say the impacts in this simulation are randomly distributed or distributed by a pattern?

6. Think about the connections between the card sequence and the likelihood of bolide collisions. Cards in the deck are randomly distributed, so the chance of a card with the selected number appearing is the same at any step in the sequence. Asteroids and comets are randomly distributed in space. The cards with the selected number are relatively rare (4 cards in 40). Huge asteroid and comet collisions are extremely rare.

a. Does a chance of an impact every hundred million years mean that if an impact occurred now another one won't occur for the next 99,999,999 years?

b. Does a chance of an impact every hundred million years mean that one *must* occur once within every hundred million year interval? (Does every interval of 10 cards have one and only one "X"?)

7. Check the prediction you made in Data Box 1. Would you like to revise your estimate?

8. Are numbers appearing at regular intervals or do they seem to be randomly distributed?

9. The impacts that have occurred in Earth's history occurred at particular times. But if you could rewind time and start again, would you expect to have catastrophic impacts appearing at the same time on the second, third, or fourth run? Does this pattern or lack of pattern have implications for the history of life on our planet?

ONE IN A MILLION

MATERIALS

Students work in pairs. Each pair will need

◆ pencil

◆ deck of cards

WHAT IS HAPPENING?

Students often have poor intuitions about probability, and this can lead to confusion when probability statements are discussed—as they were in Activities 18 and 19. Commonly, students come to the *mistaken* belief that if an event has a probability of occurring once every one hundred million years then they should expect to see that event happening at evenly spaced intervals—e.g., 1 million years ago, 101 million years ago, 201 million years ago, and so on. This activity uses a simple exercise to replace that misconception with an intuition-based understanding of probabilistic events.

IMPORTANT POINTS FOR STUDENTS TO UNDERSTAND

◆ Random events do not occur in regular intervals even when probabilities are given as "once every so many years."

◆ Saying an event has a probability of, for example, one in ten means that during *each trial* the likelihood of the event is one in ten.

◆ Saying an event has a probability of, for example, one in ten does *not* mean that the event must happen once in every ten trials.

PREPARATION

Be sure you are familiar with basic probability theory prior to starting this activity. You should review such concepts as random distribution and sampling with and without replacement. Also, you might want to have several pairs of dice available to aid your discussion. The master table used in this activity can be made on either a chalkboard or overhead transparency. It should list the numbers in the sequence 1 through 40 and have enough room for all teams to record their data.

SUGGESTIONS FOR FURTHER STUDY

After this activity, return your students to the issues discussed in Activities 18 and 19. Ask them to reconsider their conclusions in light of their increased understanding of probabilistic events.

Studying probability using cards is relatively straightforward and can be extended easily. Probability plays an important role in the creation of card games. Encourage students to investigate this.

CONNECTIONS

Students can explore how probabilities are determined for other life risks: automobile accidents, different kinds of cancers, earthquakes, and so on. What do these statements really mean to us? How are they calculated? What can be done to reduce the likelihood of these events? Compare these to the likelihood of impact events (see Morrison readings in Resources List).

ANSWERS TO QUESTIONS FOR STUDENTS

1. In this activity, occurrence of particular cards in the sequence is at random. Students should *not* see a clear pattern, although some certainly will try to create one. (Seven is the minimum number of shuffles needed to guarantee a random distribution of cards.) The main point is that there is no regular spacing or periodicity; there will be some clumping.

2. Students might guess that the next "X" should come ten cards later. This is *not* correct, but you can see why this would be their prediction. The correct prediction is that the selected number is equally likely to appear at all subsequent positions in the sequence because they were randomly distributed during the shuffle.

3. The dealer has 4 opportunities out of 40 (4 per 40, or 4/40) to get the selected number. In other words, 1 chance in 10.

4. This calculation can be tricky. What students are estimating here is actually "what is the probability that the shuffling left one of the selected cards in the second position." Without more shuffling, the probability remains 4 in 40, or 1 in 10—the same as for the first card. This is an important point for students not to miss. With enough shuffling to create a random distribution of the cards before the counting starts, each card is equally likely to be left at a particular place in the deck's sequence. As a result, the probability remains the same. (With shuffling after each count, the probability is more complicated: for the first card it is 1 in 40. For the second, there are 39 cards left. If a selected card appeared on the first tick, the probability for a second one is 3 in 39; if it did not, the probability for a first one is 4 in 39. This is called sampling without replacement.)

5. By this point, students should see a random distribution in the sequence.

6 a. It does not. This is a common misconception.

   b. It does not. This is a common misconception.

7. Be sure to emphasize that making predictions and later revising them is a normal part of scientific research. Hypotheses and predictions are made on the basis of the best information available at the time. Learning more is crucial to progress in science. Revision of predictions is perfectly normal and expected.

8. As the number of trials increases, the histogram will produce an increasingly random distribution.

9. If impacts are occurring on Earth at randomly spaced intervals, then if time were rewound and replayed, the resulting impact history might be quite different. For example, the impact at the K/T boundary most likely would not have occurred, one more likely would have occurred at another time, and the history of life—especially those creatures pushed to extinction as a result of such impacts—would have faced considerably different challenges.

APPENDICES

IMAGE FROM CRATERS!-CD

View of the Moon being lit by Earth. Image taken by the Star Tracker camera aboard the U.S. spacecraft Clementine. On Craters!-CD this is a full-color image as file MoonM15.tif.

BACKGROUND TO CRATERING

by William K. Hartmann

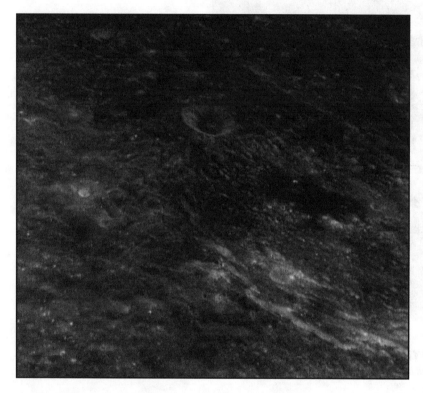

Oblique view of the lunar surface taken from the Apollo 8 spacecraft showing typical lunar farside terrain. The sharp crater near the center of the scene is 25 km in diameter. That crater is on the rim of a larger crater. On Craters!-CD this is image MoonM18.tif.

Huge circles have appeared throughout nature at a rate that has been, for most of the solar system's history, fairly constant but random. Each circle represents the explosive impact of a piece of interplanetary debris—an asteroid or comet, or fragment of either. The discovery that this process happens on all worlds, including Earth, gives us a way of understanding evolution of the awesome, pock-marked landscapes that our generation has found on other planets and moons. It also offers a way to understand some of the mysterious catastrophes that have punctuated the long, slow march of biological evolution on Earth.

Galileo discovered craters on the Moon in 1609. We designed Activities 1 and 2 to let students simulate this important discovery. Galileo's work solidified the Copernican revolution, which allowed human beings to realize that Earth is not at the center of the solar system, but rather just one world among many.

We've come a long way since then, with much of the progress being made since the 1960s. Until the 1960s, meteorite-impact craters were known only on the Moon and, grudgingly, in Arizona. Scientists originally thought Arizona's Barringer Crater was volcanic, and even the lunar craters were thought to be volcanic by many astronomers until the 1950s. Students can learn more about the Arizona crater in Activity 11. Activities 3 to 5 enable students to learn some of the kinds of evidence that finally convinced scientists in the 1950s and 1960s that each lunar crater marks the impact of an interplanetary body. Through those activities, students can make craters of their own and see "landscapes" that look similar to photos of the Moon.

In the 1960s and 1970s, space probes such as the Mariner and Voyager missions began to reveal vistas of craters on Mars, Mercury, Phobos, Jupiter's moons, and other worlds. Much of this material is covered in Activity 10, which lets students make the leap from what they learned about the Moon to the landscapes of other planets. During the time of the space probes, researchers in Canada and elsewhere documented dozens of hitherto-unrecognized, eroded, sediment-buried impact scars dotted across the older regions of Earth. The impact scars represent millions of years of geologic time. Students will gain an appreciation for craters that mostly eroded away in Activities 11 and 12.

Now we accept that nearly all worlds in the solar system bear impact craters—the scars of ancient explosions caused by the force of interplanetary debris. Most moons and planets, including the Moon, Mercury, Mars, Phobos, Deimos, Ganymede, Callisto, Mimas, Tethys, Rhea, Miranda, and Aerial, have many craters in at least some regions. Some regions of the asteroids Gaspra and Ida are also heavily cratered. The only worlds with few craters, such as Venus, Earth, and the icy moons Europa and Triton, are the ones where internal geological activity has led to resurfacing. For example, Jupiter's satellite Io, the most volcanically active world in the solar system, is resurfaced continually by ongoing volcanic eruptions. Its young surface hinders the discovery of any major impact crater.

The only other worlds without known impact craters are those whose cloudy atmospheres hinder our study of their surfaces. These include Saturn, Uranus, Neptune, and Saturn's moon, Titan. Giant Jupiter probably has no well-defined surface at all, because its extreme gravity, pressure, and heat in its lower atmosphere result in a smooth transition from compressed gas to mushy liquid.

Apollo astronauts photographed these craters on the Moon. Note the size differences among the craters.

USING CRATERS TO ESTIMATE AGES

The fact that craters accumulate at a steady rate means that we can count the number of them (per square kilometer) and estimate surface ages. For example, lava flows on Venus have obliterated craters on all but the most recent surfaces. The small number of craters per square kilometer allows scientists to estimate that the mean characteristic age of the surface plains of Venus is about 500 million to 800 million years. This is approximately twice the average age of continental surface formations on Earth.

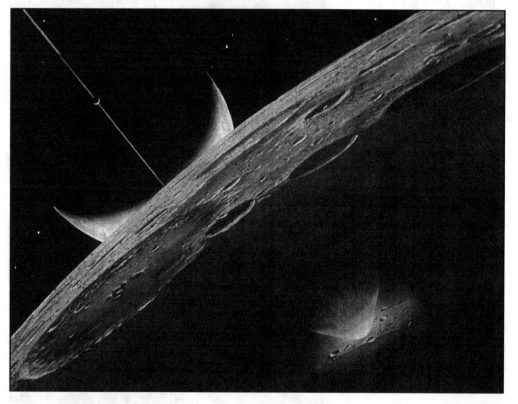

Artist's rendering of an impact on Rhea, a moon of Saturn.

The main uncertainty is the rate of crater formation on other worlds. Lunar rocks and soil samples brought back by astronauts from six Apollo landing sites, and by Russian robotic probes from three landing sites, gave dates for several regions of the Moon. These dates in turn allowed good calibration of the number of craters formed per millennium in the Earth-Moon system, averaged over 3 billion years. That number was consistent with estimates for Earth in more recent times, based on Canadian craters and on numbers of known asteroids intersecting Earth's orbit.

By adjusting this rate of crater formation to accommodate conditions on other planets, we can estimate surface ages on other worlds. These estimates allow us to understand the evolution of those bodies. For example, on Mars, nearer the asteroid belt than Earth, the rate of crater formation may be roughly twice the rate on Earth. In 1981 a NASA team called the Basaltic Volcanism Study Project used this figure to estimate that broad lava plains on Mars had a most probable age of around 1.6 billion years. A few years later other scientists discovered that a handful of lava-composed meteorites were rocks blasted off of Mars; most of these meteorites were around 1.2 to 1.4 billion years, fairly consistent with our earlier estimate.

As a rule of thumb, consider that all heavily cratered terrain is about 4 billion years old. Impact rates were highest during the era of solar-system formation, which began 4.55 billion years ago and dwindled by 4 billion years ago. In the first 50 million years (4.55 to 4.5 billion years ago), based on meteorite dates, most of the planets had accumulated their current masses by aggregation of dust grains and debris left over from formation of the sun. In the next 500 million years (4.5 to 4 billion years ago), most of the remaining interplanetary debris and fragments of shattered asteroids were swept up by the planets, making an intense cratering rate. Craters essentially saturated the landscapes. Thus, the heavily cratered landscapes date from the end of that era. By 3.5 billion years ago, the cratering rate had dropped essentially to its current value.

If a lava flow resurfaced a large area 3.5 billion years ago among the dark lava plains of the Moon, for example, the modern cratering rate was sufficient to scatter many craters on it, but insufficient to re-saturate it with craters.

IMPACT EXPLOSIONS

Impact events appear as spectacular explosions, as humans learned in 1908 when an interplanetary body exploded over Siberia, and again in 1994, when comet fragments hit Jupiter. The explosion, not a nuclear or even chemical reaction, represents an example of transformation of kinetic energy into heat and mechanical explosive energy. Interplanetary bodies usually hit planets at speeds of tens of kilometers per second, far beyond the speed of sound. Just as with a sonic boom from an aircraft, the impact creates a shock wave when the compression wave (which travels only at the speed of sound) can't get out of the way of the bolide. Energy "piles up" and becomes concentrated in front of the bolide. As the bolide enters the ground and stops, the shock wave blasts through the ground at the speed of sound, melting, fragmenting, and blasting pieces outward, forming a crater.

We obviously can't create all these phenomena in Activity 3. When we drop or throw projectiles into a powder target, we can create an analogy to these events. The fine particles of powder are analogous to rocks, and the "blast" of air blowing powder out of the impact site, compressed during the moment the projectile hits the surface, is analogous to the shock wave blasting rocky debris out of a meteorite crater.

CLASSES OF CRATERS

Studies of cratering, starting with lunar data in the early 1970s and later confirmed by the examination of other planets, revealed that as the size of craters increased, the form of the craters changed. The smallest craters, called "simple" or "bowl-shaped" craters, have the form of a simple bowl, as the name implies. At larger sizes, gravitational forces on the massive walls and rim of the crater come into play, slumping walls and distorting shapes.

Because these effects depend on gravity, they begin at different sizes on different planets. Starting at diameters of a few kilometers on Earth—but 10 kilometers on the Moon—the weight of the walls depresses the rim and forces material up in the center, forming a "central mountain peak" in the crater. Rocks deform plastically during the high pressures achieved in the impact, which aids the effect. In some ways the central peak resembles the rebound of a droplet as it strikes water, although this analogy is not exact. Most of the larger lunar craters are thus "central peak craters."

At still larger sizes, the central peak opens up into a cluster of peaks, and a rather rare crater form is established, called a "peak ring crater." In this form, starting at roughly 30 to 50 kilometers on Earth and 200 kilometers on the Moon, no central peak exists, but a well-defined ring of peaks forms on an otherwise flat floor. One such inner ring, although eroded, can be seen in the larger Clearwater Lakes crater in Canada. Several of the 100-kilometer scale craters on Venus show beautiful examples of this, and the so-called Cretaceous/Tertiary boundary (or K/T boundary from its abbreviation on geologic maps) probably showed it, also (see cover paintings).

At larger scales above about 500 km on the Moon, beautiful patterns of multiple concentric rings develop, rather than a single rim. These are called "multi-ring basins," and often show radial fracture patterns, as well. These rings resemble the concentric/radial patterns developed around a bullet hole in glass. These ancient scars represent the largest and grandest records of cratering in the solar system. They were caused by impacts of asteroid-like bodies as large as 100 to 200 kilometers in diameter!

The different forms of craters are not stressed in this book, because the experiments in the early activities can simulate only bowl-shaped craters. However, a survey of photographs in this book will demonstrate other kinds of craters.

TERMINOLOGY

In discussing the origins of craters and their effects, terminology can get confusing. Studies of asteroids, comets, meteorites, solar system origin, etc., developed independently over the last 200 years, each with their own terminology. Only today do we realize their connection in one "big picture." A summary of some terms that are useful follows. Generally, in the student lessons, we have tried to simplify this terminology and minimize jargon, but this list will help you in your reading here and elsewhere.

ASTEROID An interplanetary body of rocky and/or metallic composition. Most are in the asteroid belt, but many are known in other parts of the solar system, including Earth-crossing orbits.

COMET An interplanetary body with a substantial amount of ice. When a comet is closer to the sun than Jupiter or the asteroid belt, the ice sublimes into gas, blowing dust off the surface, and creating a tail of gas and dust particles. Until a decade or so ago, scientists thought that comets were a wholly distinct phenomenon from asteroids. Now we see more of a continuum from low ice content (asteroids) to high ice content (comets).

PLANETESIMAL A general term for asteroids, comets, and dust grains, but usually reserved for discussions of conditions 4.5 billion years ago as the planets were forming. For example, planetesimals aggregated during collisions to form planets.

METEOROID A fragment of an asteroid or comet in interplanetary space.

BOLIDE Nearly the same as meteoroid, but usually reserved for a body about to hit a planet, or, better yet, passing through a planet's atmosphere just before impact. In Craters! we use "bolide" as a generic term for any falling body, whether it be a comet, meteorite, or other body.

METEOR A small bolide (pea-sized or smaller) that burns up in the atmosphere and never hits the ground. Same as a "shooting star."

Asteroid Ida is densely pocked by craters like asteroid Gaspra on page 83. This image is Other643.tif on Craters!-CD.

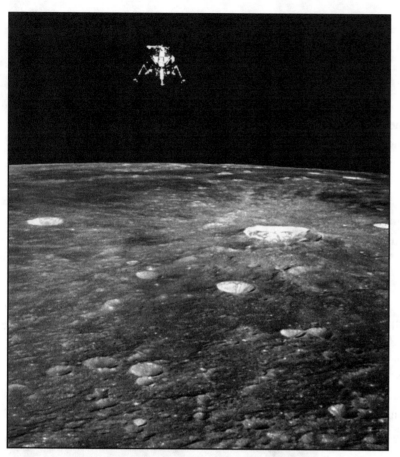

The Apollo landing craft sails over craters on the Moon during a lunar expedition.

FIREBALL A larger, brighter bolide that breaks up in the atmosphere and may drop pieces on the ground, i.e. meteorites.

METEORITE A fragment of a bolide that reaches the ground. Meteorites have three broad composition groups: carbonaceous (carbon rich, with substantial moisture content; they come from known carbonaceous-class black asteroids, and some may come from comets); rocky (fragments of rocky asteroids or mantles and crusts of parent bodies); and iron (more correctly, nickel iron alloy; they are fragments of metallic asteroids or iron cores of fragmented parent bodies).

PARENT BODY A general term for the hypothetical larger, original body of which a given asteroid or meteorite is just one fragment.

CRATER This has been used for depressions formed either by impact or by volcanoes.

IMPACT CRATER This is a better term to specify non-volcanic craters formed by impacts of interplanetary debris.

VOLCANIC CRATER General term for any depression formed by volcanism, such as the pit at the top of a cinder cone.

CALDERA The term for large steep-walled, flat-floor volcanic craters greater than 1/2 mile in diameter, formed at least in part by the collapse or subsidence of the surface into the volcanic chamber below.

IMPACT CRATERING AS A GEOLOGIC PROCESS: THE LINK TO ASTEROIDS

On any world that lacks internally driven geologic or atmosphere-related erosion, the dominant landform will be craters. If you landed on a solid surface on a randomly chosen world in the solar system, you most likely would see the characteristic rolling hills and intersecting rims of overlapping impact craters.

During the several billion years of geologic history, Earth and all the planets have been hit by the asteroids and comets that are drifting throughout interplanetary space. Every hit forms a crater. Small craters are more common because there are more small asteroids and comets than large ones. Earth gets hit by many boulder-sized meteorites every year. Statistically, Earth receives a megaton-sized impact explosion every century or so, and a massive climate-changing impact about every hundred million years. A surprising, yet obvious, link exists between the craters and the asteroids. If most craters come from asteroid impacts, the size distributions of craters ought to fit the size distributions of asteroids. Activities 6 and 7 let students make this leap from "routine" photos of the Moon to the nature of asteroids in space.

ASTEROIDS AS DEBRIS FROM THE PLANET-FORMING ERA

Here a more subtle link exists. For years, astronomers had concluded that asteroids formed at the same time as the solar system. Contrary to popular opinion, asteroids in the belt are not fragments of a single planet. Studies of meteorites, which are fragments of asteroids, reveal the existence of several distinct parent bodies, probably ranging from 300 to 1,000 kilometers in width. In other words, asteroids are debris that never quite assembled into a single planet. Several parent bodies formed as the other planets were forming. But then, as Jupiter reached its enormous size, Jupiter's gravity disturbed motions in the asteroid belt, increasing the mean asteroid collision velocity. Instead of gently coalescing on impact, the asteroids shattered each other. Today's asteroids represent the fragments. Jupiter's gravity kicks some of them out of the asteroid belt, where they may cross Earth's orbit and collide with Earth. The abundant small ones become our meteorites; the rare large ones blast craters and occasionally wreak havoc.

The subtle link comes from thinking about the size distribution of craters and asteroids, and linking this to the process of fragmentation that produced the asteroids when their parent bodies smashed together. If you take a rock, concrete mass, plaster asteroid model, or other solid body and smash it by hitting it with another body, with a hammer, or by

Artist's rendering of an impact crater on the Moon. The crater's diameter is 1 km.

dropping it onto a hard surface, it ought to shatter in a way similar to that of an asteroid. The size distribution of fragments ought to show some similarities to that found among asteroids, and among craters made by the asteroids.

In general terms, the size distribution produced by fragmentation makes many small fragments and few large ones. The smaller the fragment size, the more fragments. The nature of the curve is such that if you decrease size by a factor of two, you increase the number by about a factor of four. It is fairly simple to confirm this among lunar craters and by smashing up model asteroids—and thus tie together an entire realm of cosmic phenomena. That is the point of Activities 6 through 9.

CRATERING AS AN IMPORTANT PROCESS IN BIOLOGICAL EVOLUTION ON EARTH

The Earth was a planet of dramatic change 65 million years ago. Approximately 76 percent of all species died in a few million years; large dinosaurs became extinct and were replaced by mammals. The break was so dramatic that most geologists defined a new era and chose this boundary layer to mark the end of the Mesozoic ("Middle-life") Era and beginning of the Cenozoic ("New-life") Era.

In geology books of a few decades ago, the biological revolution was vaguely ascribed to faster-than-normal climate change. But in the 1980s, in a dazzling upheaval of geological and biological thinking, researchers realized that the thin stratum dividing the two eras (the K/T boundary) contained debris produced by a large asteroid impact on Earth. With the new discoveries, many scientists theorized that the biological change coincided with a tremendous impact that left debris all over the world. Most scientists have now accepted that at least one moderately large asteroid or comet (about 10 kilometers across) struck Earth 65 million years ago. The resulting explosion ejected enough debris to darken the atmosphere and even ignite fires around the world. This is discussed in Activities 13 through 18.

Recognition of the importance of impacts leads to recognition of the importance of the interplanetary debris—asteroids and comets—in long-term future human history. We know that atom-bomb-size explosions occur in the high atmosphere on a time scale of decades. During the next 10,000 years or so a much larger impact appears likely, one that could disrupt agriculture and civilization over wide areas.

IMPLICATIONS AND APPLICATIONS

These facts alone should ensure the study of cratering and collisions in science courses. Cratering, however, has innumerable ramifications in the other sciences. For example, these activities relate to the concept of kinetic energy and the conversion of potential energy into kinetic energy and then into heat and mechanical motion. We emphasize this physics lesson in Activities 8 and 9.

Applications in chemistry seem slightly less obvious, but nonetheless interesting. For one thing, geochemists discovered the K/T impact by measuring iridium abundances in soil layers of different depths and ages. Entirely unexpectedly, they found abnormally high concentrations of iridium at the K/T boundary layer, and realized that because meteorites are enriched in iridium, a giant meteorite may have been the source. This is emphasized in Activities 14, 16, and 17. Iridium has a strong affinity for iron; as a result, during the formation of the planet most of it had been drawn deep into the iron-rich core of Earth. Thus, consideration of iridium's abundance alone gives another valuable lesson in chemistry.

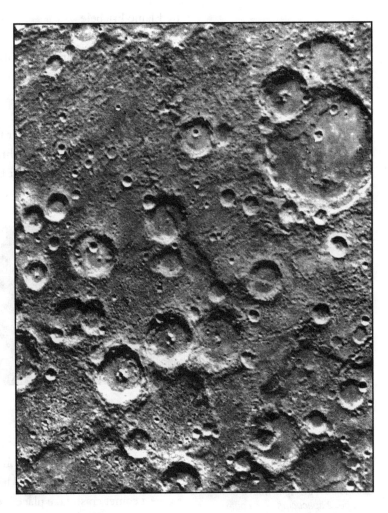

There are other chemical lessons in the phenomenology of impacts, including recent work on changes in nitrogen-oxygen compounds in the atmosphere resulting from impact phenomena.

What more dramatic subject could be offered to students than the prospect of a mile-wide or ten-mile-wide asteroid crashing through Earth's atmosphere in a dazzling flash of light, making an explosion bigger than the biggest bomb, blasting out a crater many kilometers across, blanketing the atmosphere with a many-months supply of sooty debris, and wiping out dinosaurs, civilizations, or whatever else happens to inhabit the unfortunate planet at that fateful moment?

Mercury's heavily cratered highlands resemble the highlands of our own Moon. This image is Other644.tif on Craters!-CD.

For all of these reasons impact cratering works well as a unifying theme in science teaching. It illustrates fundamental principles, teaches us about the larger world, and lets us have fun —all at the same time!

THE SMASH-UP OF THE MILLENNIUM: COMET SHOEMAKER-LEVY 9

by Elaine Friebele

Throughout the solar system, planets and moons bear the pock marks of past asteroid and comet crashes. Though rarely observed, the heavy bombardment continues, and even our own planet risks an occasional large impact. Several years ago, an asteroid about 300 m across sped by the Earth at only twice the distance of the Moon. This near miss was discovered—after the fact—from photographs taken by Henry Holt of Northern Arizona University through the 18-inch telescope on Mount Palomar, California. Had the asteroid hit Earth, it would have made an explosion with somewhat more energy than the largest H-bomb. As it turns out, our planet was lucky to be in the right place at the right time. The asteroid missed us by only six hours.

Discovering a comet or asteroid against the vast backdrop of stars and planets in the night sky is not easy. Over a 19-year period, amateur astronomer David Levy spent 917 hours searching the skies before he discovered his first comet ten years ago. (Now he has discovered 19.) Finding a comet hurtling toward a planet or watching the impact is even less likely. Eugene Shoemaker has devoted his life to studying impact craters on the Moon and the Earth. "I've seen the objects and I've seen the resulting craters," he said. "I have always wondered what it would be like to see a comet crash take place." Until the summer of 1994, no one in history had ever caught a comet in the act of crashing into a planet. Then, amateurs and professionals both witnessed the fiery death of comet Shoemaker-Levy 9 (discovered only a year earlier by Levy, Shoemaker, and his wife Carolyn) as it crashed into the planet Jupiter. The observations changed some traditional scientific theories about comets and how they impact planets and other bodies.

Artist depictions of Shoemaker-Levy 9 impacting Jupiter from four different perspectives: at left, from the viewpoint of Earth; second from left, from one of Jupiter's moons; second from the right, from the Voyager 2 spacecraft in the outer reaches of the solar system; and, at right, from Jupiter's south pole. On Craters!-CD, this is file OtherS01.tif. (Courtesy of NASA/Jet Propulsion Laboratory)

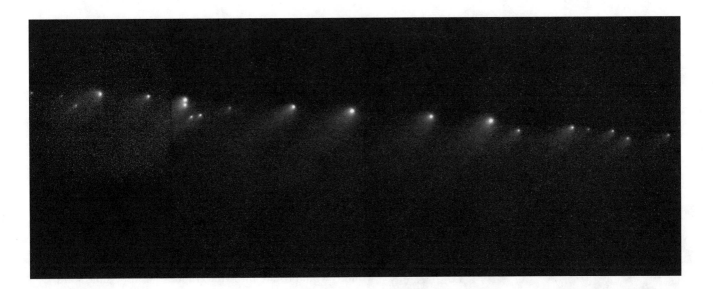

A "STRING OF PEARLS" IS DISCOVERED

In March 1993, David Levy joined the Shoemakers and French astronomer Phillipe Bendjoya at the 18-inch telescope on Mount Palomar for a night of sky watching. The sparkling night sky presented a perfect opportunity to take pictures with the telescope camera.

Comet hunters typically take two images of every field of sky and scan the pictures for signs of moving comets, which appear to float above the background of distant stars. The Shoemakers and Levy were not confident about getting a second picture, because drifting clouds had begun to obscure the sky. After waiting for several hours, Levy took the badly needed second exposure—just before the clouds came in for good.

As Carolyn Shoemaker scanned the films, she exclaimed, "This looks like a squashed comet!" Instead of having a nice round head, this one looked like a bar.

Since the sky was too cloudy to observe the comet from Mount Palomar, the astronomers called Jim Scotti at the University of Arizona's Spacewatch telescope atop Kitt Peak. He positioned the telescope and snapped a picture. In his years of observing the solar system's most exotic objects, Scotti had never seen anything like this. The "bar" turned out to be a series of several comets side by side, traveling across the sky.

Over the next two months, astronomers around the world trained their telescopes on the comet, named Shoemaker-Levy 9, and counted at least 21 comet fragments in the string of pearls. The pieces were lettered "A" through "W," leaving out "I" and "O" to avoid confusion with "one" and "zero." Gradually, astronomers began piecing together the comet's history. More than 100 years ago, the comet was captured by the giant planet of Jupiter as it circled the Sun. It then revolved around Jupiter in a

A mosaic of images from the Hubble Space Telescope on January 24-27, 1994. Twenty fragments are visible. Each has its own coma and tail. The fourth from the left (the first bright one) is apparently starting to separate into at least two pieces. On Craters!-CD, this is file OtherS15.tif. (Courtesy of NASA/Jet Propulsion Laboratory)

narrow orbit that resembled a rubber band stretched between two fingers. Every time the comet came to one end of the rubber band, it ventured close to Jupiter and its huge pull of gravity.

Traveling in this close part of the orbit in July 1992, the comet whizzed only 32,000 km from Jupiter's mass of swirling clouds. The force of the giant planet's gravity proved too much for the comet—a conglomeration of rock and ice that astronomers often call a "dirty snowball." Shoemaker-Levy fell apart, and the fragments, emitting gas and dust, spread out along the orbit like soldiers marching in a column.

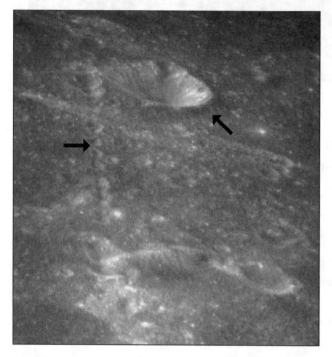

An Apollo 11 view of the Moon's farside. The line of small craters is located within the large I.A.U. crater no. IX. Some scientists believe crater chains such as these are caused by the impact of a string of fragments from a comet that has come apart, as happened with Shoemaker-Levy 9. This crater chain is approximately 55 km in length, and the large crater adjacent to the crater chain is about 17 km in diameter. On Craters!-CD, this is file MoonSL01.tif. (Courtesy of NASA)

Scientists predicted that the comet would finally surrender to the giant planet's gravity, crashing into the far side of Jupiter on July 16, 1994. Minutes after the collision, Jupiter's new wounds would rotate into view. Jupiter has no visible solid surface, only a cloudy atmosphere. How much would the huge explosions disturb the atmosphere?

"It's the scientific event of the century," exclaimed comet expert Michael A'Hearn of the University of Maryland. On the average, a comet 10 km across plows into Jupiter once every 1,000 years. This extraordinary collision would not only occur in our lifetime, it would happen when Jupiter was visible from Earth.

FORECASTS FOILED BY HAZY VIEW

Using what they had learned from studying craters on the Earth and the Moon, astronomers proposed theories about how the comet pieces would smash into Jupiter's atmosphere. Though basing their predictions on scientific theories, the researchers may have longed for the magic of a crystal ball. No one had ever observed comet impacts. Neither had they measured collisions of such large objects at such high speeds and fiery temperatures.

The scientists were also frustrated by what they didn't know about Shoemaker-Levy: its size, what it was made of, its brittleness, and how well it was "glued" together.

Pictures taken through Earth-based telescopes provided hazy images of the Shoemaker-Levy fragments, 630 million km away. Even the Hubble Space Telescope could only clearly distinguish objects bigger than 300 km across—much larger than the fragments, which were several km in size. Still, astronomers hoped that if they could see the contrast between light reflected from the ice nuclei and light scattered from the dusty clouds around each piece, they could calculate the size of the fragments. A July 1993 Hubble Space Telescope picture of Shoemaker-Levy showed hazy bright spots, representing the comet nuclei, surrounded by a coma of dust. By visually subtracting the comas, astronomers estimated that the largest fragments were about 4 km in diameter. Strangely enough, images taken six months later (after the Hubble's optics were improved) contained no trace of individual nuclei. Theories blossomed, suggesting everything from comets with no solid nuclei—"snowballs without ice"—to the nuclei being concealed by growing clouds of dust grains.

Astronomers concluded that since the parent comet is not visible in any photographs or images taken before the Shoemaker-Levy discovery, it was no larger than 10 km in diameter. Other reviews relating the fragment train's length to the size of the original object concluded that the original comet was small—only 1 to 2 km in diameter—

This mosaic shows the evolution of the G impact site on Jupiter. The images from lower left to upper right show the impact plume about 5 minutes after impact; the fresh impact site 1.5 hours after impact; the impact site after evolution by the winds of Jupiter (left), along with the L impact (right), 3 days after the G impact and 1.3 days after the L impact; and further evolution of the G and L sites due to winds and an additional impact (S) in the G vicinity, 5 days after the G impact. On Craters!-CD, this is file OtherS12.tif. (Courtesy of NASA/HST Comet Science Team)

and crumbled like a loose cookie. All comets contain ice, but was the ice-rich material solid and strong or weak and crumbly? Some researchers described it as a "rubble pile" of half a million house-size blocks with room-size spaces between them.

If the comet was loosely put together, its continued break up was likely. And that is what observers saw. In fact, it was becoming difficult to keep up with the fragments as they split and split again.

Certainly, most astronomers thought, bigger comet fragments would create bigger blasts. Striking at 60 km/s, a solid ice nucleus 1 km across would deliver energy equal to 500 billion tons of TNT or 50,000 hydrogen bombs. If the fragment were 5 km in diameter, it would pack a wallop 600 times stronger. The more energy entering the crash, researchers believed, the brighter and hotter the flash. On the other hand, if the comet fragments were weak and continued to fall apart, Jupiter might be pelted with a cosmic hailstorm instead of individual blasts.

The comet pieces might explode as they hit the cloud tops with a brilliant flash of light, or the nuclei, if they survived, would penetrate into the mysterious clouds. Some people thought each fragment would break up, spreading horizontally like a pancake in the cloud layers.

The bigger blasts were predicted to release flashes of light as brilliant as the Sun, as seen from satellites. They would heat the surrounding gas to 10,000° to 30,000° K, igniting massive fireballs that would quickly rise above the stratosphere (the upper layer of Jupiter's atmosphere) and be visible from Earth.

Scientists also proposed that if the solid material reached Jupiter's dense lower atmosphere, the shock of some impacts could create a pulse of gravity waves detectable from Earth. The gravity waves, appearing as concentric rings of fluctuating temperatures, might last one or two days. Short-lived sound waves, as well as tsunamis, or gigantic surface waves, would roll through Jupiter's atmosphere like ripples spreading over a pond after a pebble is dropped.

Some researchers were reluctant to expect big fireworks. "Jupiter will swallow these comets up without so much as a burp," said radio astronomer Alexander Dessler of the University of Arizona, referring to the effect on Jupiter's magnetic field. But others were more hopeful. "I predict that the impact will produce at least one major effect that no one has thought of," said Richard West of the European Southern Observatory.

FIREWORKS GALORE, AND MORE

In fact, the collision of Shoemaker-Levy with Jupiter held many surprises. Both professional astronomers and amateurs with backyard telescopes observed dark plumes rising from the bruises on Jupiter—rather than white puffs expected from "snowballs being blown apart." The dark hue seems to have come from fine dust and something like soot thrown up by the impacts.

"I feel sorry for Jupiter," joked Heidi Hammel, planet specialist at Massachusetts Institute of Technology. "It's really getting pummeled."

With a full but very distant view of the fireworks, the spacecraft Galileo recorded a comet impact—that of fragment G—for the first time in history. As each fragment collided with Jupiter, there were three brightenings. The first was the entry flash when the fragment shock-heated Jupiter's atmosphere to incandescence. The second flash came from the fireball and plume that rose from the explosion of the fragment in Jupiter's atmosphere.

A time sequence showing the impact of the first Shoemaker-Levy 9 fragment. The upper left frame shows Jupiter just before impact. The bright object to the right is the moon, Io. In the second frame, the fireball appears above the southeast (lower left) limb of the planet. The fireball flared to maximum brightness within a few minutes, at which time its flux surpassed that of Io. The final frame shows Jupiter approximately 20 minutes later when the impact zone had faded somewhat. These images were taken at the German-Spanish 3.5 meter telescope on Calar Alto in southern Spain. On Craters!-CD, this is file OtherS08.tif. (Courtesy: Max Planck Institut fur Astronomie, and others)

The third flash occurred when the expanding, cooling plume fell back to the upper atmosphere, violently heating that region.

Some of the brightest—and largest—comet fragments turned out to be duds when they hit. Bewildered observers named fragments B and F, two of the brighter comets, "bust" and "fizzle" because of their puny impacts. Astronomers were unable to explain the unexpectedly bright crash of the smaller fragment A. Most surprisingly, the plumes rising from each impact—whether the smash-up of a small fragment or a large one—were the same size, rising to a height of 3300 km. This observation has made space physicists rethink what happens when material explodes and its kinetic energy is converted to heat an explosive motion in Jupiter's atmosphere.

"The data has raised more questions than we had before the impact," said astronomer Heidi Hammel of the Massachusetts Institute of Technology. "That's the way science actually is. It's easy to make simple models when you don't have much data. The comet crash has given us so much data we're in data shock, and it makes the models a lot more complicated."

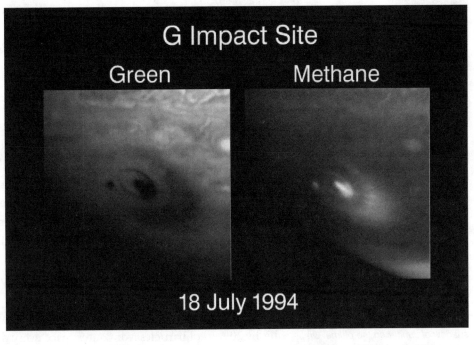

Astronomers expected that much of the cometary dust would miss Jupiter, eventually forming a new ring around Jupiter in about 10 years. In fact, they thought that Jupiter's radio emissions might decrease because the dust would take up some of its energetic electrons. Yet amateur ham radio operators who built a special backyard antenna for the event picked up a strong pulse of radio emission signals from the impact of fragment A. Radio scientists observed that Jupiter's total radio emissions peaked 20–30 percent above normal during the week of bombardment. They concluded that particles in Jupiter's atmosphere were energized by the impacts.

This Hubble Space Telescope image shows two views of the impact zone on Jupiter of fragment G, obtained in the early morning of July 18, 1994. The impact site is visible as a complex pattern of circles seen in the lower left. The small dark feature to the left of the pattern of circles is the impact site of fragment D. The dark, sharp ring at the site of the fragment G impact is 80% of the size of Earth. On Craters!-CD, this is file OtherS17.tif. (Courtesy of NASA/ HST Jupiter Imaging Science Team)

A sharply defined ring in the Hubble images of the G impact, traveling at a velocity of 800 m/s, was thought to be evidence of a sonic boom generated by the explosion. Researchers also observed waves spreading out from 5 different impact sites at speeds of 450–500 m/s. Although scientists are still trying to decide exactly what these waves are, the speeds are consistent with gravity waves—atmospheric ripples that cause the debris from the impact to bob up and down.

Atmospheric scientists, who wanted to know if new compounds could form when comets crash into planets, used special instruments to detect chemical compounds in the billowing hot plumes. They detected water vapor for a brief period after the impact. The water may have come from ice in the comet or from Jupiter. But the amount of water detected—the equivalent of a 400 m diameter ball of ice—was too great in relation to the other chemicals the scientists measured to have come from Jupiter. Planetary researchers concluded that the water came from the Shoemaker-Levy fragments, or that it was newly formed by the explosion from hydrogen molecules in Jupiter's atmosphere and oxygen molecules in the comet's ice. They also saw a variety of sulfur compounds, which probably came from a sulfur-rich atmospheric layer beneath Jupiter's mysterious clouds.

It may take years for astronomers, physicists, and planetary scientists to understand the data from one of the rarest events in scientific history. We have new evidence about the nature of comets, the formation of rings around planets, multi-million megaton atmospheric explosions, and Jupiter's atmosphere. New theories will sprout from the fertile field of new information. Our knowledge of the universe and our understanding of processes on Earth will be expanded. Perhaps we will learn more about what comets are made of and whether some of the compounds on Earth came from comets. The important thing is that the comet crash let us witness the general type of large-scale collision that sculpted the cratered landscapes of most moons and planets. The observations from the impact of Shoemaker-Levy might even help us understand the catastrophe that doomed the dinosaurs 65 million years ago.

As we go about the business of our daily lives, we are unaware that the Earth is being hit by 20 tons of particles from outer space every day. Though most of the particles are the size of grains of sand and pebbles, some are as large as golf balls, bread boxes, and even desks. Could a comet the size of Shoemaker-Levy hit the Earth? Would it happen in our lifetime? According to Eugene Shoemaker, the Earth is likely to be struck once every 100,000 years by an asteroid at least 1 km across—an impact that, judging by Shoemaker-Levy's collision with Jupiter, could be disastrous for life on this planet. However, as David Levy put it, instead of worrying about a catastrophe in this world, we were privileged to watch—and learn from—a rare event on another.

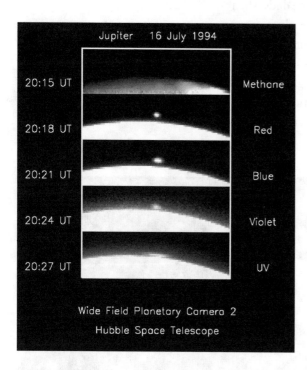

A plume near the terminator of Jupiter at the time of the impact. A bright feature appears 1000–1500 km above the limb of Jupiter at 20:18:17. (An image at 20:15:17 did not show a detached feature.) One interpretation is that the feature is visible by reflected sunlight, and the apparent detachment is due to the shadow of Jupiter on the plume. On Craters!-CD, this is file OtherS06.tif. (Courtesy of NASA/HST Jupiter Imaging Science Team)

MASTER MATERIALS LIST

ACTIVITY 1

for each group:

- assortment of lenses
- pair of cardboard tubes
- blank sheet of paper
- marker or dark pen
- ruler or meter stick
- scissors
- tape
- clay or lens holder

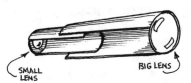

SMALL LENS   BIG LENS

ACTIVITY 2

- telescope or binoculars
- paper and pencils for sketches

ACTIVITY 3

for each group:

- bag of simulated planetary bedrock (light colored). Choices include mortar powder, white flour, or grout.
- cup of simulated planetary surface (dark colored). Choices include dark-colored grout, yellow cornmeal, or chocolate powder.
- broad, shallow box, such as pizza box or lid from a paper box
- sieve or large spoon
- simulated bolides, labeled and of assorted masses
- drop cloth or floor cover
- ruler
- leveling device
- chair or stepladder
- string (2 meters long) with a weight on the end
- balance

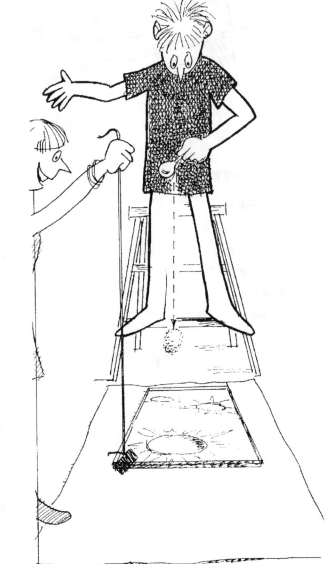

ACTIVITY 5

for each group:

- ◆ copies of crater photographs (two for each group)
- ◆ drawing paper
- ◆ pencils
- ◆ model craters

ACTIVITY 6

for each group:

- ◆ image of the Moon's surface
- ◆ ruler
- ◆ freshly-sharpened pencil
- ◆ graph paper (optional)

ACTIVITY 4

for each group:

- ◆ crater sample
- ◆ modeling clay
- ◆ cardboard base
- ◆ ruler
- ◆ lamp or spotlight
- ◆ protractor
- ◆ calculator with tangent function

ACTIVITY 7

for each group:

- ◆ box containing fragments from a simulated asteroid collision
- ◆ rulers (one for each student)
- ◆ graph paper

for collision simulation:

- ◆ sledge hammer
- ◆ mat
- ◆ burlap or heavy canvas bag with tie
- ◆ safety goggles for all participants
- ◆ simulated asteroids (molded from concrete or plaster or use concrete block or brick)

ACTIVITY 8

for each group:

- ◆ plastic tube at least 50 cm long
- ◆ stoppers to close both ends of the tube
- ◆ balance
- ◆ thermometer (-10° to 110° C)
- ◆ plastic foam cup
- ◆ 250 ml beaker
- ◆ 600g dry sand, at room temperature
- ◆ balance
- ◆ graph paper

ACTIVITY 10

- images of surfaces from different planetary bodies
- materials from selected previous activities

ACTIVITY 11

- image of Barringer Crater
- instructions for research

ACTIVITY 9

for each group:

- bag of simulated planetary bedrock
- cup of simulated planetary surface
- container
- sieve or large spoon
- simulated bolides, assorted sizes (Table tennis balls or super balls refilled with lead weights, reusable ice balls, BBs cast in plaster molds, and slingshot ammunition work well.)
- drop cloth or floor cover
- ruler
- chair
- string with a weight on the end
- graph paper
- safety goggles for all participants

ACTIVITY 12

for each student:

- at least one topographic or geologic map of an area on Earth
- one sample image of the Moon's surface
- blank map of North America (provided)

ACTIVITY 13

- instructions for student research

ACTIVITY 14

- pencil
- ruler
- protractor
- colored pencils (optional)

ACTIVITY 15

for each pair of students:

◆ Dino Data Sheet (provided)

◆ blank Species Lifetime charts (1 per student; provided)

◆ blank higher-level Diversity Diagrams (4 or 5 per student; provided)

◆ colored pencil or marker

◆ scissors

ACTIVITY 16

for each student:

◆ 2 sheets of graph paper

ACTIVITY 17

◆ no special materials are needed for this activity

ACTIVITY 18

◆ no special materials are needed for this activity

ACTIVITY 19

◆ no special materials are needed for this activity

ACTIVITY 20

for each pair of students:

◆ pencil

◆ deck of cards

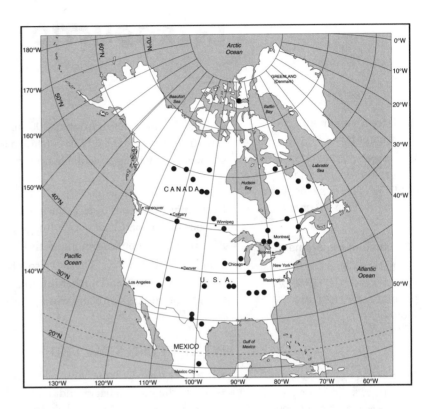

INTRODUCTION TO CRATERS!-CD

CD-ROM

Macintosh® minimum requirements:

Macintosh® 68030 (LC III, or higher) with double-speed CD-ROM, gray scale or color monitor. System 7.0 or higher.

PC minimum requirements:

386 33Mhz with 4 Mb RAM, double speed CD-ROM, gray scale or color monitor. Microsoft Windows™.

To use *Craters!-CD* begin at the Windows File Manager. The File Manager gives you a graphical view of the contents of directories.

The directories on the selected drive appear in the window on the left. When you select a directory its contents appear in the window on the right.

If you manipulate the image in any way, when you exit the application will ask you if you want to save changes. Unless you wish to save copies of files on your hard drive, select No.

Craters!-CD includes more than 200 supplementary images for use with the activities in *Craters!*. A CD icon (shown at right) tells you there are related supplementary images available on *Craters!-CD*.

Everything you need to start viewing images with *Craters!-CD* is included here. There are four folders on *Craters!-CD*: Images, DinoData, a text folder (called Mactext or PCtext), and an application folder (NIH Image for the Macintosh®, LViewPro for the Windows™-based PC). There is also a ReadMe text file, which includes more thorough instructions for use and further information about the files on *Craters!-CD*. You can read text files on the CD with any word processing program.

PC GETTING STARTED

✦ Insert *Craters!-CD* into your CD-ROM drive (using a disc caddy if appropriate).
✦ Locate the File Manager and double click on it. From the File Manager you can access the contents of other disk drives, including the CD-ROM drive. You can also view the contents of directories, such as the Images and LViewPro application directories. All the drives your computer has access to are represented by icons displayed below the menu bar in the File Manager.
✦ Select your CD-ROM drive.
✦ Select the directory "lviewpro." Executable files, or applications, have a suffix of ".exe" at the end of the filename.
✦ Double-click on the file lviewp1a.exe in the directory contents window on the right. This launches LViewPro, the application you will use to view images on *Craters!-CD*.

✦ The blank LViewPro window will appear, with a column of tools on the right. Select Open... from the File menu. The Open Image File window appears. Shown at right are the drive letter and the selected directory, LViewPro.
✦ To show all directories on the drive, double click on the drive folder (letter).
✦ Select the file Images and double click on it. A list of viewable files appears.
✦ Select All Files in the List Files of Type box at the left.
✦ Double click on any of the files named below Images at the right.
✦ Double click on any of the files listed in the top left window to see an image.
✦ To see a different image, select Open... from the File menu and repeat procedure. The previously opened image file will close automatically.

- Either from within the File Manager or the Program Manager locate a word processor application icon and double click on it.
- Select Open... from the File menu.
- Select the PCtext directory on the CD-ROM drive.
- Double click on the file that corresponds to the general subject (Moon, Earth or Other) and Activity number (following the subject) of the image file about which you wish to see information.

For more information, open the Readme.txt file the same way. The ReadMe file on *Craters!-CD* contains information about the organization of the image files, as well as directions for printing the images, and adjusting the window size for a full view of an image. The files in the Dinodata directory correspond to Activity 15. It has its own Readme.txt file with information on how to use the dinodata.doc file.

Text descriptions of each image are located in the directory PCtext. Text files and image files have identical names, but text files have the suffix "txt." The text descriptions are grouped by Activity number, with individual image descriptions listed therein. There are five images of the Moon for use with Activity 4; thus, the text file Moon4.txt contains five text descriptions.

MACINTOSH GETTING STARTED

- Double click on the CD icon to display the contents of the CD.
- Open the NIH Image V1.57/68k folder, then double click on the NIH Image icon (it looks like a microscope). NIH Image is the application you will use to view images on *Craters!-CD*.

When you insert *Craters!-CD* into your CD-ROM drive (using a disc caddy if appropriate), the *Craters!-CD* icon appears on the desktop.

- Select Open from the File menu.
- Locate the Images folder on *Craters!-CD*.
- Double click on any of the images folders, then double click on any image file to open it. To conserve memory, close each image before opening a new one. If you manipulate the image in any way, the application will ask you if you want to save changes. Unless you wish to save copies of files on your hard drive, select No. Because some of the image files are very large, you may encounter memory shortage notices when attempting to open an image. There are specific remedies listed in the ReadMe file on *Craters!-CD*.

Within the Images folder there are many separate folders that contain the image files.

- Launch a word processor program by locating its icon on your hard drive and double clicking on it.
- Select Open from the File menu.
- Select the Mactext folder on *Craters!-CD*.
- Double click on the file that corresponds to the general subject (Moon, Earth or Other) and Activity number (following the subject) of the image file about which you wish to see information.

For more information, open the ReadMe file the same way. The ReadMe file on *Craters!-CD* contains information about the organization of the image files, as well as directions for printing and manipulating the images. The files in the DinoData folder correspond to Activity 15. There is a ReadMe file in the DinoData folder with information on how to use the DinoData file.

Text descriptions of each image are located in the folder Mactext. Text files and image files have identical names, but text files have the suffix "txt." The text descriptions are grouped by Activity number, with individual image descriptions listed therein. There are five images of the Moon for use with Activity 4; thus, the text file Moon4.txt contains five text descriptions.

RESOURCES LIST

This annotated bibliography lists resources for extending classroom activities on topics presented in this book. For convenience, it is divided into several categories—first, general curriculum and background materials; second, materials for specific topics. In addition, this appendix provides a listing of CD-ROMs related to subjects in this book. You'll also find a directory of contacts to NASA education programs and resources. This bibliography is not intended to be comprehensive, however, it will give you a great set of starting points.

With the rapid expansion of on-line and Internet services, teachers and students can find a wide range of information sources using their computers and modems. The resources are especially rich on the World Wide Web, which combines text, graphics, and hyperlinks. Almost every major data center and many smaller ones maintain publicly accessible Web sites (for example, NSTA's Web site is http://www.nsta.org). The best way to locate Web sites related to this book is through any of the various Web search tools—e.g., Yahoo, World Wide Web Worm, and WebCrawler. Ideal starting points for planetary topics are the NASA Web sites listed below.

CURRICULUM MATERIALS

◆ *The Content Core* (Washington, DC: National Science Teachers Association, 1993 revised edition).

Organizes subject matter of science education according to tenets of Scope, Sequence, and Coordination (SS&C) project.

◆ Linda Crow, et al., *Earth and Sky* (expected 1995).

Activity-based, SS&C-sponsored teaching manual developed for 7th grade classroom use. Teaches relationships of the sky, stars, Moon, and Earth and is a useful guide for SS&C presentation style.

◆ Richard D'Alli, Ron Greeley, and Peter Schultz, *Activities in Planetary Geology* (Washington, DC: NASA, 1982). NASA Publication EP-179.

Extremely useful activity-based manual for studies of the Moon, cratering, and other topics.

◆ Nahum Kipnis, *Rediscovering Optics* (Minneapolis, MN: BENA Press, 1993).

High-school activity book in optics. Emphasizes inexpensive—though historically-accurate—recreations of famous experiments.

◆ John and Ruth Lewis, *Space Resources: Breaking the Bonds to Earth* (New York: Columbia University Press, 1987).

Fine starting point for student research in planetary and space exploration.

◆ *Relevant Research* (Washington, DC: National Science Teachers Association, 1992).

Collection of research papers and respected philosophical statements on how secondary students learn science best. Serves as a basis for SS&C project.

◆ G. Jeffrey Taylor (coordinator), *Exploring the Moon* (Washington, DC: NASA, 1994).

Teacher's guide with activities for Earth and space science topics using the Moon. Also examines special topics related to the Moon itself. Grades 4–12.

BOLIDE SOURCES AND CRATERING

◆ Tom Gehrels, *Hazards Due to Comets and Asteroids* (Tucson, AZ: University of Arizona Press, 1994).

Exceptional discussion of cratering, especially on Earth. Provides good starting point for extending activities in this book. Has many good data tables but high technical level.

◆ Ronald Greeley, *Planetary Landscapes* (Boston: Allen & Unwin, 1987).

General introduction to craters and other planetary features.

◆ William Hartmann, *The History of Earth: An Illustrated Chronicle of an Evolving Planet* (New York: Workman, 1991).

Popular introduction to Earth history, geologic periods, impacts, and the evolution of life. Well illustrated. High school level.

◆ William Hartmann, *Moons & Planets*. (Belmont, CA: Wadsworth, 1993).

College-level introduction to planetary science, including cratering, asteroids, comets, and surface landscapes.

◆ B. Mason, *Meteorites* (New York: Wiley, 1962).

Provides both popular and technical introduction to meteorites.

◆ H.J. Melosh, *Impact Cratering: A Geologic Process* (New York: Oxford University Press, 1989), Oxford Monographs on Geology and Geophysics, number 11.

Technical study of physics and mechanics involved in the cratering process.

◆ J.T. Wasson, *Meteorites* (New York: Springer Verlag, 1974).

Technical introduction to different types of meteorites.

MOON

◆ Alan Boss, "The Origin of the Moon," *Science*, 24 January 1986, volume 231, pp. 341–345.

Describes theory of the origin of the Moon as a result of an impact between a Mars-sized body and the proto-Earth.

◆ G. Jeffrey Taylor, "The Scientific Legacy of Apollo," *Scientific American*, July 1994, pp. 40–47.

Discusses theories about origin of the Moon, especially idea that the Moon formation was a result of a collision between proto-Earth and a giant meteor roughly 4.5 billion years ago.

IMPACTS ON EARTH

◆ Richard Grieve, "Terrestrial Impact: The Record in the Rocks," *Meteoritics*, 1991, volume 26, pp. 175–194.

Extensive database of approximately 130 impact craters on Earth. Discusses biases in impact record *toward* geologically young and *away from* small (<20 kilometer diameters) craters. Earlier surveys can be found in: Richard Grieve, et al., *Astronaut's Guide to Terrestrial Impact Craters* (Houston, TX: Lunar and Planetary Institute, 1988), LPI Technical Report 88-03; and Richard Grieve, "Terrestrial Impact Structures," *Annual Review of Earth and Planetary Sciences*, 1987, volume 15, pp. 245–270. (Grieve 1988 served as the basis for Activity 12.)

◆ Paul Hodge, *Meteorite Craters and Impact Structures of the Earth* (New York: Cambridge University Press, 1994).

General overview of impact craters on Earth. Provides good set of original data and images. Repeats much that is found in Grieve's writings.

◆ Richard Grieve, "Impact Cratering on the Earth," *Scientific American*, April 1990, volume 262, pp. 66–73.

General overview of impact sites on Earth. Discusses implications if impacts occurred in the past with greater frequency and intensity than previously thought.

◆ F. Kyte, et al., "New Evidence on the Size and Possible Effects of a Late Pliocene Oceanic Asteroid Impact," *Science,* 1988, volume 241, pp. 63–65.

Presents evidence for an impact at the end of the Pliocene epoch in the South Pacific. Also see S. Margolis, et al., "Microtektites, Microkrystites, and Spinels from a Late Pliocene Asteroid Impact in the Southern Ocean," *Science*, volume 251, pp. 1594–1597.

◆ P. Olsen, et al., "New Early Jurassic Tetrapod Assemblages Constrain Triassic–Jurassic Tetrapod Extinction Event," *Science*, 1987, volume 237, pp. 1025–1029.

Presents evidence for an impact occurring at the end of the Triassic period in Manicouagau, Canada. The impact crater is 100 km.

◆ Annika Sanfilippo, et al., "Late Eocene Microtektites and Radiolarian Extinctions on Barbados," *Nature,* 1985, volume 314, pp. 613–615.

Presents evidence for an impact at the end of the Eocene epoch.

◆ Peter Schultz and Ruben Lianza, "Recent Grazing Impacts on the Earth in the Rio Cuarto Crater Field," *Science,* 16 January, 1992, volume 355, pp. 234–237.

Presents evidence for a series of impacts where a meteorite skidded over a 34 kilometer range. Impact probably occurred at an angle of less than 15 degrees.

◆ Anonymous, "Earth's Cosmic Dusting," *Sky and Telescope*, March 1994, vol. 87, p. 13.

Space isn't empty. Researchers have analyzed panels of NASA's Long Duration Exposure Facility, which spent more than five years in orbit. The results suggest that about 40,000 metric tons of microscopic debris fall to the Earth each year.

◆ Anonymous, "The Hard Rain," *Economist*, 11 September 1993, volume 328, pp. 81–84.

Introduces public policy issues relating to Earth-crossing asteroids and comets. Provides both critical and supportive perspectives of *Spaceguard Survey*.

◆ Anonymous, "The Threat From Space," *Economist*, 11 September 1993, volume 328, pp. 13–14.

Editorial discusses conclusions of *Spaceguard Survey* report and public policy options.

◆ Clark Chapman and David Morrison, "Impacts on the Earth by Asteroids and Comets: Assessing the Hazard," *Nature*, 6 January 1994, volume 367, pp. 33–40.

Overview of threats posed by Earth-crossing asteroids and comets. Compares risks of impacts to other low frequency, high-consequence events. Superb starting point for classroom discussions of public policy issues.

◆ Christopher Chyba, "Death from the Sky," *Astronomy*, December 1993, volume 21, pp. 38–45.

Summarizes information known about the 1908 Tunguska explosion in the sky over Siberia, attributed to a rocky asteroid exploding before it hit the ground. Uses this as an example of how bolide impacts can affect Earth's history and human populations.

◆ David Morrison, "The Spaceguard Survey: Protecting the Earth from Cosmic Impacts," *Mercury,* May 1992, volume 21, pp. 103–106+.

Easy-to-follow summary of *Spaceguard Survey* report.

◆ David Morrison (chair), *The Spaceguard Survey: Report of the NASA International Near-Earth-Object Detection Workshop* (Pasadena, CA: Jet Propulsion Laboratory/California Institute of Technology, 1992).

Fundamental NASA study of Earth-crossing asteroids and comets. Includes discussion of public policy options.

◆ *The New York Times,* articles on surveys of asteroids and the possibilities of future Earth impacts:

March 25, 1992 (page A23), April 1, 1992 (page A18), April 6, 1992 (page A18), April 7, 1992 (page C1), April 18, 1992 (page A18), January 4, 1993 (page B12), June 24, 1993 (page A21), September 17, 1993 (page A1), November 9, 1993 (page C6), January 25, 1994 (page C1), March 24, 1994 (page A20), August 1, 1994 (page A1).

BOLIDES AS FUTURE THREAT TO EARTH

MASS EXTINCTIONS

- Eugene Shoemaker, "Asteroid and Comet Bombardment of the Earth," *Annual Review of Earth and Planetary Sciences*, 1983, volume 11, pp. 461-494.

Detailed technical overview of possible future impacts on Earth of Earth-crossing asteroids. This article provides the foundation for much of Shoemaker's subsequent work.

- Eugene Shoemaker, Ruth Wolfe, and Carolyn Shoemaker, "Asteroid and Comet Flux in the Neighborhood of Earth," in Sharpton and Ward, *Global Catastrophes in Earth History*, pp. 155–170.

Updated (from Shoemaker, 1983) discussion of possible future impacts on Earth. Expanded list of Earth-crossing asteroids. Source of data in Activity 18.

- Luis Alvarez, et al., "Extraterrestrial Cause for the Cretaceous-Tertiary Extinction," *Science*, 1980, volume 208, pp. 1095–1108.

Original paper in which the Alvarez team proposed bolide impact as the explanation for K/T extinction.

- Luis Alvarez, "Mass Extinctions Caused by Large Bolide Impacts," *Physics Today*, 1987, volume 40, pp. 24–33.

Summarizes evidence in favor of impact theory for K/T extinction. Good discussion of predictions from theory and evidence in favor of them. Also see Walter Alvarez and Frank Alvarez, "An Extraterrestrial Impact," *Scientific American*, 1990, volume 263, pp. 79–92, for a nontechnical summary of the evidence.

- W.G. Chaloner and A. Hallam, *Evolution and Extinction* (London: Royal Society of London, 1989).

Collection of technical articles on effects of extinction on history of life. Detailed discussion of groups around K/T boundary.

- Richard Cowen, *History of Life, 2nd edition* (Cambridge, MA: Blackwell, 1994).

Popular introduction to paleontology for non-scientists. Up-to-date summaries from the origin of life to humans and the ice age.

- Stephen Donovan, *Mass Extinctions: Processes and Evidence* (New York: Columbia University Press, 1989).

Excellent starter for studying mass extinctions other than that around the K/T boundary. Provides chapter summaries of research for each of the major mass extinctions in fossil record.

- David Elliott (ed.), *Dynamics of Evolution* (New York: John Wiley and Sons, 1986).

Collection of technical papers about mass extinctions. Good material on fossil record during K/T transition in both marine and land environments.

- Douglas Erwin, *The Great Paleozoic Crisis: Life and Death in the Permian* (New York: Columbia University Press, 1993).

Detailed study of the mass extinction at the end of the Permian Era, roughly 225 million years ago. Considers implications of what happened and examines how it could have happened.

◆ Karl Flessa, "The 'Facts' of Mass Extinctions," in V.L. Sharpton and P.D. Ward (eds.), *Global Catastrophes in Earth History*, GSA Special Paper 247, 1990.

Discusses problems of how best to study extinction and record its extent in the history of life. Discusses problems of measuring duration, magnitude, and breadth.

◆ William Hartmann and Ron Miller, *The History of Earth* (New York: Wolkman Publishing Co., 1991).

◆ Alan Hildebrand and others, "Discovery of the K/T Boundary Impact Crater, 'Chicxulub,' in Yucatan," *Geology*, 1991, volume 19, p. 867.

Also see Virgil Sharpton and 9 others, "Chicxulub Multi-Ring Impact Basin: Size and Other Characteristics from Gravity Analysis," *Science*, 1993, volume 261, pp. 1564–1567, for a summary of data on the discovery of the crater.

◆ David Jablonski, "Extinctions: A Paleontological Perspective," *Science*, 16 Aug. 1991, volume 253, pp. 754–757.

Technical analysis of extinction's effect on the history of life. Concludes that widespread genera survive mass extinctions preferentially, whereas geographically-restricted genera are particularly vulnerable. Leaves implication that widespread, weedy species—such as rats, ragweed, and cockroaches—are the least vulnerable to extinction.

◆ David Norman, *Dinosaur!* (New York: Prentice Hall, 1991).

Based on 4-part television series on dinosaurs. Good overview of dinosaur biology, classification, extinction, and origin of birds.

◆ Donald Prothero, *Paradise Lost* (New York: Columbia University Press, 1993).

Tells fascinating story of the mass extinctions that took place in the Eocene and Oligocene periods (40–34 million years ago) as the result of changes in oceanic and atmospheric circulation patterns.

◆ Virgil Sharpton and Peter Ward, *Global Catastrophes in Earth History: An Interdisciplinary Conference on Impacts, Volcanism, and Mass Mortality* (Boulder, CO: Geological Society of America, 1990), GSA Special Paper 247.

Collection of scientific papers on all aspects of mass extinctions, especially impact theory and K/T extinction.

◆ James Valentine, *Phanerozoic Diversity Patterns: Profiles in Macroevolution* (Princeton, NJ: Princeton University Press, 1985).

Standard source of information on history of life expressed in diversity diagrams. Chapter 1 is especially useful.

◆ David Weishampel, et al., *The Dinosauria* (Berkeley: University of California Press, 1984).

Comprehensive scientific overview of information on dinosaurs. Discusses biology, distribution, taxonomy, and evolution (but few drawings). Surveys extraordinary expansion of information about dinosaurs in last two decades. Served as source for Activity 15.

♦ E.O. Wilson (ed.), *Biodiversity* (Washington, DC: National Academy Press, 1988).

Collection of technical papers on current biodiversity and extinction issues. Contains useful data and analyses for comparison of present crisis to those during mass extinction events.

♦ Wendy Wolbach, R. Lewis, and E. Anders. "Cretaceous Extinctions: Evidence for Wildfires and Search for Meteoriteic Material," *Science*, 1985, vol. 230, pp. 167–170.

VOLCANISM AS ALTERNATIVE TO IMPACT THEORY FOR K/T EXTINCTION

♦ Dewey MacLean, "K/T Transition into Chaos," *Journal of Geological Education*, 1988, volume 36, pp. 237–243.

Discusses K/T transition with emphasis on volcanism and role of volcanic activity as destabilizer of Earth's biosphere. Good bibliography of volcanism at K/T boundary.

♦ Charles Officier, C.L. Drake, and J.L. Pindell, "Cretaceous-Tertiary Events and the Caribbean Caper," *GSA Today*, 1992, vol. 2, pp. 69–75.

Detailed examination of evidence for Caribbean impact site at K/T boundary. Weighted towards volcanism. *GSA Today* is published by the Geological Society of America.

♦ Charles Officier, "Extinctions, Iridium, and Shock Minerals Associated with the Cretaceous/Tertiary Transition," *Journal of Geological Education*, 1990, vol. 38, pp. 402–425.

Detailed discussion of evidence used to defend impact theory. Heavily weighted towards volcanism.

HISTORICAL

♦ Luis Alvarez, *Alvarez: Adventures of a Physicist* (New York: Basic Books, 1987).

Autobiography of Nobel prize-winning physicist who was deeply involved in developing original form of modern impact theory for the K/T extinction.

♦ Leonard Bruno, *Landmarks of Science from the Collections of the Library of Congress* (New York: Facts on File, Inc., 1989).

Superb introduction to original sources in the history of science. Astronomy chapter discusses early observations of the Moon by Galileo, Hevelius, and others.

♦ Galileo Galilei, *Sidereus Nuncius, or, The Sidereal Messenger* (Chicago: University of Chicago Press, 1989), translation by Albert Van Helden.

English language translation of Galileo's 1610 report of observations of the sky using his newly made telescope. Introduction describes early history of telescope and provides biographical sketch of Galileo.

◆ Ursula Marvin, "Meteorites, the Moon and the History of Geology," *Journal of Geological Education*, 1986, vol. 34, pp. 140–165.

Historical discussion of meteorites, from early eyewitness accounts (e.g., 861 A.D. in Japan, and 1942 in Alsace, France). Extensive bibliography.

MAPS

◆ The U.S. Geological Survey can provide many kinds of maps for classroom use. These include maps of the Moon, topographic maps, satellite image maps, and photo image maps. For more information, contact one of the USGS's Earth Science Information Centers. These are located in every region of the country.

Earth Science Information Centers
1-800-USA-MAPS

◆ Free map indexes and catalogs of USGS books, circulars, and leaflets also can be obtained through the USGS Map Distribution Center.

USGS Map Distribution
Box 25286, Building 810
Denver Federal Center
Denver, CO 80225
(303) 236-7477 voice
(303) 236-1972 fax

◆ The USGS also has a service dedicated to answering public inquiries about geological topics (such as crater sites on Earth).

Geologic Inquiries Group
U.S. Geological Survey
907 National Center
Reston, VA 22092
(703) 648-4383 voice
(703) 648-6684 fax

PLANETARY IMAGES ON CD-ROM

◆ *Welcome to the Planets Educational CD-ROM,* version 1.1., NASA.

For additional information, contact Jet Propulsion Laboratory, Planetary Data System, PDS Operator, 4800 Oak Grove Drive, Mail Stop 525-389, Pasadena, CA 91109. Phone: (818) 306-6130. Internet: pds_operator@jplpds.jpl.nasa.gov

◆ *The Mars Educational Multimedia CD-ROM,* The Center for Mars Exploration with the NASA Ames Space Science Division, NASA Headquarters Mission from Planet Earth, SETI Institute, and the Planetary Society.

For additional information, contact The Center for Mars Exploration, Mail Stop 245-1, Moffett Field, CA 94035-1000. Phone: (415) 604-0421. Internet: cmex_cd@barsoom.arc.nasa.gov

- *Mars Explorer,* Virtual Reality Labs.

- *Redshift Multimedia Astronomy,* Maris Multimedia.

- *Venus Explorer,* Virtual Reality Labs.

- *Astronomy Village: Investigating the Universe,* NASA, 1995.

ADDITIONAL CRATER IMAGES

- Many additional crater images, other photographs of planetary bodies, or more background information can be found on World Wide Web sites throughout the world. Use a Web searching tool using a planetary body's name or planetary probe's name as a key word.

- NASA sponsors a number of regional Planetary Image Facilities, which contain research-quality archives of planetary images taken from space probes and Earth-based telescopes. These facilities contain an enormous variety of planetary images and are used by astronomers and space scientists for research. They are located throughout the United States. Teachers are welcome to visit these facilities by appointment. Two of these facilities are

Center for Earth and Planetary Studies
National Air and Space Museum
4th and Independence Ave., S.W.
Room 3773, MRC 315
Smithsonian Institution
Washington, DC 20560
(202) 357-1457

Jet Propulsion Laboratory
California Institute of Technology
Mail Stop 202-01
4800 Oak Grove Drive
Pasadena, CA 91109
(818) 354-3343

- To meet public interest in cratering, The Planetary Society has created *Impact Craters: A Slide Set,* a 20-slide collection for use in classrooms. Among the slides included are the paintings used for this book's cover. A descriptive guide to the images accompanies this set.

The Planetary Society
65 North Catalina Avenue
Pasadena, CA 91106
(818) 793-5100

- The Astronomical Society of the Pacific offers a slide set (25 slides) and booklet for studies of Shoemaker-Levy 9. These slides are of high quality and include a good range of images.

Astronomical Society of the Pacific
390 Ashton Ave.
San Francisco, CA 94112
(415) 337-1100

NASA RESOURCES FOR EDUCATORS

NASA's Central Operation of Resources for Educators (CORE) was established for the national and international distribution of NASA-produced educational materials in audiovisual format. Educators can obtain a catalog of these materials and an order form by written request (on school letterhead) to:

NASA CORE
Lorain County Joint Vocational School
15181 Route 58 South
Oberlin, OH 44074
(216) 774-1051, ext. 293 or 294

CENTRAL OPERATION OF RESOURSES FOR EDUCATORS (CORE)

NASA's Teacher Resource Center (TRC) Network was created by the NASA Education Division to make additional information available to the education community. TRCs contain a wealth of information for educators: publications, reference books, slide sets, audio cassettes, videotapes, tele-lecture programs, computer programs, lesson plans, and teacher guides with activities. Because each NASA field center has its own area of expertise, no two TRCs are exactly alike. Phone calls are welcome if you are unable to visit the TRC that serves your geographic area. For the TRC in your region, follow this guide:

TEACHER RESOURCE CENTER (TRC) NETWORK

AK, AZ, CA, HI, ID, MT, NV, OR, UT, WA, WY
    NASA Teacher Resource Center
    Mail Stop T12-A
    NASA Ames Research Center
    Moffett Field, CA 94035-1000
    (415) 604-3574

CT, DE, DC, ME, MD, MA, NH, NJ, NY, PA, RI, VT
    NASA Teacher Resource Laboratory
    Mail Code 130.3
    NASA Goddard Space Flight Center
    Greenbelt, MD 20771-0001
    (301) 286-8570

CO, KS, NE, ND, OK, SD, TX
    NASA Teacher Resource Room
    Mail Code AP-4
    NASA Johnson Space Flight Center
    Houston, TX 77058-3696
    (713) 483-8696

FL, GA, PR, VI
> NASA Educators Resource Laboratory
> Mail Code ERL
> NASA Kennedy Space Center
> Kennedy Space Center, FL 32899-0001
> (407) 867-4090

KY, NC, SC, VA, WV
> Virginia Air and Space Museum
> NASA Teacher Resource Center for
> NASA Langley Research Center
> 600 Settler's Landing Road
> Hampton, VA 23669-4033
> (804) 727-0900 ext. 757

IL, IN, MI, MN, OH, WI
> NASA Teacher Resource Center
> Mail Stop 8-1
> NASA Lewis Research Center
> 21000 Brookpark Road
> Cleveland, OH 44135-3191
> (216) 433-2017

AL, AR, IA, LA, MO, TN
> U.S. Space and Rocket Center
> NASA Teacher Resource Center for
> NASA Marshall Space Flight Center
> P.O. Box 070015
> Huntsville, AL 35807-7015
> (205) 544-5812

MS
> NASA Teacher Resource Center
> Building 1200
> NASA John C. Stennis Space Center
> Stennis Space Center, MS 39529-6000
> (601) 688-3338

Serves inquiries related to space and planetary exploration
> NASA Teacher Resource Center
> JPL Education Outreach
> Mail Stop CS-530
> NASA Jet Propulsion Laboratory
> 4800 Oak Grove Drive
> Pasadena, CA 91109-8099
> (818) 354-6916

CA cities near the facility:
> Public Affairs Office (Trl. 42)
> NASA Teacher Resource Center
> NASA Dryden Flight Research Facility
> Edwards, CA 93523-0273
> (805) 258-3456

VA and MD's Eastern Shores
> NASA Teacher Resource Lab
> Education Complex—Visitors Center
> Building J-17
> NASA Wallops Flight Facility
> Wallops Island, VA 23337-5099
> (804) 824-2297/2298

REGIONAL TEACHER RESOURCE CENTERS (RTRCS)

Regional Teacher Resource Centers (RTRCs) offer more educators access to NASA educational materials. NASA has formed partnerships with universities, museums, and other educational facilities to serve as RTRCs in many states. Teachers may preview, copy, or receive NASA materials at these sites. A complete list of RTRCs is available through NASA CORE.

NASA QUEST

NASA Quest is the on-line home for the NASA K–12 Internet Initiative. This resource houses curriculum supplements for teachers, original Internet-related documents, information about educational reform, and archives of interactive projects. Quest also is rich in pointers to other NASA and education resources. It is a good starting point for on-line NASA explorations.

> World Wide Web: http://quest.arc.nasa.gov
> Gopher: quest.arc.nasa.gov

For more information, send an E-mail message to:
> listmanager@quest.arc.nasa.gov

NASA Spacelink is another on-line resource for K–12. It houses a large collection of current (updated daily) and historical information about NASA's projects and missions, including the space shuttle. It also contains materials for NASA education programs, images, and other materials useful in the classroom. Spacelink may be accessed by computer through direct-dial modem or the Internet.

NASA SPACELINK

     Modem line: (205) 895-0028
     Terminal emulation: VT-100 required
     Data format: 8-N-1
     Telnet: spacelink.msfc.nasa.gov

Spacelink fully supports the following Internet services:
     World Wide Web: http://spacelink.msfc.nasa.gov
     Gopher: spacelink.msfc.nasa.gov
     Anonymous FTP: spacelink.msfc.nasa.gov
     Internet TCP/IP address: 192.149.89.61

For more information, contact:
     Spacelink Administrator
     Education Programs Office
     Mail Code CL01
     NASA Marshall Space Flight Center
     Huntsville, AL 35812-0001
     (205) 544-6360
     E-mail: comments@spacelink.msfc.nasa.gov

NASA Educational Satellite Videoconferences for Teachers is offered as an in-service education program for educators through the school year. The content of each program varies but includes aeronautics or space science topics of interest to elementary and secondary teachers. NASA program managers, scientists, astronauts, and education specialists are featured presenters. The videoconference schedule is available on NASA Spacelink and through NASA CORE.

NASA EDUCATIONAL SATELLITE VIDEO-CONFERENCES

The video conference is free to registered educational institutions. To participate, the institution must have a C-band satellite receiving system, teacher release time, and an optional long distance telephone line for interaction. Arrangements may also be made to receive the satellite signal through a local cable television system. The programs may be videotaped and copied for later use.

For more information, contact:
     Videoconference Producer
     NASA Teaching from Space Program
     308 A CITD
     Oklahoma State University
     Stillwater, OK 74078-0422
     E-mail: nasaaedutv@smtpgate.osu.hq.nasa.gov

IMPROVE YOUR IMAGE WITH

CRATERS!-CD

WHAT'S ON CRATERS!-CD AND WHY WOULD I WANT IT?

Craters! puts images of real impacts in the hands of your students. Printed versions of the most useful images accompany these activities. As a bonus, we assembled an additional 200 impact-related images from just about every kind of planetary body in our solar system, including Earth. We put these images onto a companion CD-ROM. Use these images to supplement those printed in the book and for additional projects. With easy-to-use viewers for both Windows™ and Macintosh®, *Craters!-CD* lets you display and manipulate images on-screen or print high resolution copies for classroom use. Forget photocopies. Use *Craters!-CD* to produce fresh, clear, easy-to-replace images every time. *Craters!-CD* is yours for no additional charge!

DO I HAVE TO USE CRATERS!-CD?

No. About half the activities in *Craters!* use images. The book contains printed versions of all the images you will need. *Craters!-CD* also includes copies of those images, plus supplemental ones to *complement* those in the book. Using *Craters!-CD* adds variety. Plus, in contrast to photocopies, *Craters!-CD* will give you high-quality, first generation versions of the images you want every time.

HOW DO I KNOW WHAT IMAGES TO USE?

Images on *Craters!-CD* are linked to activities in two ways. When you see the CD-ROM icon on a page, you'll know supplemental images are available, and you'll see the file names for the images we recommend. Plus, the images on *Craters!-CD* are organized with names and directories that link directly to the activities. You'll know at a glance exactly where to look for more images.

CD-ROM

WHAT KIND OF COMPUTER DO I NEED?

Craters!-CD runs in either Macintosh® or Windows™ environments. It has viewers that work on each platform. There are directions in the book for getting it started. We chose basic viewers to make this easy-to-use, but you can use other viewers if you want. You'll need a computer that can read a CD-ROM. For printing, we recommend a laser printer.

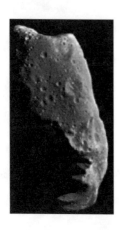